HOMERIC QUESTIONS

GREGORY NAGY

HOMERIC
QUESTIONS

University of Texas Press   Austin

Requests for permission to reproduce material from this work should be sent to Permissions, University of Texas Press, P.O. Box 7819, Austin, TX 78713-7819.

∞ The paper used in this publication meets the minimum requirements of American National Standard for Information Sciences—Permanence of Paper for Printed Library Materials, ANSI Z39.48-1984.

Library of Congress Cataloging-in-Publication Data

Nagy, Gregory.
    Homeric questions / Gregory Nagy. — 1st ed.
        p.   cm.
    Includes bibliographical references (p.   ) and index.
    ISBN 0-292-75561-9 (cloth : alk. paper). — ISBN 0-292-75562-7 (pbk. : alk. paper)
    1. Homer—Technique. 2. Epic poetry, Greek—History and criticism—Theory, etc. 3. Oral formulaic analysis. 4. Oral tradition—Greece.
    I. Title.
    PA4037.N345   1996
    883'.01—dc20   95-39353

To the memory of Albert Bates Lord

Contents

Preface

The core of this book is a speech, the Presidential Address of the 1991 convention of the American Philological Association, which was later developed into an article.[1] All along I thought of this article as a companion piece to two other articles I have published elsewhere.[2] Now I have finally rewritten all three articles to suit the original idea of the book. The introduction and the epilogue, which frame the four chapters of the book, come closest to the original speech. That speech, and this whole book, pose some Homeric questions to an audience of classical philologists. These questions, I think, are relevant to the legacy of "the classics," of philology itself. More than that: if I am right that philology is a focal point of humanistic studies, these questions may be relevant in one way or another to all students of the humanities.

1. N 1992a.

2. N 1992b, 1994a.

HOMERIC QUESTIONS

Introduction

The title of this work is marked by the word *Questions,* in the plural. It takes the place of the expected singular, along with a definite article, associated with that familiar phrase, "the Homeric Question." Today there is no agreement about what the Homeric Question might be. Perhaps the most succinct of many possible formulations is this one: "The Homeric Question is primarily concerned with the composition, authorship, and date of the *Iliad* and the *Odyssey.*"[1] Not that any one way of formulating the question in the past was ever really sufficient. Who was Homer? When and where did Homer live? Was there a Homer? Is there one author of the *Iliad* and the *Odyssey,* or are there different authors for each? Is there a succession of authors or even of redactors for each? Is there, for that matter, a unitary *Iliad,* a unitary *Odyssey?*

I choose *Homeric Questions* as the title of this book both because I am convinced that the reality of the Homeric poems, the *Iliad* and the *Odyssey,* cannot possibly be comprehended through any one Question, and because a plurality of questions can better recover the spirit of the Greek word *zḗtēma,* meaning the kind of intellectual "question" that engages opposing viewpoints. In Plato's usage, *zḗtēma* refers to a question or inquiry of a philosophical nature. This is the word used in the title of Porphyry's *Homeric Questions,* a work that continues in a tradition that can be traced as far back as Aristotle. As Rudolf Pfeiffer writes, "Probably over a long period of time Aristotle had drawn up for his lectures a list of 'difficulties' [*aporḗmata* or *problḗmata*] of interpretation in Homer with their respective 'solutions' [*lúseis*]; this custom of *zētḗmata probállein* may have prospered at the symposia of intellectual circles."[2]

---

1. Davison 1962:234.

2. Pfeiffer 1968:69.

2   A number of quotations from Aristotle's work are preserved, mostly in Porphyry's *Homeric Questions*.[3] In one of these, Aristotle is disputing the assertion, as found in Plato's *Republic* (319b), that it cannot be true that Achilles dragged the corpse of Hektor around the tomb of Patroklos; Aristotle contradicts this assertion by referring to a Thessalian custom, still prevalent, he says, in his own time, of dragging the corpses of murderers around the tombs of those they had murdered (F 166 Rose).[4] As Pfeiffer goes on to say, "It is an example of the way [Aristotle] used the stupendous treasures of his collections for the correct interpretation of the epic poet against less learned predecessors who had raised subjective moral arguments without being aware of historical facts."[5] Among the historical facts used by Aristotle is diction, *léxis*.[6] For my own approach to Homeric Questions, diction is the primary empirical given.

We will return to the topic of diction presently. For now let us continue with the account by Pfeiffer:

> Although certain circles of the Alexandrine Museum seem to have adopted this "method" of *zētémata,* which amused Ptolemaic kings and Roman emperors, as it had amused Athenian symposiasts, the great and serious grammarians disliked it as a more or less frivolous game. . . . It was mainly continued by the philosophic schools, Peripatetics, Stoics, Neoplatonists, and by amateurs, until Porphyry (who died about 305 [C.E.]) arranged his final collection of *Homérika zētémata* in the grand style, in which he very probably still used Aristotle's original work.[7]

The title *Homeric Questions* reaffirms the original Aristotelian seriousness of *Homérika zētémata,* avoiding the accretive implications of frivolity. To this extent it matches the seriousness of scholarship in the period of the Renaissance and thereafter concerning the Homeric Question. But my title also affirms the need to pose the question in such a way that it will not presuppose the necessity of any

---

3. Hintenlang 1961; Pfeiffer 1968:69.

4. Hintenlang 1961:22–23; Pfeiffer 1968:69.

5. Pfeiffer 1968:70.

6. See ibid.

7. Pfeiffer 1968:70–71, with reference to Lehrs 1882:206.

single answer or solution, *lúsis*. And even if a unified answer were to be achieved in the long run, the result is likely to be a blend achieved from a plurality of different voices, not the singular strain of a monotone edict emanating from the unquestioned authority of accepted scholarship to which some would assign the title of philology.

For purposes of my argument, we need to turn back to earlier understandings of the very idea of *philology*. Let us consider, for example, the report of Suetonius that Eratosthenes of Cyrene, who succeeded the scholar-poet Apollonius of Rhodes as head of the Library of Alexandria, was the first scholar to formalize the term *philólogos* in referring to his identity as a scholar, and that in so doing he was drawing attention to a *doctrina* that is *multiplex variaque,* a course of studies that is many-sided and composed of many different elements.[8]

The era of the great Library of Alexandria reflects a link between our new world of philology and the old world of the actual words that are studied in philology, like the *ipsissima verba* credited to Homer. Those who presided over the words, as texts, were the Muses: the very name of the Library of Alexandria was, after all, the Museum, the place of the Muses, and its head was officially a priest of the Muses, nominated by the king himself.[9] These Muses of the text had once been the Muses of performance.

The members of the Museum, which was part of the royal compound, have been described by Pfeiffer: "They had a carefree life: free meals, high salaries, no taxes to pay, very pleasant surroundings, good lodgings and servants. There was plenty of opportunity for quarrelling with each other."[10] One might say that the Museum itself was a formalization of nostalgia for the glory days when the Muses supposedly inspired the competitive performance of a poet. The importance of *performance* as the realization of the poetic art will become clear as the discussion proceeds.

Another head of the Alexandrian Library, Aristarchus of Samothrace, perhaps the most accomplished philologist of the Hellenistic era, was described by Panaetius of Rhodes, a leading figure among the Stoics, as a *mantis* 'seer' when it came to understanding the words of

---

8. Suetonius *De grammaticis et rhetoribus* c. 10 (Pfeiffer 1968:158 n. 8); see the definitive edition of Kaster 1995.

9. Testimonia collected by Pfeiffer 1968:96.

10. Ibid., 97.

4   poetry (Athenaeus 634c).[11] In this concept of the seer, we see again
the nostalgia of philology for the Muses of inspired performance.

The beginnings of a split between *philology* and *performance*—a split
that had led to this nostalgia, ongoing into our own time—are evident in an account of Herodotus that I have examined at length elsewhere, concerning two ominous disasters that befell the island of
Chios, a reputed birthplace of Homer.[12] In the earliest attested mention of schools in ancient Greece, Herodotus 6.27.2, the spotlight
centers on an incident that occurred on the island of Chios around
496 B.C.E., where a roof collapsed on a group of 120 boys as they were
being taught *grámmata* 'letters'; only one boy survived. This disaster is
explicitly described by Herodotus as an omen presaging the overall
political disaster that was about to befall the whole community of
Chios in the wake of the Ionian Revolt against the Persians (6.27.1),
namely, the attack by Histiaios (6.26.1–2), and then the atrocities resulting from the occupation of the island by the Persians (6.31–32).

The disaster that befell the schoolboys at Chios is directly coupled
by the narrative of Herodotus with another disaster, likewise presaging the overall political disaster about to befall all of Chios: at about
the same time, a *khorós* 'chorus' of 100 young men from Chios, officially sent to Delphi for a performance at a festival there, fell victim
to a plague that killed 98 of them. Only two of the boys returned
alive to Chios (6.27.2).

In this account by Herodotus, then, we see two symmetrical disasters befalling the poetic traditions of a community, presaging a general political disaster befalling the community as a whole: first to be
mentioned are the old-fashioned and elitist oral traditions of the
chorus, to be followed by the newer and even more elitist written
traditions of the school. The differentiation between the older and
newer traditions, as we see it played out in the narrative of Herodotus, can be viewed as the beginnings of the crisis of philology, ongoing in our own time.[13]

It is as if the misfortune of the people of Chios had to be presaged
separately, in both public and private sectors. The deaths of the

---

11. Ibid., 232.

12. N 1990c, restating an earlier discussion in N 1990a:406–413. On Chios as birthplace
of Homer, see Acusilaus FGH 2 F 2.

13. N 1990c. See especially p. 40 on Sophocles as composer *and* performer.

chorus-boys affected the public at large, in that choruses were inclusive, to the extent that they represented the community at large. The
deaths of the schoolboys, on the other hand, affected primarily the
elite, in that schools were more exclusive, restricted to the rich and
the powerful.

For our own era, the scene of a disaster where the roof caves in on
schoolboys learning their letters becomes all the more disturbing because schools are all we have left from the split between the more
inclusive education of the chorus and the more exclusive education
of the school. For us it is not just a scene: it is a primal scene. The
crisis of philology, signaled initially by the split between chorus and
school, deepens with the conceptual narrowing of *paideía* as education over the course of time.

The narrowing is signaled by exclusion. In the *Protagoras* of Plato,
we are witness to a proposal that girl musicians be excluded from the
company of good old boys at the symposium. Even as slave-girls,
women lose the chance to contribute to, let alone benefit from, the
new *paideía*. Meanwhile, the traditions of the old *paideía,* where aris-
tocratic girls had once received their education in the form of choral
training, become obsolete. Obsolete too, ironically, is the old *paideía*
of boys, both in the chorus and in the schools. The new schools as
ridiculed in the *Clouds* of Aristophanes seem to have lost the art of
performing the "classics," and the classics have become written texts
to be studied and emulated in writing. Gone forever, in the end, are
the performances of Sophocles. Gone forever is the possibility of
bringing such performances back to life, even if for just one more
time, at occasions like the symposium. Gone forever, perhaps, is the
art of actually *performing* a composition for any given occasion.

As I have said, the era of the Museum at Alexandria represents a
grand humanistic effort to preserve, even as texts, the *ipsissima verba*.
To that extent, it also represents an attempt to reverse the narrowing
of *paideía*. Our own hope lies in the capacity of philology, as also
of schools, to continue to reverse such a pattern of narrowing, to
recover a more integrated, integral, *paideía*. The symptom of a nar-
rowed education can be described as the terminal prestige of ar-
rested development, where schoolboys, instead of getting killed, grow
up to be the old boys of an exclusive confraternity that they call
philology, *their* philology.[14] The humanism of philology, which must

---

14. N 1990b:47. On the concept of *terminal prestige,* see McClary 1989.

6   surely counter such a narrow modern view, depends on its inclusive-
ness, its diversity of interests. We come back to the ancient scholarly
ideal of a *doctrina* that is *multiplex variaque,* a course of studies that
is many-sided and composed of many different elements. Such a
course of studies, I argue, is essential for pursuing Homeric Questions, not to mention other classical questions.

One small but troubling sign of narrowing, of a movement away
from a course of studies that is ideally many-sided, is the way in which
we contemporary classics scholars—certainly not just Homerists—
tend to use the words "right" and "wrong": this kind of value judgment seems to operate on the assumption that the reader already
accepts the argument being offered and rejects all others. The implications are discouraging, because a cumulative plurality of scholars
who say "I am right" and "most of you are wrong" suggests that most
of those who make this claim are wrong and only some, if any, are
right. I propose to write instead, here and elsewhere, that I agree or
disagree, without presupposing the ultimate judgment. Or, better,
my arguments either converge with or diverge from those of others.
I cannot presuppose that I am right, since even a "right" formulation
may need to be reformulated in the future, but I, along with all other
classicists, need to be wary of a style of criticism that seeks to reformu-
late our formulations in a style of one-upmanship, where the latest
word pretends to be the last word.[15]

The idea of a *zḗtēma* or 'question', in the usage of those earliest
scholars of Homeric poetry, assumes an ongoing conflict of views in
an ongoing debate of scholars. It is in that spirit of open-endedness
that I take up my own set of questions, Homeric Questions, making
clear my disagreements as well as agreements with other scholars.
My goal is to offer a set of answers, *sine ira et studio,* that must in the
long run be tested by further questions. In my search for answers,
I am striving for a definitive formulation of my own thinking on
Homeric poetry as it has evolved since my earliest published formulations, which appeared over twenty years ago.[16] Whatever answers I

---

15. Phillips (1989:637) makes the following remarks on the "scientific model" of classical
scholarship: "The most recent work becomes the most truthful, with the exceptions either
of older views which agree with contemporary conceptualizations (hence becoming glim-
merings of truth) or which through their apparent 'error' provide a point of departure for
interpretational polemic or which offer compilations of data as yet not reedited. This ahis-
torical view of contemporary 'truth' makes classical studies akin to the natural sciences."

16. Householder and Nagy 1972b, esp. pp. 19–26, 35–36, 48–54, 62–70. In my earlier
publications, I consistently refer to this work according to the pagination of version 1972a,

propose, however, leave open-ended the need for further answers—
and questions.

The ideal in the academic discourse of my Homeric Questions is
respect for the positive efforts of others. Polemics tend to be reserved
for occasions where I countercriticize some criticisms that seem intended to displace or exclude results and views.[17] But I hope in general to transcend the kind of internal battles in classical scholarship
where the intensity of contentiousness over the rights and wrongs
of interpretation seems at times symptomatic of a specially virulent
strain of *odium philologicum,* likely to shock even the most cynical specialist in other areas of the humanities. Such marked levels of contentiousness among classicists may be excused as an indirect reflex
of the agonistic striving toward the definition of value in ancient
Hellenic poetics. Excuses should not distract, however, from a basic
shortcoming that seems to result from such strife, namely, an avoidance of new or different methods for fear of being condemned as
unorthodox. Such a pattern of avoidance can lead to narrow and
consequently oversimplified approaches to complex problems. My
goal is to apply a wide enough variety of inductive approaches to do
justice to the complexity of the problems addressed.

Failure to apply a broad enough spectrum of empirical methods
to a given question is oftentimes not recognized as a failure by the
very ones who fail. Ironically, it is sometimes they who will blame
newer scholars who may have succeeded in deploying a wider variety
of approaches. It is as if the newcomers were rival heirs to a domain
called philology. The blame can take the form of accusing newcomers of not having proved what they are seeking to prove. What the
blamers may be thereby admitting, however unintentionally, is that
they do not know how to use methods that others have found to
advance their own arguments. In this connection I am reminded of

---

because of a troublesome typographical error on p. 20 of version 1972b. Still, the latter
version is now more easily available and more often cited (e.g., Palmer 1980:72, 74, 105,
316; and Janko 1992:8 n. 2, 11 nn. 10 and 13, 16 n. 27, 17 n. 30, 303); accordingly, I will
simply correct the error at p. 20 of version 1972b (εὐρέα πόντον and εὐρὺν πόντον at
line 5, εὐρέι πόντῳ at line 6) and refer to this version hereafter.

17. An example that comes to mind is this statement by Griffin (1987:103 n. 36: "On the
phrase κλέος ἄφθιτον [*kléos áphthiton* 'imperishable fame'], on which too much has been
based, I share the reservations of Finkelberg (1986)." Cf. N 1974, which is indeed based
on the Homeric expression *kléos áphthiton* (*Iliad* 9.413). I offer some counterarguments to
Finkelberg 1986 in N 1990a:244–245 n. 126. Cf. Edwards 1985a:75–78 and Martin
1989:182–183.

8   Terry Eagleton's formulation, "Hostility to theory usually means an opposition to other people's theories and an oblivion of one's own."[18]

Yet another problem that can lead to a narrowing of resources in
pursuing Homeric Questions has to do with a negative attitude toward the study of earlier stages of Greek literature, deriving from the
inference that the further one goes back in time, the less one may really know. This attitude, as I find it articulated by some classicists,
comes dangerously close to shunning the study of older evidence on
the ground that there is not enough information to prove anything.
In resisting such a stance, I take my inspiration from a philologist
who studies Greek texts that are even older—as texts—than the Homeric poems. I quote the words of John Chadwick, as he speaks
about the Linear B tablets of the second millennium B.C.E.:

> Some of my colleagues will doubtless think I have in places gone
> too far in reconstructing a pattern which will explain the docu-
> ments. Here I can only say that some pattern must exist, for these
> are authentic, contemporary sources; and if the pattern I have pro-
> posed is the wrong one, I will cheerfully adopt a better one when it
> is offered. But what I do reject is the defeatist attitude which re-
> fuses even to devise a pattern, because all its details cannot be
> proved. The documents exist; therefore the circumstances existed
> which caused them to be written, and my experience has shown
> me that these are not altogether impossible to conjecture.[19]

In the case of the Homeric poems, it can be said even more forcefully: not only does the text exist, but even the ultimate reception of
the Homeric poems is historically attested, ready to be studied empirically. As I have already indicated, the primary given in my own
work is the *léxis*, or diction, of the Homeric poems. What, then, is the
primary question? For me, it is vital that the evidence provided by
the words, the *ipsissima verba*, reflect on the context in which the
words were said, the actual performance. The essence of performing
song and poetry, an essence permanently lost from the *paideía* that
we have inherited from the ancient Greeks, is for me the primary
question.

---

18. Eagleton 1983:viii.

19. Chadwick 1976:x.

In choosing language and text as my primary empirical given, I hope to stay within a long preexisting continuum of philologists. In choosing *performance,* the occasion of performance, as my primary question, I go beyond this continuum in relying on two other disciplines. These disciplines are linguistics and anthropology.

Let us start with linguistics. Here we can make a distinction between two kinds, descriptive and historical. In the case of descriptive linguistics, the problematic word *structuralism* tends to take pride of place in the discourse of classicists, even displacing the very use of the term *linguistics.* Too much has been said about structuralism, both for and against, by those who are unfamiliar with the rudiments of descriptive linguistics. For one who was initially trained as a linguist and only later as a classicist, the point is this: the observation that language is a structure is not a matter of theory, not someone's brilliant insight, but the cumulative result of inductive experience in descriptive linguistics.[20]

Now we turn to historical linguistics, a method that I have used extensively in my earlier work on Homer.[21] Here, too, we may confront a problematic word: this time, it is *etymology.* For example, it has been said about my approach that it "regards alleged etymologies from the distant linguistic past to be some kind of key to Homeric epic."[22] This is to underrate the value of historical linguistics in the study of tradition: the purpose of connecting the etymology of a Homeric word with its current usage in the Homeric poems is to establish *a continuum of meaning within tradition.*[23] An etymology may be a "key"

---

20. As Meillet (1925:12) points out, each linguistic fact is part of a system ("chaque fait linguistique fait partie d'un ensemble où tout se tient"). We need not expect, however, any such system to be perfect: it is fitting to recall the succinct formula of a noted American linguist and anthropologist: "All grammars leak" (Sapir 1921:38). See discussion of linguistic models in Householder and Nagy 1972b:17; also N 1990a:4–5. Few studies in Homer apply linguistics with the degree of intellectual rigor and flair that this field requires. An exception is Miller 1982a and 1982b: the author reveals a thorough grounding in linguistic theory and praxis. Here I record my own debt to my linguistics teachers, Fred Householder and Calvert Watkins; also to former students, many of whom have published monographs that apply the methods of linguistics (e.g., Bers 1974, Bergren 1975, Shannon 1975, Muellner 1976, Frame 1978, Sinos 1980, Lowenstam 1981, Martin 1983, Sacks 1987, Crane 1988, Caswell 1990, Edmunds 1990, Kelly 1990, Roth 1990, Stoddart 1990, Lowry 1991, Slatkin 1991, Vodoklys 1992, Batchelder 1994, Petropoulos 1994).

21. Especially N 1974, 1979, 1990b.

22. Taplin 1992:116 n. 12, commenting on N 1979.

23. N 1990b:20–21.

10   to the diachronic explanation of some reality, as in the case of a cultural continuum, but it cannot be equated with some clever novelty in literary criticism.[24]

As for the second of the two disciplines that I propose to apply, anthropology, I should note simply that this discipline has as yet exerted so little influence in the field of classics, with a few notable exceptions, that it is seldom mentioned even by those classicists who are given to issuing admonitions against the intrusion of supposedly alien disciplines. Ironically, the field of anthropology has as much to benefit from the currently construed field of classics as the other way around. We find ourselves in an era when the ethnographic evidence of living traditions is rapidly becoming extinct, where many thousands of years of cumulative human experience are becoming obliterated by less than a century or so of modern technological progress, and where the need to reaffirm the humanistic value of tradition in the modern world often cannot be met by the members of endangered traditional societies, who are sometimes in the forefront of embracing the very progress that threatens to obliterate their traditions. The field of classics, which lends itself to the empirical study of tradition, seems ideally suited to articulate the value of tradition in other societies, whether or not these societies are closely comparable to those of ancient Greece and Rome.

The primary Homeric question at hand, that of performance, is not only to be articulated in terms of linguistics and anthropology. It is also to be linked with the past research of two scholars whose training stemmed not directly from these two disciplines but from the classics. It is essential that I invoke these two scholars, both deceased, as we approach the centerpiece of my Homeric Questions. Their names are Milman Parry and Albert Lord. On the occasion of delivering my presidential address at the 1991 convention of the American Philological Association, I stressed what a humbling experience it was for me to be given an honor—and an opportunity—that others before me, who had their own Homeric Questions, would have deserved far more. In particular, I had in mind these two scholars, Milman Parry and Albert Lord, neither of whom was ever awarded such an honor by the American Philological Association. Parry died young, and there was little opportunity for the American Philological

---

24. See further debate in N 1994b. More below on the term *diachronic*. On traditionality as an instrument of meaning, see Slatkin 1991.

Association to recognize the lasting value of his contributions to
the study of Homer and to the field of classics in general.[25] In the
case of Albert Lord, Life Member of the American Philological Association, whose own important research continued his earlier work
with his teacher, Milman Parry, I hope to honor his contributions to
classical philology by way of my Homeric Questions, which are meant
to serve as extensions of the questions that he had asked in his
Singer of Tales[26] and, shortly before his death, in *Epic Singers and Oral
Tradition*.[27]

---

25. The collected papers of Milman Parry have been published by his son, Adam: Parry
1971.

26. Lord 1960.

27. Lord 1991. I sense that there is a special need to put on record, for the institutional
memory of the American Philological Association, the honor that is Lord's due. This need
is prompted not only by the value of his scholarship but also because, as I still remember
clearly, one particular APA presidential address, delivered in a previous year on the subject
of Homeric composition, seemed to go out of its way to slight Lord's work.

 CHAPTER 1

Homer and Questions of Oral Poetry

Parry and Lord studied oral poetry, and their work provides the key to the primary Homeric question of *performance,* as we are about to see. It can even be said that their work on oral poetry permanently changed the very nature of any Homeric question.

The term *oral poetry* may not fully capture the concept behind it, in view of the semantic difficulties conjured up by both individual words, *oral* and *poetry*. Still, the composite term *oral poetry* has a historical validity in that both Parry and Lord had used it to designate the overall concept that they were developing. I propose to continue the use of this term, with the understanding that *oral* is not simply the opposite of *written* and that the *poetry* of *oral poetry* is here meant in the broadest possible sense of the word, in that *poetry* in the context of this expression is not necessarily to be distinguished from *singing* or *song*.[1] If indeed *oral* is not to be understood simply as the opposite of *written,* it is even possible to speak of *oral literature,* a term actually used and defended by Albert Lord.[2] Where I draw the line is at the usage of "write" instead of "compose" as applied to figures like Homer. There is more to be said about this usage presently.

Pertinent to this question is a work by Ruth Finnegan, entitled "What Is Oral Literature Anyway?"[3] We may note the contentious tone in this question, as it is framed and developed by Finnegan. It

---

1. Cf. N 1990a:17–51.

2. See Lord 1991:2–3, 16. On the disadvantages of the term, see Martin (1989:4), who also quotes Herzfeld 1985b:202: "Even the recognition of folk texts as 'oral literature'. . . merely projected an elegant oxymoron: by defining textuality in terms of 'literature,' a purely verbocentric conception, it left arbitration in the control of 'high culture.' "

3. Finnegan 1976.

14 has to do with her understandable intent, as an anthropologist who specializes in African traditions, to broaden the concept of oral poetry or oral "literature" as developed by Parry and Lord in order to apply it beyond the specific instances studied by them, certainly beyond Homer and beyond Greek civilization. We may also note a downright hostile tone toward the work of Parry and Lord when the same sort of question is invoked by some classicists who seek not a broader application of the term *oral poetry* but rather a discontinuation of any application at all in the case of Homer, let alone any later Greek literature. I write this in an era when scholarly works are produced with titles like *Homer: Beyond Oral Poetry.*[4]

The question of formulating the dichotomy of oral and written seems to me in any case irrelevant to another question, whether Homeric poetry can actually refer to writing. It seems to me self-evident that even an oral tradition can refer to a written tradition without necessarily being influenced by it. I should add in this regard my own conviction that Homeric poetry does indeed refer to the technology of writing, and that such references in no way require us to assume that writing was used for the creation of Homeric poetry. The most striking example is the mention of a diptych containing "baneful signs" (*sēmata lugrá*) that Bellerophon is carrying to the king of Lycia (*Iliad* 6.168, 176, 178).[5] Another example, to be discussed later on, is a reference made by Homeric poetry to the wording of an imagined epigram commemorating a fallen warrior (*Iliad* 7.89–90).[6]

Having considered the implications of *oral poetry,* let us move to a more precise term, *oral traditional poetry.* I propose to use the concept of *tradition* or *traditional* in conjunction with *oral poetry* in such a way as to focus on the perception of tradition by the given society in which the given tradition operates, not on any perception by the outside observer who is looking in, as it were, on the given tradition. My approach to *tradition* is intended to avoid any situations where "the term is apparently also used (and manipulated?) in an emotive sense, not seldom linked with deeply felt and powerful academic,

---

4. Bremer, de Jong, and Kalff 1987.

5. N 1990b:207. For an archaeological attestation of a writing tablet in the format of a diptych made of boxwood, with ivory hinge, dated to the late fourteenth or early thirteenth century B.C.E., see Bass 1990.

6. See p. 36 below.

moral, or political values."[7] Whereas a given tradition may be perceived in absolute terms within a given society, it can be analyzed in relative terms by the outside observer using empirical criteria: what may seem ancient and immutable to members of a given society can in fact be contemporary and ever-changing from the standpoint of empiricist observation.[8] Moreover, I recognize that tradition is not just an inherited system: as with language itself, tradition comes to life in the here-and-now of real people in real situations.[9] A particularly compelling example of the changeability of tradition is the case of orally transmitted genealogies among the Tiv of Nigeria:

> Early British administrators among the Tiv of Nigeria were aware of the great importance attached to these genealogies, which were continually discussed in court cases where the rights and duties of one man towards another were in dispute. Consequently they took the trouble to write down the long lists of names and preserve them for posterity, so that future administrators might refer to them in giving judgement. Forty years later, when the Bohannans carried out anthropological field work in the area, their successors were still using the same genealogies. However, these written pedigrees now gave rise to many disagreements; the Tiv maintained that they were incorrect, while the officials regarded them as statements of fact, as records of what had actually happened, and could not agree that the unlettered indigenes could be better informed about the past than their own literate predecessors. What neither party realized was that in any society of this kind changes take place which require a constant readjustment in the genealogies if they are to continue to carry out their function as mnemonics of social relationships.[10]

---

7. Finnegan 1991:106.

8. It is from this perspective that I have used the word *tradition* in my previous work as well, e.g., N 1979:3, and more explicitly in N 1990a:57–61, 70–72 (cf. pp. 349, 411). *Pace* Peradotto 1990:100 n. 2. I would add the observation, derived from my reference to my own work just given, that there can be different levels of rigidity or flexibility in different traditions, even in different phases of the same given tradition. Also, that there are situations where the empirical methods of disciplines such as linguistics can be applied to determine what aspects of a given tradition are older or newer.

9. Cf. N 1990a:17 n. 2, with bibliography on the useful concepts of *parole* and *langue*.

10. Goody and Watt 1968:32, following the work of Bohannan 1952; cf. Morris 1986:87. Further discussion can be found in Jensen 1980:98–99 and Thomas 1989:178–179 n. 58 and 188 n. 85.

16   In sum, there is certainly no need to think of tradition as rigid and unchanging. Still, there is a need to develop empirical criteria for determining what is older and what is newer within tradition, and for the past twenty years or so I have been publishing works that apply historical linguistics as well as other approaches for the purpose of coming to terms with the archaeology, as it were, of tradition. This is just the opposite of romanticizing tradition as a concept.[11] The aim, rather, is to study tradition empirically, and thereby to determine objectively both what is being preserved and what is being changed.

I approach my Homeric Questions by applying the concept of oral traditional poetry to Homer. For this purpose, I find it essential to introduce an inventory of ten further concepts. Each of these ten concepts derives from the necessity of having to confront the reality of performance in oral poetry, either directly in living oral traditions or indirectly in texts that reveal clear traces of such traditions. The centrality of performance to the concept of oral poetry will become apparent as the discussion proceeds.

Some of the terms used in the inventory that follows will be new to those who have not worked with oral poetry. Most of these terms I have taken from the disciplines of linguistics and anthropology. Other concepts that I use may be traditional for classicists but still require some reassessment in terms of oral poetry.

1. FIELDWORK

The fundamental empirical given for the study of oral poetry is the procedure of collecting evidence about the *performance* of living oral traditions as recorded, observed, and described in their native setting. Let us call this procedure fieldwork.[12] "Although much talked about in negative criticism," Lord says in his introduction to *Epic Singers and Oral Tradition,* "living oral-traditional literature is still not very well known, and I try over and over again in the course of this book to acquaint the reader with some of the best of what I have had the privilege to experience and to demonstrate the details of its excellence."[13] Lord spoke from experience,

---

11. *Pace* Lloyd-Jones (1992:57), who claims that my approach romanticizes tradition; his arguments have been anticipated by the counterarguments in N 1990a:1.

12. For an enlightening introduction to the term, see Nettl 1983:6–7, 9.

13. Lord 1991:2.

and this background of experience is his fieldwork. It is this background that confers on him an authority that the vast majority of his critics who are classicists utterly lack. Paradoxically, Lord's modesty about his experience in fieldwork, which is a salient feature of his scholarship, is matched by the arrogance displayed by those of his critics who at times seem to take a grim sort of pride in their unfamiliarity with nonclassical forms of poetry like the South Slavic oral traditions. It is as if such marvels of the so-called Western world as the Homeric poems should be rescued from those who truly understand the workings of oral traditions. Lord's *Epic Singers and Oral Tradition* lays claim, once and for all, to the legitimacy and importance of exploring the heritage of "Western" literature in oral traditional literature.

2. SYNCHRONY VERSUS DIACHRONY

The terms *synchrony* and *diachrony* come from linguistics.[14] Fieldwork in the study of oral poetry as it is performed requires a synchronic perspective, for purposes of describing the actual system perpetuated by the tradition. When it comes to delving into the principles of organization underlying the tradition, that is, the reality of cultural continuity, the diachronic perspective is also needed. Techniques of linguistic reconstruction can help explain otherwise opaque aspects of the language as it is current in the tradition: that is to say, the diachronic approach is needed to supplement the synchronic, as well as vice versa.[15]

3. COMPOSITION-IN-PERFORMANCE

The synchronic analysis of living oral traditions reveals that composition and performance are in varying degrees aspects of one process. The Homeric text, of and by itself, could never have revealed such a reality. The fundamental statement is by Lord: "An oral poem is composed not *for* but *in* performance."[16]

---

14. For a useful summary, with bibliography, see Ducrot and Todorov 1979:137–144; cf. N 1990a:4.

15. N 1990b:20–21.

16. Lord 1960:28. My use of the term *performance* is not intended to convey any connotations of a stage presence, as it were, on the part of the performer. I have in mind rather the *performative* dimension of an utterance, as analyzed from an anthropological perspective. For a pragmatic application of the word *performative,* see, for example, Tambiah 1985: 123–166. Cf. Martin 1989:231: "authoritative self-presentation to an audience."

4. DIFFUSION

Both synchronic and diachronic perspectives reveal this aspect of oral tradition, interactive with the aspects of composition and performance. Patterns of diffusion can be either centrifugal or centripetal. (See the discussion in Chapter 2.) [17]

5. THEME

For purposes of this presentation, a working definition of *theme* is *a basic unit of content.*[18]

6. FORMULA

Another working definition, to be debated at length in the discussion that follows: the *formula* is *a fixed phrase conditioned by the traditional themes of oral poetry.*[19] The formula is to the form as the theme is to the content.[20] This formulation presupposes that form and content conceptually overlap. Parry's own definition is worded as follows: the formula is "a group of words which is regularly employed under the same metrical conditions to express a given essential idea."[21]

7. ECONOMY (THRIFT)

As Parry argues, Homeric language tends to be "free of phrases which, having the same metrical value *and expressing the same idea,* could replace one another."[22] This principle of *economy* or *thrift* is an observable reality on the level of performance.[23]

---

17. The word will not be used in the sense of a "diffusionist" approach, familiar to linguists and folklorists.

18. Cf. N 1990b:9 n. 10, following Lord 1960:68–98; for an altered working definition, see Lord 1991:26–27.

19. N 1990b:29.

20. Cf. Lord 1991:73–74.

21. Parry 1930 [1971:272].

22. Parry 1930 [1971:276] (italics mine).

23. N 1990b:24, following Lord 1960:53.

8. TRADITION VERSUS INNOVATION

To repeat, oral tradition comes to life in performance, and the here-and-now of each new performance is an opportunity for innovation, whether or not any such innovation is explicitly acknowledged in the tradition.[24]

9. UNITY AND ORGANIZATION

In terms of oral poetics, the unity and organization of the Homeric poems is a *result* of the *performance* tradition itself, not a *cause* effected by a *composer* who is above tradition.[25] (Related concepts are unitarians versus analysts, and neoanalysts.)

10. AUTHOR AND TEXT

In terms of oral poetics, authorship is determined by the authority of performance and textuality, by the degree of a composition's invariability from performance to performance. The very concept of text can be derived metaphorically from the concept of composition-in-performance.[26]

In the wake of this inventory of ten concepts that I find essential for approaching my Homeric Questions, I also offer, before proceeding any further, a list of ten examples of usage that I find commonly being applied in misleading ways by some contemporary experts in Homeric poetry. My aim is not to quarrel with anyone in particular but rather to promote more precise usage concerning oral poetics in general. The sequence of the following ten examples of what strikes me as misleading usage corresponds roughly to the sequence of the preceding inventory of ten crucial concepts pertaining to oral poetics.

1. "Oral theory."

It is a major misunderstanding, I submit, to speak of "the oral theory" of Milman Parry or Albert Lord. Parry and Lord had investigated the

24. Cf. N 1990a:55–56.

25. N 1979:6–7.

26. N 1990a:53; see further discussion below. It is hazardous to retroject to the ancient world our contemporary notions of the "author"—notably the *individual* author. On the semantic problems of retrojecting our notions of the individual, see Held 1991.

20 *empirical reality* of oral poetry, as ascertained from the living traditions of South Slavic oral poetry as well as other living traditions. The existence of oral poetry is a fact, ascertained by way of fieldwork. The application of what we know inductively about oral poetry to the text of the *Iliad* and the *Odyssey*, or to any other text, is not an attempt to prove a "theory" about oral poetry. If we are going to use the word *theory* at all in such a context, it would be more reasonable to say that Parry and Lord had various *theories* about the affinity of Homeric poetry with what we know about oral poetry.

2. "The world of Homer."

To say in Homeric criticism that the "world" or "worldview" that emerges from the structure of the *Iliad* and the *Odyssey* is the construct of one man at one time and place, or however many men from however many different times and places, risks the flattening out of the process of oral poetic creation, which requires analysis in the dimensions of both diachrony and synchrony.[27] This caveat is relevant to the question of whether the overall perspective of Homeric poetry is grounded in, say, an age dating back to before the middle of the thirteenth century B.C.E. or, alternatively, in the eighth century B.C.E.[28]

3. "Homer + [verb]."

To say in Homeric criticism that "Homer does this" or "the poet intends that" can lead to problems. Not necessarily, but it can.

---

27. A model for a combined synchronic and diachronic approach is Sherratt 1990. Reacting to Martin's application (1989:7–10), with regard to the problem of Homeric composition/performance, of a wide range of comparative evidence about different kinds of performer-audience interaction, Griffin (1991:5) invokes "the unambiguous evidence, on the subject of Homeric performance, of the Homeric poems," referring to the descriptions of performances like those of Phemios in *Odyssey* 1. One response is to ask this question: how exactly are such performances as those of Phemios "Homeric"? In other words, how does the Homeric representation of poetry correspond to the essence of Homeric poetry itself? Can we simply assume that there is no gap between the two kinds of "poetry"? The results of my own study of the question suggest that there is indeed a gap (see especially N 1990a:21, 14, where I develop the concept of "diachronic skewing").

28. On the world of Homeric poetry in the second millennium B.C.E., see Vermeule 1986, esp. p. 85 n. 28. For the perspective of the eighth century B.C.E., see Morris 1986. Commenting on Moses Finley's title, *The World of Odysseus* (1977), Catenacci (1993:21) suggests that a more apt title would be *The Possible World of Odysseus*, citing further bibliography on theories of "possible worlds."

Granted, such usage corresponds to the spirit of conventional Greek references to the creation of epic poetry by Homer. For the ancient Greeks, however, Homer was not just the creator of epic par excellence: he was also the culture hero of epic itself.[29] Greek institutions tend to be traditionally retrojected, by the Greeks themselves, each to a protocreator, a culture hero who is credited with the sum total of a given cultural institution.[30] It was a common practice to attribute any major achievement of society, even if this achievement may have been realized only through a lengthy period of social evolution, to the episodic and personal accomplishment of a culture hero who is pictured as having made his monumental contribution in an earlier era of the given society.[31] Greek myths about lawgivers, for example, whether the lawgivers are historical figures or not, tend to reconstruct these figures as the originators of the sum total of customary law as it evolved through time.[32] So also with Homer: he is retrojected as the original genius of epic.[33]

Thus the usage of saying that "Homer does this" or "the poet intends that" may become risky for modern experts if they start thinking of "Homer" in overly personalized terms, without regard for the traditional dynamics of composition and performance, *and* without regard for synchrony and diachrony.[34] To say that "Homer wrote" is the ultimate risk.

Suffice it to note for now that the generic characterizations of Homer and other early poets seem to be a traditional function of the

---

29. N 1990a:78–81. On the meaning of *Hómēros*, see Chapter 3, pp. 89–90.

30. Cf. Kleingünther 1933.

31. For an illuminating discussion of culture heroes in Chinese traditions, see Raphals 1992:53: Yi invents the bow; Zhu, armor; Xi Zhong, the carriage, Qiao Chui, the boat.

32. N 1985:33, and N 1990a:170, 368.

33. Cf. N 1990a:55, especially with reference to Plato *Ion* 533d–536d. In the Homeric *Hymn to Apollo*, the dramatized first-person speaker claims the identity of Homer: see the detailed discussion in N 1990a:375–377 (expanding on N 1979:8–9) and N 1990b:54 (cf. Clay 1989:53 with n. 111 and p. 55 with n. 116).

34. Carey (1992:285) argues that, "in his approach to Greek literature in general, Nagy overemphasizes the tradition at the expense of the individual." I would counterargue that my approach gives due credit to tradition in contexts where many contemporary classicists overemphasize the individual poet at the expense of tradition: see especially N 1990a: 79–80.

22   poetry that represents them. This is not to say that the poetic tradition actually creates the poet; rather, the tradition has the capacity to transform even historical figures into generic characters who represent and are represented by the tradition.[35] We may recall the formulation of Paul Zumthor: "Le poète est situé dans son langage plutôt que son langage en lui."[36]

4. "Homer's poetry is artistically superior to all other poetry of his time."

The preeminence of the *Iliad* and the *Odyssey* as the definitive epics of the Greeks is a historical fact, at least by the fifth century. Or, as can be argued, it is a historical eventuality. The attribution of their preeminence, however, to artistic superiority over other epics is merely an assumption. What little evidence we have about other epics comes from the fragments and ancient plot-outlines of the so-called Cycle. If the poetry of the Cycle were fully attested, it is quite possible that we would conclude that the *Iliad* and the *Odyssey* are indeed artistically superior. The question, however, might still remain: by whose standards? The more basic question is not *why* but *how* the *Iliad* and the *Odyssey* became preeminent.[37] One available answer, explored further below, is based on the concept of greater *diffusion* for the epic traditions of the *Iliad* and the *Odyssey* in comparison to other epic traditions.

5. "The formula made the poet say it that way."

Such a requirement of oral poetry is often assumed, without justification, by both proponents and opponents of the idea that Homeric poetry is based on oral poetry. I disagree. To assume that whatever is being meant in Homeric poetry is determined by such formal considerations as formula or meter (as when experts say that the formula or meter made the poet say this or that) is to misunderstand the relationship of form and content in oral poetics. Diachronically,

---

35. N 1990a:79, in response to Griffith 1983:58 n. 82.

36. Zumthor 1972:68.

37. N 1990a:72 and n. 99, with bibliography.

the content—let us call it *theme*—determines the form, even if the   23
form affects the content synchronically.[38]

6. "The meter made the poet say it that way."

I suggest that this kind of reasoning stems from misunderstandings
of Parry's definition of the formula as "a group of words which is regularly employed under the same metrical conditions to express a
given essential idea," which I have already quoted above. I have written at length about the relationship of formula and meter, and I start
here by repeating my central argument that formula shaped meter,
from a diachronic point of view, rather than the other way around.[39]

A convenient way to examine any possible misunderstandings
about the relationship between formula and meter is to consider
the attempted refutation of Parry's concept of the formula in Ruth
Finnegan's book on oral poetry.[40] Ironically, Finnegan's book seems
to be misreading Parry's concept at the very point where it attempts
to undermine its validity. In her description of Homeric epithets,
Finnegan says that they "are often combined with other formulaic
phrases—repeated word-groups—which have the right metrical qualities to fit the [given] part of the line."[41] She adduces the words of
Parry himself: "In composing [the poet] will do no more than put together for his needs phrases which he has often heard or used himself, and which, grouping themselves *in accordance with a fixed pattern
of thought* [italics mine], come naturally to make the sentence and
the verse."[42]

As one critic has noticed, "We see here that Parry is saying much
more than Finnegan."[43] The formula is "not just a phrase that the
poet is free to choose according to his metrical needs, since the for-

---

38. See a detailed discussion in N 1990b:18–35, explaining the results of N 1974.

39. N 1990b:18–35.

40. Finnegan 1977.

41. Ibid., 59.

42. Parry 1930 [1971:270].

43. Davidson 1994:62.

24   mulas are regulated by the traditional themes of the poet's composition."[44] By contrast, as this critic has pointed out,[45] Finnegan assumes that formulas have a life independent of themes: "*As well as* formulaic phrases and sequences [italics mine], the bard has in his repertoire a number of set themes which he can draw on to form the structure of his poem."[46] The assumption here is that formulas are merely stock phrases repeated simply to fill metrical needs: the oral poet "can select what he wishes from the common stock of formulae, and can choose slightly different terms that fit his metre . . . and vary the details."[47] Such a definition overvalues traditional form and undervalues, in contrast to the views of Parry and Lord, the role of traditional content.[48] Using the premise that formulas are simply a matter of repeated phraseology that fits the meter, Finnegan faults the Parry-Lord approach to oral poetry: "Does it really add to our understanding of the style or process of composition in a given piece to name certain repeated patterns of words, sounds or meanings as 'formulae'? Or to suggest that the characteristic of oral style is that such formulae are 'all-pervasive' (as in Lord [1960]:47)?"[49] In light of what can be adduced from the writings of Parry and Lord, however, Finnegan's criticism seems unfounded.

If we may understand the formula as "the building-block of a system of traditional oral poetic expression,"[50] then it seems no longer

---

44. Ibid., in response to the claims of Finnegan 1977:62 about the metrical conditioning of formulas. On the relationship of formula and meter, see N 1990b:18–35; cf. Lord 1991:73–74. For further criticism of Finnegan's interpretation of Parry's understanding of the formula, see Miller 1982b:32.

45. Davidson 1994:62.

46. Finnegan 1977:64.

47. Ibid., 62.

48. See Davidson 1994:60–62 and N 1990b:18–35; cf. Lord 1991:73–74. For a wide-ranging critique of various definitions of the formula, with special reference to Austin 1975 (11–80), Finnegan 1977 (54–55, 73–86), Kiparsky 1976, and Nagler 1974 (23), see Miller 1982a:35–48. (I leave open, however, the question of whether or not there was a distinct Aeolic phase in the development of Homeric diction.)

49. Finnegan 1977:71.

50. Davidson 1994:62.

reasonable to find fault with Lord's observation that formulas are "all-pervasive" in oral poetry.[51]

7. "The poet had only one way of saying it."

Once again, such a requirement of oral poetry is often assumed, without justification, by both proponents and opponents. But the principle of economy or thrift is a tendency, not a constant, as I have argued in earlier work.[52]

8. "Homer had a new way of saying it."

This is a specific instance of number 3 above. Granted, to the extent that the performer controls or "owns" the performance in conjunction with the audience, the opportunity for innovation is there. Such innovation, however, takes place within the tradition, not beyond it. Given that performance itself is a key aspect of oral tradition, and that tradition comes to life in the context of performance and in the person of the performer, I disagree with those who concentrate so much on the person that they forget about the tradition in which that person performs—a tradition that can be inductively observed from the rules inherent even in the context of performance.[53] As in

---

51. Martin (1989:92) observes: "Only a deracinated, print culture would view Homeric formulas as devices to aid the composition of poetry." Rather, formulas "belong to the 'composition', if you like, of personal identity in a traditional world" (ibid.). All this is not to say that we cannot find gaps in Parry's argumentation. For an attempt at pinpointing such gaps, I cite the subtle arguments of Lynn-George 1988:55–81. The issues raised by Lynn-George call for an Auseinandersetzung, the scope of which would surpass what is being attempted in this presentation.

52. N 1990b:24 (first written in 1976). See also Martin 1989:8 n. 30 disputing Shive 1987 on the questions of *economy* and *extension*. I notice that Janko (1982:24) uses the expression "the tendency to economy" in the following formulation: "The tendency to economy is only properly applied within the poetry of the same composer, and even there, as Edwards has shown [Janko (p. 241 n. 16) cites Edwards 1971: Ch. 5], it was less strict than has been thought." Actually, the more basic point is that the principle of economy is to be observed on the level of *individual performance:* Lord 1960:53–54; cf. Lord 1991:73–74. For a demonstration of the remarkable degrees of economy in Homeric composition, see also Visser 1987, who shows that each of twenty-five expressions for "he killed" in the *Iliad* occupies a distinct metrical slot.

53. Again, N 1990a:79. There are, of course, areas where rules do not apply, inviting free variation. I borrow the concept of *free variant* from the field of descriptive linguistics. This concept is particularly useful for describing those aspects of tradition where innovation is

the case of number 3, the risk is to make "Homer" overly personalized, without regard for the traditional dynamics of composition and performance, *and* without regard for synchrony and diachrony.

9. "The poem is so obviously unified and organized that the poet must have become somehow emancipated from the oral tradition."

Such a reaction stems from descriptions of oral poetry in terms of *improvisation* (or *extemporization*)—terms that can easily be misunderstood. To many, for example, such terms suggest that "anything goes." A most useful response, with vigorous criticism of a wide variety of misunderstandings, is the work of D. Gary Miller.[54] His key argument is this: "Mental operations 'generate' as little as possible; they search for stored expressions of varying degrees of suitability to the speaker's goal."[55] Also valuable is his refutation of the following three common assumptions about "improvising oral poets":

1. "Oral poets do not plan."

2. "Oral poetry is characterized by a 'loose,' unorganized structure."

3. "An oral poet could not see the whole epic sequence in the beginning."[56]

---

most likely to take place (thanks to Loukia Athanassaki, Dec. 30, 1990); see also Martin 1989:151 n. 16.

54. Miller 1982b:5–8.

55. Ibid., 7.

56. These three assumptions are restated and then refuted by Miller (1982b:90–91). I agree with Miller (p. 46) that "much paper has been wasted" on the "pseudo-issue" of "whether improvisation-composition involves memorization or not" (he provides bibliography), "partly out of misunderstanding Lord, and partly out of misconceptions about the nature of language in general and improvisation in particular." For more on the pitfalls of using the concept of memorization, see Lord 1991:236–237. I am sympathetic, however, to the idea of a dichotomy of improvisation versus memorization as discussed by Jensen 1980:13, provided that the two terms are used in a diachronic context, referring respectively to relatively more fluid versus more static phases of oral tradition. On the distinction of fluid versus static phases, see pp. 41, 111 below.

Refusing to consider the possibility that there are principles of unity and organization at work in a living oral tradition is symptomatic of a lack of appreciation for oral tradition itself, with emphasis on the word *tradition*. There is a common pattern of thinking that serves to compensate for this lack: it is manifested in the assumption that the poet must have somehow broken free of oral tradition. This assumption entails an unquestioning elevation of a reconstructed single individual to the rank of a genius or at least a transcendent author, who can then be given all or most of the credit for any observable principles of unity and organization.[57] Unity and coherence may be the *effect* of something traditional, rather than the *cause* of something untraditional.[58]

10. "Homer wrote."

This is the most extreme version of the reaction described in number 9. This way of thinking, as I will argue below, does not stem solely from a lack of firsthand knowledge about oral poetry. Those who make this claim, or those who simply make this assumption, have conceptualized authorship without having first thought through the historical realities of the era that produced Homeric poetry.

Having come to the end of this list of ten examples of what I consider misleading usage concerning oral poetics, let us return to the primary question of my Homeric Questions, concerning *performance*. For me, the key element in the triad of composition, performance, and diffusion will throughout be the second. Without performance, oral tradition is not oral. Without performance, tradition is no longer the same. Without performance, the very idea of Homer loses its integrity. More than that, the very essence of the classics becomes incomplete.

---

57. The concepts of *unity* and *single author* are not necessarily the same thing. I can justify, at least in terms of my "evolutionary model," to be discussed below, the doubts expressed by Sealey (1957:330) about a "single author" of the *Iliad* and the *Odyssey*—as if he were a historical reality. Still, I have no doubts that the *notion* of such a single author was indeed a historical reality in the ancient world. Further, I will argue that this notion was connected with the notion of a unified and singular corpus of heroic poetry.

58. N 1979:41, 78–79. On unity and coherence in the structure of evolving institutions like the Olympics, cf. ibid., 7.

 Chapter 2

An Evolutionary Model for the Making of Homeric Poetry

The massive accumulation of new or newly appreciated comparative evidence about the nature of epic in oral poetry demands application to the ongoing study of individual epic traditions. I propose here to apply some of this evidence, as collected over recent years by a broad variety of experts investigating an array of societies in Eastern Europe, Central Asia, the Indian subcontinent, and Africa, to the study of Homer in general and the Homeric *Iliad* and *Odyssey* in particular. From the start, I stress the importance of the comparative evidence of the South Slavic tradition of epic in Eastern Europe: though it is different in many ways from what we see in the Homeric poems, this tradition, as Richard P. Martin argues, "still has a claim to being one of the best comparanda."[1]

In earlier work, my starting point has been the central comparative insight of Milman Parry and Albert Lord, gleaned from their fieldwork in South Slavic oral epic traditions, that *composition* and *performance* are aspects of the same process in the making of Homeric poetry.[2] Let us continue to call this process *composition-in-performance*. Starting with the comparative evidence about composition-in-performance, I added the internal Greek evidence about the early *diffusion* of the *Iliad* and the *Odyssey* in the archaic period of Greece, positing

---

1. Martin 1989:150. Cf. Miller 1982b:26: "To avoid further absurd comparisons [criticized in Miller's previous paragraph; even more vigorous criticism at p. 97 in his book], Homer must be compared with epic poems from typologically and culturally similar epic traditions that share the characteristics of the Homeric texts, and *all of Homer's improvised oral characteristics must be considered together simultaneously.*" See also Miller 1982b:98–99. On Miller's use of the term *improvise*, see Chapter 1, note 56 above.

2. See in general Lord, *The Singer of Tales* (1960), whose formulations represent the legacy of his own fieldwork and the earlier work of Parry (collected papers, published 1971).

30   a model for the development of Homeric poetry that requires not
       two but three interacting aspects of production: *composition, perfor-*
       mance, and *diffusion.*[3] Here I move on to apply comparative evidence
       for the interaction of composition, performance, and diffusion in at-
       tested living oral epic traditions.

       My original reasons for concentrating on the role of diffusion-in-
       performance in the development of Homeric poetry had to do with
       the need to reconcile the comparative insight of Parry and Lord
       about composition-in-performance with the historical reality of an
       integral and unified Homeric *text* inherited from the ancient world.
       How the concept of diffusion helps to account for Homeric textuality
       is a question that will be taken up presently. But first, let us consider
       the implications of the historical "given," the survival of the Homeric
       text.

       For some classicists, the very nature of this written text has been a
       source of extreme skepticism concerning the validity of applying
       comparative insights about oral poetics. It is the opinion of not a few
       of these skeptics that the artistry, cohesiveness, and sheer monumen-
       tality of the *Iliad* and the *Odyssey* rule out the role of oral poetics—
       and supposedly prove that such marvels of artistic achievement must
       have required the technology of writing.[4] There are others who even
       go so far as to argue that Greek alphabetical writing was devised pri-
       marily for the purpose of writing down Homeric poetry.[5] Such at-
       titudes toward Homeric poetry tend to be associated with a more
       general view, shared by some anthropologists, that writing is the basic
       prerequisite for a major breakthrough in human cognitive capacity,
       providing the key impetus toward creative thinking and critical judg-

       ---

       3. N 1981; see further argumentation in N 1979:5–9 and N 1990a:53–55, 79–80.

       4. A notable example is the son of Milman Parry: Adam Parry, "Have We Homer's *Iliad?*"
       (1966); for a critique, see Jensen 1980:90–92. For further criticism of such views, cf.
       Taplin 1992:36. As my discussion proceeds, it will become clear that I agree with the rea-
       soning of Miller (1982a:8), who concludes: "The distant symmetry (including intricate
       verbal parallelisms), frequently adduced as evidence for a written composition (e.g.,
       Kiparsky 1976:103ff.; Goold 1977:32ff.), is irrelevant." See also Miller 1982b:100.

       5. Wade-Gery 1952:13–14. Cf. Robb 1978. For a critique of such arguments, see Harris
       (1989:45 n. 3), who also warns in particular against the "fallacy" of assuming "that early
       texts were not utilitarian because the earliest surviving texts are not." For an ambitious new
       attempt to connect Homer and the alphabet, see Powell 1991.

ment.[6] For such skeptics, then, oral poetry and literacy are clearly incompatible.

For other skeptics, oral poetry may not after all be incompatible with literacy, provided we assume that the art of oral poetry became appropriated altogether by the art of written poetry. This way, we may allow for an oral heritage in the Homeric tradition, but whatever we admire as high art in this tradition must still be attributed to literate authorship.[7]

Either way, whether or not oral poetry is supposed to be compatible with literacy, both these lines of skeptical thinking avoid the comparative insight of Parry and Lord about composition-in-performance, and they assume either explicitly or implicitly that the technology of writing was key to the composition of the actual Homeric text. My own position is that there is no proof that the technology of alphabetic writing was needed for either the composition or the performance of the Homeric poems.[8]

Given that the poetry of the *Iliad* and the *Odyssey* has indeed survived as a written text, Albert Lord offered a solution for retaining the model of composition-in-performance by postulating that these poems had been dictated.[9] There have been recent attempts to extend this dictation theory,[10] but they run into problems when it

---

6. For an explicit formulation of this view by an anthropologist, see Goody 1977:37 (also Goody and Watt 1968). For a critique of Goody's formulation, see Harris (1989:40–42), who distances himself from "woolly and grandiose" conceptualizations of writing as the key to human rationality (p. 41). For a further critique, see Thomas 1989:25.

7. See, for example, Griffin 1980:xii–xiv. A variation on this kind of outlook is the notion of a mode of composition that is *transitional* between oral and literate. For bibliography on this notion of a transitional text, with counterarguments, see Jensen 1980:89–92, expanding on the arguments of Lord 1960:129, 135–138, 154–156.

8. N 1990a:18; also pp. 8–9, 53–55, 79–80. Cf. Janko 1982:188: "If we accept, as I believe we should, that writing played no part in the *composition* (as opposed to the recording) of the Homeric and Hesiodic poems . . ."; he leaves room, however, for the possibility that writing was used for *performance* (for example, p. 276 n. 1).

9. The premier formulation of the "dictation theory" is Lord 1953; rewritten, with minimal changes, in Lord 1991:38–48 (with an "Addendum 1990" at pp. 47–48). The significance of this work was recognized by Sealey (1957:328–329).

10. See especially M. L. West 1990. Cf. Janko 1982:191: "It is difficult to refuse the conclusion that the texts [the Homeric epics] were fixed at the time when each was composed,

32 comes to explaining the early diffusion of what we now describe as the *Iliad* and the *Odyssey* in archaic Greece on both sides of the Aegean—a process that some claim was already under way as early as the fourth quarter of the seventh century before our era.[11] Any pattern of diffusion, if indeed it is to be put at so early a date, can hardly be ascribed to a hypothetical proliferation of a plethora of manuscripts, in view of the existing physical limitations on materials available for writing down, let alone circulating, compositions of such monumental size as the *Iliad* or *Odyssey*.[12] We must also reckon with the rudimentary status of writing as a technology in that period of Greek history.[13]

One solution is to imagine a situation where a single hypothetical dictated text becomes the prized possession of a special group of performers.[14] Although this modified dictation theory offers some advantages in retaining the factor of performance, there are major problems with it. For one thing, it leaves unexplained a basic question: how exactly was such a dictated text supposed to be used for the process of performance? How could a dictated text automatically become a script, a prompt, for the performer who dictated it, let alone for any other performer? In fact, such a solution does not even mesh with Albert Lord's actual experience with the phenomenon of dicta-

---

whether by rote memorisation or by oral dictated texts." Earlier applications include Jensen 1980:92. For a critical reassessment of dictation theories as they are applied to Near Eastern texts, see Hillers and McCall 1976.

11. For a formulation of such an extent of diffusion, see M. L. West 1990:33. M. L. West (1988:152) sets the terminus post quem at about 630, apparently following the lead of Friis Johansen 1967, who applies the testimony of archaic Greek art concerning narrative traditions that are comparable to what we find in the Homeric *Iliad*. At p. 84, Friis Johansen concludes that "Corinthian and Argive artists were well versed in the *Iliad* at least from around 625, not merely in selected sections, but in the entire poem." In the discussion that follows, I will argue that the iconographic evidence from the archaic period refers to epic *traditions*, including Iliadic and Odyssean traditions, but not to *written texts*.

12. For a realistic assessment of the available historical facts concerning the first 250-odd years of attested alphabetic literacy in archaic Greece, see Harris 1989:46–47, esp. p. 46: "For many generations, written texts were employed for a very limited range of purposes and by a very limited number of people." Cf. Jensen 1980:94. Pioneering works in the study of ancient Greek literacy are Havelock 1963 and 1982.

13. Again, Harris 1989:46.

14. So M. L. West 1990:34.

tion in the context of genuine living oral traditions, where the writing down of any given composition-in-performance in effect *eliminates* the performability of that particular composition. In terms of such a modified dictation theory, moreover, the technology of writing has to be invoked not only for the performance of the *Iliad* and the *Odyssey* but even for the ultimate composition of these poems, to the extent that the text is imagined to achieve its status as text at the very moment that dictation transforms a composition-in-performance into a script, as it were.

Lord's original theory of Homeric dictation does not leave room for the use of the dictated text as a mnemonic device for future performances by the singer who dictated it. Lord himself puts it this way: "Someone may suggest that it [writing] would be a mnemonic device, but this too is unrealistic. The singer has no need of a mnemonic device in a manner of singing that was designed to fill his needs without such written aids."[15] Following Lord's reasoning, Raphael Sealey argues that "the singers would hardly feel the slightest obligation to keep to the written text."[16] Sealey goes on to reject the notion of such a written text, to which he refers as a hypothetical "bardic text": he argues that, if a composition like the *Iliad* had been preserved by way of "bardic texts" in the eighth century, then it would have been preserved "by inferior poets."[17] "But audiences would surely prefer better poets," he concludes, "and a poem preserved primarily in 'bardic texts' would be likely to perish for want of popularity."[18] Reflecting on the observations made by Albert Lord about actual dictations taken in fieldwork from the South Slavic oral epic traditions,[19] Minna Skafte Jensen argues along similar lines:

> There is no reason to think that later performances of the "same" songs [underwent an influence from] the dictation in any way differing from the influence exerted by other, previous performances

15. Lord 1953 [1991:44].

16. Sealey 1957:329. Sealey (at p. 328 n. 59) actually cites Lord's 1953 article proposing the "dictation theory."

17. Sealey 1957:330.

18. Ibid.

19. Lord, in his introduction to Parry, Lord, and Bynum 1974:8–9.

of the poems. The idea that the ancient oral poet felt the written
version to be a specially important thing, to be kept afterwards,
seems to me to be culturally anachronistic, expressive of the literate person's overestimation of the importance of writing.[20]

I agree with this line of reasoning, at least as far as it applies to the
eighth or seventh century, the period of Homeric dictation according to the dictation theory as we have seen it formulated so far. As we
will find, however, attitudes toward the technology of writing in later
periods may well have changed, so that a written version, though not
necessarily a dictated version, may indeed in the course of time have
come to be perceived as "a specially important thing."

It is not so much that the use of a text as a prompt for performance is unimaginable, *once such a text exists.*[21] But an even more basic question is, how would such a hypothetical text be conceived in
eighth- or seventh-century Greece, that is, at the earliest stages in the
history of this new technology of alphabetic writing? Also, how would
we imagine that such a text ever achieved its status as text, starting
from the very moment that dictation supposedly transformed a composition-in-performance into a transcript, as it were? I ask these questions because, in terms of some current formulations of a dictation
theory, the technology of alphabetic writing has to be invoked not
only for the performance of the *Iliad* and the *Odyssey,* but even for
the ultimate composition of these poems, to the extent that dictation
supposedly creates a basic text.[22]

There are also problems with the very concept of a transcript, a
script, or a prompt supposedly coming into being in the eighth or
seventh century B.C.E. Let us consider the earliest attested uses of
alphabetic writing in Greece during the first millennium B.C.E.: Starting with the eighth century, we see brief poetic utterances being in-

---

20. Jensen 1980:87.

21. On the use of written texts as mnemonic aids in some of the living oral traditions
of modern India, see the observations of Blackburn 1988:23–26, 28–29, 93–94, on contemporary Tamil evidence. In some cultures, however, it is clear that written texts are
functionally not so much *scripts* for performance as they are *models* for recomposition-in-
performance. Cf. Davidson 1994:19–72, on medieval Persian poetic traditions.

22. M. L. West 1990:49–50. I note in passing the feelings of frustration recorded by
Radloff 1885 [1990:86] over what he felt were relatively inferior compositions when he
had the Kirghiz singers perform for dictation.

scribed in stone. On the basis of these early poetic inscriptions, it can be argued that writing was used not for the actual composition of the utterances being inscribed: "It appears that the built-in mechanics of composition, which can be ascertained from the diction of the various attested epigrams, do not necessarily correspond to the various local patterns of spelling reflected by these epigrams."[23] In other words, it can be argued that writing was needed for the recording but not for the actual composition of early poetic inscriptions.

We may ask again: was writing needed for the *performance* of poetry? As I will now argue, the language of the earliest inscribed utterances makes it clear that writing was being used as an *equivalent* to performance, not as a *means* for performance. It is evident from the language of the earliest inscriptions from the eighth century and thereafter, and the pattern holds all the way till 550 B.C.E. or so, that the speech-act of performance was thought to be inherent in the given inscription itself, which normally communicates in the first person, as if it were a talking object.[24] In this earliest attested phase of alphabetic writing, the inscription is not a transcript but a figurative performance, a speech-act that delivers its own message in the first person.[25] It is only after 550 B.C.E. or so that the language of the inscriptions begins to reveal lapses into a mode of talking that is not strictly inherent in the object inscribed, so that the generic inscription now verges on becoming a *transcript* of an utterance, poetic or

---

23. N 1990a:19 n. 7, with examples. I see no evidence to support the notion that there was extensive writing in books as early as the eighth century B.C.E., and that what we see in the early poetic inscriptions is but the tip of an iceberg. Centuries later, we can still see examples in vase paintings of anachronistic representations that show a style of lettering in books (that is, papyrus rolls) that does not match the real style of lettering in real books but is actually more appropriate to the style of lettering found in inscriptions: see Thomas 1989:31 n. 55.

24. Svenbro 1988a:33–52 (= 1993:26–43), esp. pp. 36–38 (= 29–31); cf. Day 1989. The texts studied by Svenbro fall into two main categories: 1) inscriptions on funerary markers, including seventeen dated before 600 B.C.E. (1988a:38), and 2) inscriptions on votive objects, about a thousand of them, ranging in date from the eighth century all the way to the end of the fifth (ibid., 46).

25. In one such inscription, CEG 286, the figurative voice of the inscribed letters promises that it "answers" the same thing to all men who ask their questions. The key word is *hupokrínomai*: 'I answer' πᾶσιν ἴσ' ἀνθρόποιϲ hυποκρίνομαι hόϲτιϲ ἐ[ρο]τᾶι: hόϲ μ' ἀνέθεκ' ἀνδlρõν· Ἀντιlφάνεϲ δεκάτεν 'I answer like things to all humans, whoever asks: the one, among men, who set me up, as a tithe: Antiphanes'. See N 1990a:168 n. 95.

36   otherwise, instead of being the equivalent of the utterance itself.[26] By *transcript* I mean the writing down of a composition-in-performance not as a performance per se but as a potential aid to performance. And it is only in this later period, after 550 B.C.E. or so, that we begin to see examples of the use of writing for purposes of transcribing any given composition and controlling the circumstances of any given performance.[27]

Let us return to the subject of the earliest phases of Greek poetic inscriptions, starting with the eighth century B.C.E. For an ancient reader to read such inscriptions out loud was for him to participate passively in this *fait accompli,* in that the reader's voice was being lent to the speech-act, which is in this case the very act of writing down the poetic utterance.[28] To repeat, the Greek poetic inscription in the earliest period, before 550 B.C.E., is not conceived as a transcript of performance of a short poem; it is rather conceived as a poem, because it is written down, and because this writing down is conceived as an authoritative equivalent to performance.[29] To read the inscription out loud is to become part of the performance that is the writing down: it is to hear the writing itself, not any live performance. The words of written inscriptions can therefore even be quoted in real live performance, as seems to be the case in the passage from the *Iliad* where Hektor is described as imagining the words that implicitly call out from what *sounds* like an imaginary epigram (*Iliad* 7.89–90).[30]

If indeed alphabetic writing was perceived as an equivalent to live performance already in the earliest stages of this technology in ancient Greece, and if indeed it continued to be so perceived down to

---

26. Svenbro 1988a, esp. p. 48 (= 1993:40).

27. More on this topic below.

28. Svenbro 1988:53 (= 1993:44).

29. Svenbro 1988:33–52 (= 1993:26–43); cf. Day 1989.

30. See N 1990a:18–19 n. 7, with further bibliography (especially Gentili and Giannini 1977:22–25): when Hektor is imagining that someone will say the words that he proceeds to quote, these words follow formal conventions that can be verified on the basis of genuinely attested early poetic inscriptions. Martin (1989:136) stresses "a remarkable trait" of Hektor's represented style of speaking: "the use of direct quotation . . . to dramatize for his audience what he imagines will happen." Martin continues (ibid.): "Hektor displaces memory onto an anonymous voice that speaks the language of praise or blame. . . . His rhetoric is . . . constrained by the imagined speech-acts of others."

550 B.C.E. or so, then it is justifiable to doubt the hypothesis that writing had been used, *in its earliest phases,* as a medium for recording live performance. I would therefore wish to modify slightly the wording of the suggestion that "the alphabet developed specifically or largely in order to record hexameter poetry."[31] To record epigraphical poetry: yes, maybe; but not necessarily to record epic poetry. Looking at the period before 550 B.C.E., we may well ask: why would live epic poetry have to be recorded in the first place? The fact that Homeric poetry was meant to be performed live, and that it continued to be performed live through the classical period and beyond, remains the primary historical given.[32] So we are still left, I maintain, without any internal Greek evidence to prove that the technology of alphabetic writing, as it existed during its earliest phases in the Greek archaic period, was necessary for the performance of the Homeric poems any more than it was necessary for their composition.[33]

It is in this light that I offered, in my earlier work, a different solution to the historical problem of the Homeric text. My solution combined the comparative evidence about composition and performance in attested living oral poetic traditions with the internal evidence of ancient Greek testimony about the diffusion of Homeric poetry in the archaic period of Greece. The comparative evidence from living oral epic traditions, as we are about to see, helps corroborate the internal evidence about the ancient Greek circumstances of diffusion.

Before we proceed with comparing other epic traditions with those of ancient Greece, however, a few words of background are in order about the internal Greek evidence itself. I offer here a minimalist formulation of two basic concepts, *epic* and *Homer.* For classicists, the idea of *epic* is clear in its application, if not in its definition. Following the usage of authorities like Aristotle, Hellenists can easily distinguish the poetic art-form of *epopoiía* 'making of epic' (as at the

---

31. This suggestion is recorded in passing by Janko 1982:277 n. 3, along with bibliography.

32. For a brief review of the arguments, see N 1990a:21–24, 28–29.

33. See again N 1990a:18; also pp. 8–9, 53–55, 79–80. I therefore agree with the formulation of Sealey (1957:330): "Those who hold the theory of 'oral dictated texts' suppose that, about 700 [B.C.E.], some Greeks recognized the special merit of the *Iliad;* yet, as far as can be discovered, those Greeks had learnt to recognize merit, not in songs, but in singers."

38   beginning of Aristotle *Poetics* 1447a13) from such other poetic art-
forms as *tragōidías poíēsis* 'making of tragedy' (ibid.). The application
of Homer's name to the authorship of the *Iliad* and the *Odyssey*, the
prime examples of Greek epic, is also clear. True, the earliest attested
references to *Hómēros* attribute to him not only the *Iliad* and the
Odyssey but also the epics of the so-called Cycle, such as the *Cypria*
and the *Little Iliad*.[34] In fact, the very concept of *kúklos,* usually translated as 'circle' or 'Cycle', stems from the ancient pre-Aristotelian
tradition of applying the metaphor of cycle to the sum total of epic
poetry, as if all of it were composed by Homer.[35] By the time of Aristotle, however, the epics of the Cycle are conventionally assigned to
distinct authors (*Poetics* 23.1459b1–7).[36] Such eventual disruption in
the semantics of the very concept of *Cycle* is not a matter of common
knowledge among contemporary experts in Homer.

What made decisive the differentiating of the *Iliad* and the *Odyssey*
from all other epic poems was the influence exerted by the scholars
at the Library of Alexandria, particularly by Zenodotus of Ephe-
sus: "It was of the utmost importance for the whole future that
[Zenodotus] . . . accepted the differentiation between these two
poems as Homeric and the rest of epic narrative poetry as non-
Homeric."[37] Though there were attempts to narrow down the Homeric corpus even further, as when scholars known as the "separa-
tors" or *khōrízontes* tried to separate the authorship of the *Odyssey*
from that of the *Iliad* (Proclus p. 102.2–3 Allen), the Alexandrian
verdict on Homer as the author of the *Iliad* and the *Odyssey* held firm
in the ancient world. The "Homeric Question," as reformulated in
the Renaissance and thereafter, must be viewed against this background; so also the comparative insights pioneered by Parry and Lord.

The progressive restriction of what exactly in Greek epic is to be
attributed to Homer can be connected with the historical process
that I have just highlighted, to wit, the relatively early diffusion of the

---

34. References and further discussion can be found in N 1990a:78; cf. in general
pp. 72–79 (following p. 19 n. 10).

35. For a survey, see Pfeiffer 1968:73.

36. Ibid., 73–74. Pfeiffer remarks about Aristotle that "his differentiation between Homer,
the poet of the *Iliad* and *Odyssey,* and the rest of the early epic poets, of whom he displays
intimate knowledge in chapter 23 of the *Poetics,* seems to have been final."

37. Ibid., 117. I omit Pfeiffer's phrasing ". . . followed the lead of Aristotle and. . . ."

Iliad and the *Odyssey* throughout the Greek-speaking world. In my earlier work, I adduced archaeological evidence, as assembled by Anthony Snodgrass, pointing toward a trend of pan-Hellenism that becomes especially pronounced in archaic Greece in the eighth century before our era and thereafter.[38] The epic tradition of Homer, as Snodgrass inferred from the early proliferation of the *Iliad* and the *Odyssey*, was a reflex of this trend of pan-Hellenism.[39] I extended Snodgrass's concept of pan-Hellenism, setting it up "as a hermeneutic model to help explain the nature of Homeric poetry, in that one can envisage as aspects of a single process the ongoing recomposition and diffusion of the *Iliad* and the *Odyssey*."[40] I had called this model for the text-fixation of Homeric tradition "evolutionary," without intending any Darwinian implications about progressive superiority.[41] According to this evolutionary model, as I have formulated it in my earlier work, the process of composition-in-performance, which is a matter of *recomposition* in each performance, can be expected to be directly affected by the degree of diffusion, that is, the extent to which a given tradition of composition has a chance to be performed in a varying spectrum of narrower or broader social frameworks.[42] The wider the diffusion, I argued, the fewer opportunities for recomposition, so that the widest possible reception entails,

---

38. N 1979, following Snodgrass 1971:421, 435; also pp. 352, 376, 416–417, 421, 431.

39. See an updated formulation in Snodgrass 1987:160, 165; also Morris 1986:123.

40. N 1990a:53. The recessive accent of Ἕλληνες 'Hellenes', an innovation that evidently superseded the expected *Ἑλλῆνες, indicates that the simplex form Ἕλληνες is predicated on the compound form Πανέλληνες 'pan-Hellenes', as attested in *Iliad* 2.530 and Hesiod *Works and Days* 528: see *DELG* 341. Thus the accentual history of the word for 'Hellene' shows that the very concept of *Hellene* is predicated on the concept of *pan-Hellene*.

41. N 1981. This model is an alternative to the "dictation theory," cited above at note 9. Preeminent among earlier attempts to develop an evolutionary model is Gilbert Murray's *The Rise of Greek Epic* (1934; first published in 1907). According to Murray's model, as Davison (1962:253–254) points out, the *Iliad* and the *Odyssey* "had not taken their final form until the second century B.C." Davison continues (p. 254): "There is no room in this argument for any individual Homer; and, except for Murray's high opinion of the poetic quality of the existing *Iliad* and *Odyssey* (which he shares with Wolf, Grote and his followers, and Robert), his basic theory is as nihilistic as d'Aubignac's or Lachmann's."

42. Cf. N 1979:7–9; cf. also N 1990a:53–58. For a favorable assessment of this hermeneutic construct, see Snodgrass 1987:160, 165.

40   teleologically, the strictest possible degree of adherence to a normative and unified version.[43]

I continue to describe as *text-fixation* or *textualization* the process
whereby each composition-in-performance becomes progressively
less changeable in the course of diffusion—with the proviso that
we understand *text* here in a metaphorical sense.[44] The fixity of such
a "text," of course, does not necessarily mean that the process of
composition-in-performance—let us continue to call it recomposition—has been stopped altogether. So long as the oral tradition is
alive, some degree of ongoing recomposition is still possible in each
performance, even if the tradition itself proclaims its own absolute
fixity. A case in point is the so-called "Invocation of the Bagre," a
"hymn" sung among the LoDagaa of Northern Ghana.[45] It is clear
that the expectation of both the audience and the reciters of the
"Bagre" is that each performance be exactly like every other performance, but empirical observation shows that it is not. Reaching a size
of up to 12,000 lines, the "Bagre" in fact exists in a variety of versions, and the differences among the versions can be considerable.[46]
In sum, the rate of retardation or acceleration of change in the
process of composition-in-performance depends on the stage of evolution in which we happen to find any given living oral tradition.[47]

In arguing for the notion of a single pan-Hellenic tradition of
epic—let us call it Homer—as opposed to a plethora of local traditions, I stressed the relativity of the term *pan-Hellenic* from an empirical point of view:

> It should be clear that this notion of *pan-Hellenic* is absolute only
> from the standpoint of insiders to the tradition at a given time and
> place, and that it is relative from the standpoint of outsiders, such
> as ourselves, who are merely looking in on the tradition. Each new

---

43. N 1990a:53–58 (esp. p. 56 with reference to Bausinger 1980:52; also p. 57 with reference to Zwettler 1978:221).

44. N 1990a:53. Cf. Pucci 1987:29 n. 30.

45. Goody 1972.

46. See also Goody 1977:119. This comparative evidence is applied to the question of
Homeric poetry in Morris 1986:84–85; see also p. 87 concerning the application of comparative evidence from the traditions of the Tiv in Nigeria.

47. See further discussion in N 1990a:53, 55, 60, 72, 73, 171.

performance can claim to be the definitive pan-Hellenic tradition.
Moreover, the degree of pan-Hellenic synthesis in the content of a
composition corresponds to the degree of diffusion in the performance of this composition. Because we are dealing with a relative
concept, we may speak of the poetry of the *Iliad* and the *Odyssey,*
for example, as more pan-Hellenic than the poetry of the Epic
Cycle.[48]

In other words, I am arguing that the concept of pan-Hellenism is
not at all incompatible with the factor of change. I therefore disagree
with the implications of the following assessment:

> Although a few poems may be designed to be infinitely repeatable
> and as non-local and non-occasional as possible (pan[-]Hellenic,
> even literary?)—i.e. they may aspire to say the "last word" on their
> subject, and to render all previous and future attempts futile[49]—,
> the more usual impulse is to leave loopholes for possible excep-
> tions, pegs on which to hang possible additions, open ends to
> accommodate codas or modifications desired by particular audi-
> ences in the light of other existing songs or cult traditions.[50]

To repeat, the model of pan-Hellenism is by definition not rigid, not
even for Homer.

In terms of such a model, which we may continue to describe as
evolutionary, I posit at least five distinct consecutive periods of Homeric transmission—"Five Ages of Homer," as it were—with each period showing progressively less fluidity and more rigidity:[51]

---

48. Ibid., 70–71.

49. The quoted passage at this point introduces a footnote, the contents of which I criti-
cize in note 50 below.

50. Griffith 1990:194–195. At a point that I mark with note 49 above in the quoted text,
Griffith (p. 205 n. 40) adds the following observation: "This is argued, e.g., by G. Nagy
[1990a:57–65] . . . , with reference to C. Lévi-Strauss, *The Way of the Masks* [1982] . . . ; but
it will be clear from what follows that I think few poems apart from the *Iliad* and *Odyssey*
laid much claim to pan[-]Hellenic status at the time of their composition." Here he cross-
refers to his p. 204 n. 34, where in turn he refers to his article, Griffith 1983, especially his
remarks there at pp. 46–47. For a response to those remarks, see my book *Pindar's Homer*
(N 1990a:79).

51. Cf. N 1996: Chs. 5 and 6, esp. p. 110.

42   1. A relatively most fluid period, with no written texts, extending from the early second millennium into the middle of the eighth century in the first millennium;[52]

2. A more formative or "pan-Hellenic" period, still with no written texts, from the middle of the eighth century to the middle of the sixth;[53]

3. A definitive period, centralized in Athens, with potential texts in the sense of transcripts, at any or several points from the middle of the sixth century to the later part of the fourth;[54]

4. A standardizing period, from the later part of the fourth century to the middle of the second; this period starts with the reform of Homeric performance traditions in Athens during the régime of Demetrius of Phalerum, which lasted from 317 to 307 B.C.E.;[55]

5. A relatively most rigid period, from the middle of the second century onward; this period starts with the completion of Aristarchus's editorial work on the Homeric texts, not long after 150 B.C.E. or so.[56]

A context for the definitive period in my evolutionary model is a pan-Hellenic festival like the Panathenaia at Athens, which served as the formal setting, established by law, of seasonally recurring performances of the Homeric *Iliad* and *Odyssey* (cf. Lycurgus *Against Leokrates* 102).[57] In the next chapter, we will consider in more detail

---

52. N 1990b: Ch. 1, esp. pp. 9–10. Cf. Sherratt (1990:817–821), who maps out roughly the same time-frame, with further subdivisions.

53. N 1990a:21–25, 52–81.

54. Ibid. Cf. N 1996: Ch. 5.

55. N 1996: Chs. 6 and 7.

56. Ibid.

57. N 1990a:21–25. For an inventory of primary sources, besides Lycurgus *Against Leokrates* 102, see Davison 1955a:7. See also Seaford 1994, esp. p. 73, where the "narrative development" of the Iliadic ending is correlated with "the historical development of the polis." For another view on pan-Hellenic festivals as a context for the performance of epic, cf. Taplin 1992:39. For bibliography on earlier views on the possible role of festivals as a

the question of identifying who should be given credit for shaping or, better, reshaping not only this institution of the Panathenaia but also, in particular, the institution of Homeric performances that became a featured event of this festival. At this point it is enough to highlight the involvement of the Peisistratidai—that is, of Peisistratos and his sons—who traced themselves back to the heroic-age Peisistratos, son of Nestor (as portrayed in *Odyssey* Book 3) and who ruled Athens as tyrants during the second half of the sixth century B.C.E.[58] More important for now, I argue in what follows that the Feast of the Panathenaia is a salient example of a distinct pattern of diffusion in oral traditions.

I hope to show from the comparative evidence of various oral epic traditions that there is more than one way to visualize the actual process of diffusion. Besides the pattern of an ever-widening radius of proliferation, with no clearly defined center of diffusion, there is also a more specialized pattern that can be predicated on a functional center point, a centralized context for both the coming together of diverse audiences and the spreading outward of more unified traditions. In other words, a fixed center of diffusion can bring into play both centripetal and centrifugal forces. Such a center point, as we will see, is the seasonally recurring festival of the Panathenaia at Athens.

In general as also in details, an evolutionary model for the text-fixation or textualization of the Homeric tradition is corroborated by the comparative evidence of living oral epic traditions. We may note in particular the results of recent fieldwork in the oral epic traditions

---

context for Homeric performance, see Thalmann 1984:119 plus 222 n. 19. For a discussion of the evidence of vase paintings as a criterion for determining the fixation of Homeric traditions, especially in Athens, see Lowenstam 1993a, esp. p. 216.

58. N 1990a:52–81. See also Shapiro 1983, 1990, 1992, 1993. On the claim of the Peisistratidai to be descended from the Homeric Peisistratos, son of Nestor, see N 1990a:155, citing Shapiro 1983, esp. p. 89. On the effects of the régime of the Peisistratidai on the contents of Homeric poetry, especially the *Odyssey*, see Catenacci 1993 (at pp. 7–8 n. 2, he offers a useful summary of Aloni 1984 and 1986). Cf. Cook 1995. All this is not to deny that there may well have been earlier associations of Nestor and his lineage with the lineages of other historical dynasties, such as those at Colophon and Miletus (cf. Janko 1992:134 for bibliography). See also the remarks on the Panathenaia in N 1990a:21–23, 28, 54, 73, 75, 160, 174, 192. I agree with Shapiro (1992:73) that the Panathenaia, as reorganized by the Peisistratidai of Athens, played a major role in the privileging of the *Iliad* and the *Odyssey* as the definitive poems of Homer.

44   of the Indian subcontinent.[59] In what follows, I quote extensively
from descriptions of the Indian evidence that were formulated by ob-
servers who were not at all concerned with the ancient Greek evidence to which I am now applying them.[60] The degrees of similarity
between the empirical observations of the Indian evidence, as I cite
them verbatim, and some of my constructs derived from the Greek
evidence are to my mind so striking that a casual reading could leave
the mistaken impression that the wording of the Indologists was
influenced by these constructs.

For example, researchers like Stuart Blackburn who specialize in
the oral folk epic traditions of latter-day India have developed, independent of their counterparts who specialize in ancient Greece, the
descriptive term *pan-Indian,* which they correlate with observable patterns of what they call geographical *diffusion* in epic traditions.[61]
Matching the Greek model, the descriptive term *pan-* is used in a relative sense, as we can see from the following explicit restatement
of Blackburn's position in the introduction to the book that he
co-edited: "Tracing a narrative pattern that moves from a local hero
toward a wider, more pan-Indian identity for the hero/god, [Black-
burn] concludes that this change is a response to the differing social
groups and contexts encountered as an epic spreads geographi-
cally."[62] In effect, then, Blackburn is positing an ongoing process of

---

59. For justification of the term *oral,* with specific reference to the Rajasthani epic traditions, see especially Smith 1990, who considers in detail the absence of a role to be played
by the existing technology of writing in the composition and performance of epic.

60. A key work is *Oral Epics in India* (Blackburn, Claus, Flueckiger, and Wadley 1989),
hereafter abbreviated as *OEI.* Crucial articles in the volume are Blackburn and Flueckiger
1989, "Introduction," pp. 1–11; Blackburn 1989, "Patterns of Development for Indian
Oral Epics," pp. 15–32; Flueckiger 1989, "Caste and Regional Variants in an Oral Epic
Tradition," pp. 33–54; Claus 1989, "Behind the Text: Performance and Ideology in a Tulu
Oral Tradition," pp. 55–74; Wadley 1989, "Choosing a Path: Performance Strategies in a
North Indian Epic," pp. 75–101; Kothari 1989, "Performers, Gods, and Heroes in the
Oral Epics of Rajasthan," pp. 102–117; Schomer 1989, "Paradigms for the Kali Yuga: The
Heroes of the Ālhā Epic and their Fate," pp. 140–154; and Smith 1989, "Scapegoats of
the Gods: The Ideology of the Indian Epics," pp. 176–194.

61. I draw attention to the specific use of the terms "pan-Indian" and "geographical diffusion" by Blackburn 1989:27.

62. Blackburn and Flueckiger 1989:6.

recomposition in the making of Indian epic that is analogous to an evolutionary model for the making of ancient Greek epic.

An evolutionary model is applicable also to the two great canonical Sanskrit epics of the Indian subcontinent.[63] These are the *Mahābhārata,* an epic of truly monumental dimensions that, in its ultimate form, is roughly eight times the size of the Homeric *Iliad* and *Odyssey* combined, and the relatively smaller *Rāmāyaṇa.* The performance traditions that culminated in these two Sanskrit "primary epics" extended well into the second half of the first millennium of our era.[64] It took "several centuries" for both "to reach their final forms,"[65] with the "formative period" of the *Mahābhārata* estimated at around 400 B.C.E. to 400 C.E., and of the *Rāmāyaṇa,* at around 200 B.C.E. to 200 C.E.[66]

The relative lateness of text-fixation in the case of these two canonical Sanskrit epics is illustrated by the fact that even the earlier of the two, the *Mahābhārata,* "began to take shape" at a time when the Vedas, the "priestly literature" of the Brahmin caste that had already formalized the technology of writing, had reached an advanced stage of development.[67] "Viewed against this background the *Mahābhārata* represents, as it were, a return to the beginning. It was an oral composition; it was purely heroic in character; and it dealt with people and events of which the earlier [Brahmin] literature had taken practically no notice."[68]

This dichotomy between Vedic and epic can be explained to some degree in terms of caste distinctions: "As the Vedas and their supporting

---

63. In what follows, I rely especially on the work of J. D. Smith 1980.

64. Ibid., 48. I may add that the variations attested in the textual tradition of these two monumental epics can be cited as indirect evidence for the relative lateness of text-fixation.

65. Ibid., 49.

66. Smith notes (ibid., 73) that "the *Rāmāyaṇa* had been composed in the manner of an epic, rather than having evolved as an epic"; I suggest that a similar argument could be developed about the Homeric *Odyssey,* as opposed to the *Iliad.*

67. Ibid., 49.

68. Ibid.

46 literature were the 'property' of the Brahmins, so the epic was the 'property' of the Kṣatriya-s, the caste of warriors and princes."[69] Although the Kṣatriya-s "owned" the epic, it was not composed/performed by them but by a specialized caste called the Sūta-s, performing to the accompaniment of an early form of a string instrument known as the *vīṇā.*[70] The relationship of these Sūta-s and the Kṣatriya-s is analogous to that of the medieval Cāraṇ court poets and their Rājpūt patrons.[71]

The Kṣatriya background of the Sanskrit epic tradition becomes accretively displaced and covered over, in the course of time, by a Brahmin superstructure, and the very process of this displacement can be interpreted as a sign of fluidity in an oral epic tradition. The pattern of displacement is so pervasive that the very authorship of the *Mahābhārata* is traditionally attributed to one Kṛṣṇa Dvaipāyana, a Brahmin seer who is also a major character in the plot of the *Mahābhārata.*[72] Similarly, in the *Rāmāyaṇa,* the Kṣatriya hero Rāma becomes accretively identified with the Brahmin god Viṣṇu.

Granted, experts have not yet determined to what extent such accretive patterns of displacement took place on the level of oral transmission in the two primary Sanskrit epics.[73] But, more importantly, the fact is that the living oral epic traditions in India today, affording as they do a wealth of evidence for various patterns of diffusion, pro-

---

69. Ibid. On analogies to the Brahmin/Kṣatriya distinction in the context of the emerging Greek city-state, see N 1990b:276–293.

70. The essence of the Sūta class is traditionally formulated in terms of genealogy: viewed as sons of a union between a female of the Brahmin class and a male of the Kṣatriya class, they are assigned the social roles of tending horses, driving chariots, and serving as court poets (cf. N 1990b:291–292 n. 82).

71. J. D. Smith 1980:50.

72. Ibid., 75 n. 4. It is fair to say that Kṛṣṇa becomes the god of the *Mahābhārata,* to the degree that "the epic is his theophany" (ibid., 72).

73. J. D. Smith's overview of accretive patterns in Sanskrit epic is not explicit in this regard. The work of another expert, M. C. Smith (1992), is pertinent to the question of accretion in the process of oral tradition, though I do not necessarily agree with her ultimate formulation. She posits a "nucleus" of 3,000 verses (distinguished by the epic "irregular" *triṣṭubh* meter) as opposed to the 75,000 verses in the Poona critical edition of the *Mahābhārata.*

vide comparative evidence for an evolutionary model that helps explain the actual process of accretion.[74]

As we proceed to consider in some detail the evidence of living oral epic traditions in contemporary India, it is important to stress the explicit role of religion in the very function of epic. For purposes of this presentation, a minimalist working definition of *religion* will suffice: let us consider it for the moment as simply the interaction of myth and ritual.[75] I propose further to specify "religion" in terms of *cult,* which I define for the moment as *a set of practices combining elements of ritual as well as myth.*[76] As one of the most powerful illustrations of the role of religion in the performance of Indian epic, I point to those situations where the performer presupposes the presence of an audience of gods, "watching out for errors in performance."[77]

For the first specific example of the sort of empirical evidence that has been collected by contemporary researchers concerning the role of cult in the living traditions of epic in India, let us consider the wording of a scholar specializing in Rajasthani epic, who offers the following formulation for the role of epic in the Rajasthani cultural ethos: "Concern for propitiating the powerful spirits of those who died *untimely* deaths continually feeds the epic traditions of the area."[78] In quoting this description of heroes in the Rajasthani epic traditions, I highlight the word *untimely* because of its relevance for comparison with the concept of the hero in ancient Greek epic traditions. In the case of the Herakles myth, as adduced by Greek epic itself in the retelling of *Iliad* 19.95–133, the theme of Herakles' *untimeliness* goes to the very core of the hero's essence and extends to

---

74. I should stress that, besides whatever similarities we may observe between the living oral traditions of contemporary India on the one hand and the two classical Sanskrit epics on the other, we should also expect a host of differences. One particular point of interest is the special role played by the Brahmin class in the perpetuation of the Sanskrit epics. There is also a related question: to what degree was the technology of writing an actual factor in the mnemonic traditions associated with the *Mahābhārata* and *Rāmāyaṇa*?

75. Further below, I offer minimalist working definitions of *myth* and *ritual;* cf. N 1990b:8–10, summarizing the formulations of Burkert 1979b and 1985:8.

76. So N 1990b:10.

77. Wadley 1989:79.

78. Kothari 1989:102.

the essential untimeliness of the main hero of the *Iliad,* Achilles, who in the end describes himself as the 'untimeliest of them all', *pan-a-órios* (24.540).[79] This theme of untimeliness in ancient Greek traditions is not restricted to epic: it extends to the concept of heroes in the specific context of their being worshiped in cult, as I have argued extensively elsewhere.[80] As I have also argued, the cult of heroes is a subtext, as it were, for the development of epic traditions about heroes in ancient Greece.[81] Moreover, the relationship between the cult of heroes on a local level and the epic of heroes on a pan-Hellenic level is crucial for coming to terms with the factor of diffusion in the Homeric tradition.[82] As we will see, there are striking analogies in the living traditions of India.

The ancient Greek hero's untimeliness in myth is to be contrasted with his/her timeliness in ritual, in that the cult of heroes is predicated on the central fact of seasonal recurrence, controlled by the goddess of timeliness herself, Hera.[83] The cults of heroes/ancestors in India, too, seem to operate on a cyclical principle. Although "the yearly cycle of folk epic performances has yet to be conclusively outlined for different regions and different groups within these regions,"[84] there are isolated cases where we do have specific infor-

---

79. Pötscher 1961; see further discussion in Householder and Nagy 1972b:50–52, especially on the relationship of the forms *Hḗrā* 'Hera', *Hēraklḗēs* 'Herakles', and *hḗrōs* 'hero'. These works have not been taken into account by Adams 1987. See also Davidson 1980, esp. pp. 199–200; also Sinos 1980:14, and Slatkin 1986. Further comments on the thematic connections between the heroes Herakles and Achilles can be found in Martin 1989:228–230 and N 1990b:12–15. On Achilles as *pan-a-órios* 'the untimeliest of them all', see N 1985:62. For more on *Hḗrā, Hēraklḗēs,* and *hḗrōs,* see O'Brien 1993:115–119, esp. p. 116 n. 9; see also Kazansky 1989.

80. N 1979:182–184 (with reference to *Iliad* 18.54–60, the *Homeric Hymn to Demeter,* and Adonis rituals); cf. pp. 114–121, 152–153, 174, 190–193.

81. N 1979, esp. p. 9. For a brief overview, with further bibliography, see N 1990b:10–13.

82. N 1979:7–10.

83. Cf. N 1990a:400, 136–142; also 245 n. 129 (on Herodotus 1.31.5: the goddess Hera presides over the *télos* 'fulfillment' of Kleobis and Biton, two young athletes who are "on time" to take up the task of drawing the oxcart of the priestess of Hera when the sacrificial oxen designated to draw it fail to be "on time").

84. Kothari 1989:105.

mation: a notable example is the festival of Caitrī, where the performances of epic seem to be connected with the remembrance of ancestors.[85]

Pursuing the question of the relationship between epic traditions and the cult of ancestors or heroes, let us consider in some detail the evidence from Rajasthan, starting with the following summary: "The two major Rajasthani historical epics, Pābūjī and Devnārāyaṇ, appear to have developed out of a tradition of honoring powerful spirits of the dead. A continuing concern about powerful spirits provides the framework in which these epics retain their meaning and vitality."[86] In the case of the Pābūjī regional epic tradition, it has been argued that it developed out of a local *bhomiyā* cult.[87] The *bhomiyā* have been described as "local heroes who died while defending against cattle raids, were commemorated with a carved pillar (showing a rider on a horse), and eventually became gods at the center of a cult."[88] Pābūjī himself is generally worshiped as a god.[89]

As we shall see, the semantic shift from hero to god is a peculiarly Indian phenomenon, characteristic of those stages of epic tradition that have undergone the broadest patterns of diffusion and have thus attained the most normative possible levels of the "Hindu" worldview. For purposes of comparison with the ancient Greek evidence, where the distinction between *hero* and *god* is for the most part clearly maintained, it is preferable to start with Indian patterns of cult on the most local levels, where we find the most straightforward evidence for the cult of heroes as distinct from gods. Before we begin, however, it is important to note that the ancient Greek distinction between *ancestor* and *hero*, unlike the distinction between *hero* and *god*, becomes increasingly blurred as we move further back in time.[90]

---

85. Ibid., 105–106.

86. Ibid., 102.

87. Blackburn 1989:25; cf. Kothari 1989:110.

88. Blackburn 1989:25.

89. Ibid., 26. "Indologists have often speculated that the cults of Rāma and Kṛṣṇa underwent a similar process of development" (ibid.).

90. See N 1990b:11; cf. Morris 1986:129. See also Morris 1988.

50   With this caution in place, let us return to the folk culture of Rajasthan, which has been singled out for its striking differences from the upper-caste Hindu "norm."[91] I propose to pursue our consideration of the Rajasthani *bhomiyā*, who are literally the spirits of dead warriors.[92] At the shrine of the *bhomiyā*,

> the spirit manifests himself through a medium, usually a *bhopā*. The shrine [marking where the *bhomiyā* had died] becomes active through this medium and the spirit begins to solve problems of the local people. Effective and truthful disposition by the possessed medium of the *bhomiyā* will draw people from a large area and the shrine may become an important ritual site where the hero's story is sung.[93]

As for the actual performance of the epic, "the central belief is that singing the hero's story summons him as a god, whose power is then present to protect the community."[94] What gives the hero his ultimate power is the actual fact of his death: "The death event operates as the 'generative point' for stories in local traditions. It leads to deification, to worship, to a cult, and eventually to a narrative which is ritually performed to invoke the spirits of the dead."[95]

It can be said in general about the epic traditions of India that their function is a matter of explicit ritual as well as myth: "Epic performances ritually protect and cure, while epic narratives express local ideologies and form pathways between regional and pan-Indian mythologies."[96] For the moment I simply note, for the second time now, the use of the term *pan-Indian* in this description—a subject to which we will return presently. I also note a point that may not be obvious to those unfamiliar with the perspectives of social anthropology, which is that the element of ritual in such descriptions should

---

91. See the overview, written collaboratively, in *OEI* 240–241.

92. Kothari 1989:110.

93. Ibid.

94. Blackburn and Flueckiger 1989:10.

95. Blackburn 1989:22.

96. Blackburn and Flueckiger 1989:11.

not be understood so narrowly as to exclude what we may ordinarily think of as entertainment: "Indian oral epics tend to have performance contexts that are either ritualistic or entertainment-oriented. These two performance contexts exist on a continuum because ritual and entertainment are not mutually exclusive."[97]

The relation of the local epic to the community is all-important in the Indian traditions: "Oral epics in India have that special ability to tell a community's own story and thus help to create and maintain that community's self-identity."[98] Once the local story extends beyond the community, however, there is change in content as well as form. Let us consider the following description of what happens to the theme of the death and deification of local heroes in the context of diffusion:[99]

> When a story spreads beyond its local base by attracting new patronage outside the small group that originally worshiped the dead hero, the predominance of the death motif (but not deification) weakens. In its place, new elements are added at each of the next two successively larger geographical ranges: a supernatural birth at the sub-regional level and an identification with a *pan-Indian* figure at the regional level. The overall effect of this development is to obscure the human origins of the hero/god with a prior divine existence, a process that is complete when the hero/god is identified with a *pan-Indian* figure.[100]

For the third time now, we note the use of the word *pan-Indian* in describing the ultimate stages of epic diffusion in India. We may note as well that the application of this term is reserved for the *regional* level of diffusion and beyond. The categories of *regional* and *subregional* are part of an overall taxonomy developed by Stuart Blackburn for

---

97. Blackburn 1989:20. For a perspective that stresses the aspect of entertainment at the expense of other aspects in ancient Greek poetics, see Heath 1990.

98. Blackburn and Flueckiger 1989:11.

99. The last point is illustrated by Blackburn (1989:24–25) with two examples. In the Pābūjī narrative, which counts as a regional epic in his taxonomy, the Pābūjī figure turns out to be a reincarnation of the pan-Indian figure Lakṣmaṇa, the younger brother of Rāma. In the Devnārāyaṇ narrative, another regional epic, the hero Devnārāyaṇ turns out to be none other than the god Viṣṇu himself.

100. Ibid., 21–22; highlighting mine.

52 the purpose of classifying the relative ranges of diffusion for fifteen samples of living epic traditions in India. The ranges of diffusion for these fifteen selected epic traditions, preceded by categories of description for these ranges, are as follows:

1. local (10–100-mile range);

2. subregional (100–200-mile range);

3. regional (200–300-mile range);

4. supraregional (400+-mile range).[101]

We may note in particular the observation that the breakthrough of an epic from local to subregional status is promoted by a cult where a large festival is held annually at a single temple.[102]

An ancient Greek analogy that immediately comes to mind is a pan-Hellenic festival like the Panathenaia at Athens, which, as we have already noted, served as the formal setting, established by law, of seasonally recurring performances of the Homeric *Iliad* and *Odyssey* (Lycurgus *Against Leokrates* 102). As the comparative evidence of oral epic traditions in contemporary India shows, the institution of Homeric performances at the Panathenaia can be visualized as a process of diffusion. In other words, diffusion is not restricted to the pattern of an ever-widening radius of proliferation, with no clearly defined center of diffusion. As the Indic comparative evidence shows, there is also a more specialized pattern that can be predicated on a functional center point, bringing into play both centripetal and centrifugal forces. Such a center point, to repeat, can take the form of a centralized context for both the coming together of diverse audiences and the spreading outward of more unified traditions.

For purposes of further comparison, we may observe that the more pan-Indian the epic, the more divergent it seems from the an-

---

101. Blackburn 1989:17–18. We may note the gap between the maximum assigned to the regional category, 300 miles, and the minimum assigned to the supraregional, 400 miles. This gap reflects the fact that the data-gathering is still at an early stage. The map that reflects the evidence available so far, as presented by Blackburn on p. 19, "is intended to present only the approximate spread of the traditions" (p. 17). Moreover, this map represents only the positive evidence of attestations, and the negative evidence indicating where certain epic traditions are *not* being performed is so far limited to the local and subregional traditions (p. 17). Thus the accuracy of the mapping "decreases as geographical spread increases" (ibid.).

102. J. D. Smith 1989:178.

cient Greek evidence. The actual phenomena of pan-Indianism and pan-Hellenism are comparable, but not so much the results of the respective phenomena of synthesis and diffusion. The most divergent point of comparison is the tendency of the hero's being elevated to the status of divinity in pan-Indian traditions. I have in mind such phenomena in the Indian evidence as the appropriation of epics having a ritual context by such pan-Indian trends as Vaiṣṇava veneration.[103] True, even where the hero is divinized, there can survive traces of hero-god distinctions: in the Tulu traditions, for example, there is a distinction made between the *bhūta* or deified dead and the *dēvaṟu,* that is, deities of divine origins.[104] Clearly, the deified dead represent the new and augmented phase of the hero, just one step removed from the status of deities proper. Just as clearly, there are attestations of the next logical step: "New social groups accept the hero as a god and not simply as the deified dead because they have no close link to him by blood or locale."[105]

All this is not to say that the hero's elevation to the status of divinity cannot happen on the most local level.[106] Conversely, in the case of the Lorik-Candā epic, which fits Blackburn's category of "supra-regional" epic,[107] its hero and heroine, Lorik and Candā, "are not deified and thus [this epic's] spread is not associated with that of a religious cult."[108] There are even more important exceptions: "The *Mahābhārata* heroes, like the heroes of the Ālhā, do not die in battle, are not deified, and are not widely worshiped. They, too, lack both the conditions and the need for deification."[109] Still, the general trend of pan-Indian oral epic traditions is the highlighting of the

---

103. On which see Blackburn 1989:27.

104. Ibid., 23.

105. Ibid.

106. As in the bow-song tradition of the Tampimār, on which see Blackburn 1989:22.

107. Ibid., 18.

108. Flueckiger 1989:33.

109. Blackburn 1989:30. Cf. Schomer 1989:142–143. In general, the Ālhā epic defies the typologies established by Blackburn 1989, as he concedes at p. 29. As for Blackburn's concession about the heroes of the *Mahābhārata,* there are exceptions to the exception: folk traditions can deify heroes of Sanskrit epic, as in the case of the Draupadī cults of central Tamil Nadu, on which see Blackburn p. 30 n. 23.

54   hero's immortalization and the shading over of his mortality: "As these stories *diffuse* (even to a limited extent within the local range), they *change* [highlighting mine]. The hero's death remains the central narrative event, evoking emotional responses in listeners and explaining the hero's new status as a god, but it becomes less local history and more narrative convention."[110] There is even a tendency in Indian traditions to avoid describing the actual death of the hero.[111] In the pan-Hellenic traditions of the *Iliad* and the *Odyssey*, conversely, the topic of a hero's immortalization tends to be shaded over, while his mortality and the circumstances of his death are highlighted as the centerpiece of Homeric humanism.[112]

Either way, whatever the direction of shifts in emphasis may be, both the Greek and the Indian traditions seem to become progressively less occasional or ad hoc in the process of diffusion. To discover the occasional or ad hoc applications of ancient Greek epic, of course, is largely a matter of reconstruction, or at least of inference from the surviving texts. In the case of Indian epic, on the other hand, there is a great deal of direct evidence about occasionality in the living traditions, and such testimony, as we shall see, affords valuable comparative insights that help us better understand the available testimony of the Greek traditions.

Let us begin with Indian evidence about the circumstances of performance and of performer-audience interaction. There are two basic performance-types: *song-recitation* and *dance-drama;*[113] dance-drama has been described as "a secondary form in that it only exists where song-recitation also exists."[114] Performers of epic—singers, musical accompanists, dancers, and ritual specialists—are predominantly from the middle- and low-level castes; by contrast, classical performance traditions of the Sanskrit epics were "controlled by high-

---

110. Blackburn 1989:23.

111. J. D. Smith 1989:185.

112. See, e.g., N 1990b:122–142. For more on the conventional universalization of mortality and death in Homeric poetry, see N 1990a:143 n. 40.

113. Blackburn and Flueckiger 1989:9.

114. Ibid. In this context, we may note the following important observation: "Each north Indian folk song genre usually has a distinctive textural and melodic pattern and many genres are melody-specific" (Wadley 1989:93).

level castes, often Brahmins."[115] The possibility of a performer's traveling through different districts seems to be linked with the degree of his professionalism.[116] This phenomenon of professionalization, which seems to be a key to the factor of diffusion, is analogous to the status of the ancient Greek *aoidós* 'singer' as a *dēmiourgós,* that is, an itinerant artisan (*Odyssey* 17.381–385).[117]

In the Indian traditions, the notion of *audience* is actually more appropriate in the case of professional singers' performances, whereas some more neutral term like *group* suits the sort of situation where "non-professional general caste groups sing for the group itself."[118] For purposes of comparison, the ongoing distinction between *audience* and *group* in these descriptions of Indian traditions is pertinent to the scenes of person-to-person or person-to-group interaction in Homeric narrative that seem to mirror the conventions of performer-audience interaction in the "real world" that frames the performance of the narrative.[119] It is also pertinent to the issues raised by Wolfgang Rösler's *Dichter und Gruppe,* a work that investigates the reception of archaic Greek lyric in the specific social context of archaic Lesbos.[120] We may ask, for example, on the basis of the comparative evidence, whether the interaction of Alcaeus with his group on one level simply mirrors the performance of the Alcaeus-persona to the audience on another level.[121]

In the case of the general caste group's "nonprofessional" performing of epic in the Indian traditions, even this broad category for the aspect of *performers* has its own structure. There has to be a leader,

---

115. Blackburn and Flueckiger 1989:9.

116. Wadley 1989:80.

117. Details in N 1990a:56–67. Burkert (1992) organizes his chapters along the lines of categories of *dēmiourgós* as catalogued in *Odyssey* 17.381–385. On the varying degrees of quasi-professionalism in African traditions of song, see Okpewho 1979:35–50.

118. Kothari 1989:103.

119. For a far-reaching investigation of such mirroring, see Martin 1989.

120. Rösler 1980.

121. For an illustration of the "catholic/epichoric" dichotomy in the application of nonepic compositions, see, e.g., the commentary on Theognis 367–370 in N 1990a: 374–375.

56   who generally has had more background in performance than the others, including the mastery of a musical instrument.[122] Potential leaders, who are specialists in a sense, have to compete with one another, and I infer that increasing specialization in the performance of epic is a functional correlate of increasing formalized competition among performers.[123] A comparable correlation of professionalization and competition is discernible in archaic Greek songmaking traditions.[124]

In the course of this brief survey of occasionality in the living epic traditions of India, we may note in passing that epic, as a form of public activity, is performed almost exclusively by male singers.[125] The rarely found exceptions, however, are particularly revealing. For background to the case about to be cited, we may note that the Ahir caste of Uttar Pradesh appropriates the Lorik-Candā epic;[126] this epic "helps to maintain the Ahirs' image of themselves as a warrior caste."[127] "It is primarily Ahirs who sponsor performances at occasions such as weddings and the birth of a child. The Lorik-Candā epic is also sung at various festivals, during the harvest season, and at village or town fairs."[128] In Chhattisgarh, the corresponding epic is called Candainī, and it is with the background of reference to this tradition that we turn to an exceptional case of performance by women. The researcher reports as follows: "One night as I was recording an elderly Gond (tribal) woman singing a variety of narrative songs, she began singing about the wedding of the epic heroine and her first husband. But the woman did not consider this to be Candainī singing."[129] The narrative content in fact corresponds to

---

122. Kothari 1989:103.

123. Cf. ibid. For the attestation of competition events in Ḍholā epic performance in western Uttar Pradesh, see Wadley 1989:98.

124. N 1990a:22–24, 77, 137 n. 7, 353–354, 386, 401–403. Cf. Martin 1989:227.

125. Blackburn and Flueckiger 1989:9.

126. Flueckiger 1989:36.

127. Ibid., 41.

128. Ibid., 37.

129. Ibid., 40.

Candainī, but the form is different: a distinct *rāg* 'tune' and style.[130]
In this case, we find a striking ancient Greek parallel in Sappho frag-
ment 44, the "Wedding of Hektor and Andromache": this song, composed in a meter that is cognate with but distinct from the epic
dactylic hexameter, deals in a nonepic manner with themes that are
otherwise characteristic of epic.[131] We have here a particularly striking example of the effects of a given occasion on the very nature of
epic composition. Just as the song of Sappho about the wedding of
Hektor and Andromache is exceptional in the history of Greek literature, so also the song of the elderly Gond woman proved to be exceptional in one particular researcher's survey of living Indian oral
epic traditions. It may well be worth asking whether this discovery
about women's traditions in India would have been possible if the
researcher in this case, Joyce Flueckiger, did not happen to be a
woman. The question is whether a woman researcher would be
deemed by her women informants to be more suitable for the reception of distinctly women's traditions.[132]

In the many epic traditions of India, there are striking examples of
selectivity in choosing not only which topics to highlight or shade
over in a given sequence but also which *variant* of a given topic to use
within that sequence. Such choices are tuned to the narrowness or
breadth of audience reception. Let us consider two situations, one
where the local aspects of an epic tradition have to be highlighted
and another where the same aspects are shaded over. We begin with
the Kordabbu epic tradition of the Tulu-speaking area of Karnataka,
a tradition where parts of the narrative are recited by the possessed
priest "in a voice characteristic of the spirits"; this stretch of narrative
is marked by a switch from the third to the first person, and is known
as the Words of the Hero.[133] "In his performance the possessed priest
must not only recite Kordabbu's story, but also assume his character

---

130. Ibid.

131. See N 1974:118–139 ("The Wedding of Hektor and Andromache: Epic Contacts in
Sappho 44LP").

132. I asked John D. Smith, an expert in this field, for his opinion (May 11, 1993, at the
University of Cambridge), and his answer was "yes."

133. Claus 1989:60. For typological parallels to such a convention, where the hero communicates directly with the audience through the performer, see Martin 1989:234.

58 and dramatically portray his exploits for several hours on end."[134] This description applies to the Mundala caste. But there is also another performance tradition, called the *kōla,* maintained by the Nalke caste, which is "a professional bardic caste."[135] It has been reported about these performers:

> Together with their recitation, they perform a costumed dance-drama, acting out the major incidents of the spirit's life while in a state of possession. Nalkes perform *kōlas* for many other deities besides Kordabbu and thus know a sizable repertoire of different *pāḍḍanas* [a generic term for multistory tradition]. The Nalke have no greater ties to the Mundala or Kordabbu than they do to any other caste or any other caste's heroes.[136]

I save the most important detail for last: the Nalke "are not likely to elaborate specific details that might offend the sensibilities of a particular group in a village and give rise to a dispute. The Nalke leave the details of the hero's life and his relationship to other castes to the villagers concerned."[137] An analogy that immediately comes to mind is the screening out of local traditions from the repertoire of *aoidoí* 'singers' as itinerant artisans in archaic Greece, with the result that the subject matter controlled by such performers becomes a sort of least common denominator appropriate to the most generalized kinds of audience.[138]

In contrast to the distinct nonoccasionality of attested ancient Greek epic, we have by now seen a great deal of comparative evidence for occasionality on the level of local performance in the living oral epic traditions of India. There is ample evidence also from the epic traditions of Central Asia.[139] It will suffice here to quote a particularly revealing description of occasionality in Kirghiz epic tra-

---

134. Claus 1989:60. For instances of switching from third to second to first person, see ibid., 74.

135. Ibid., 72.

136. Ibid., 60.

137. Ibid., 72.

138. See extensive discussion in N 1990a:56–57.

139. See, e.g., Hatto 1980:307; cited, with further analogies, by Martin 1989:6–7. See also Reichl 1992:113–117.

ditions from a report published in 1885 by a pioneer in the study of
oral epic traditions, Wilhelm Radloff:

> The singer's competence (*innere Disposition*) depends on the num-
> ber of themes (*Bildteile*) he knows, but this alone is insufficient for
> singing, as I said before; encouragement from the outside is neces-
> sary. Such encouragement comes naturally from the crowd of lis-
> teners surrounding the singer. Since the singer wishes to earn the
> crowd's applause, and since he is not concerned only about fame
> but also about material benefits, he always attempts to adjust his
> song to the audience around him. If he is not directly called upon
> to sing a specific episode, he begins his song with a prelude that is
> supposed to introduce the audience to the ideas of his song. By
> linking the verses in a most artful way, and by making allusions to
> the most prestigious persons present, he knows how to entertain
> his audience before he goes on to the actual song. When he can
> tell from the audience's vocal approbation that he has gained their
> full attention, he either goes on to the plot directly or gives a brief
> sketch of specific events that preceded the episode he is about to
> sing, and then he begins with the plot.[140] The song does not pro-
> ceed at an even pace. The excited applause of the audience con-
> tinually spurs the singer on to new efforts, and he knows how to
> adjust his song to audience circumstances. If wealthy and noble
> Kirghiz are present, he knows how to skillfully weave in praises of
> their dynasties, and he sings about those episodes which he ex-
> pects will stir the nobility's applause in particular.[141]

Such testimony is pertinent to the comparative information about
the living oral epic traditions in Africa, where we see a similar correlation of occasionality and local contexts. Let us consider the epic
traditions of Manding society, marked by "both a vigorous pan-
cultural tradition and a constant pull toward diversity," crossing as
it does several linguistic and modern political boundaries.[142] "The

---

140. My addendum: we may compare the conventions of the ancient Greek *prooímion* or
'prelude', which afford the most distinct opportunities for the performer to refer to the
occasion of performance: see N 1990a:79 n. 133, 353–360. Cf. N 1990b:53–61.

141. Radloff 1885 [1990:85].

142. The apt description of Sienkewicz 1991:184. For a general assessment of his work,
see Tompkins 1992:157: "Sienkewicz is not simply, in the condescending manner of many
classicists, dragging in Sunjata as a 'test case' or 'parallel' to the *Iliad:* if the *Iliad* had never
been composed, Sienkewicz's study of this important epic would remain substantial and

60   Manding peoples believe that their oral stories retell the experiences
of their common past, yet the diversity of their multiforms shows the
ability of these stories to adapt to changes of time and locality."[143]
The centerpiece of Manding oral poetry is an epic tradition about a
historical figure called Sunjata, a powerful chieftain whose lifetime is
historically dated to the thirteenth century C.E. and who is recognized as the founder of the Manding empire.[144] Recorded versions of
the *Sunjata* narrative range in length from a single evening's performance to a thirty-hour stretch.[145] In some of these recorded versions,
we can find explicit documentation of the singer's selective use of
available narrative versions that tie in directly with such details as the
genealogies of members of his audience.[146] The degree of occasionality in the performance of *Sunjata* epic traditions justifies a formulation such as this one: "The epic is more than the tale of its characters;
it is at the same time about its audience."[147]

To the existing comparative information about epic in Africa we
may add still further information from the realm of praise poetry.
When we take an overall look at the evidence collected in Africa, it
appears that praise poetry, in the process of diffusion from local toward more regional contexts of performance, progressively takes on
the characteristics of what we might otherwise call epic. This trend is
markedly noticeable, for example, in the traditions of praise poetry
in Xhosa society.[148] Here we may adduce the internal evidence of
Greek civilization concerning the relationship of epic with praise po-

---

meritorious. . . . There is a clear parallel with Wickersham's [1991] essay, in the sense that
both [essays] view epics as continuously evolving, never frozen."

143. Sienkewicz 1991:184.

144. Ibid., 186.

145. References in ibid., 187.

146. Ibid., 187–188.

147. Ibid., 194.

148. A key work is Opland 1989. Cf. Opland 1988. In Manding oral poetry, we may note
that the *Sunjata* epic tradition features distinct characteristics of praise poetry in the context of quoting direct address, which is "sung in a style different from the narrative sections of the epic" (Sienkewicz 1991:195, following Innes 1974:17–20).

etry. Following the formulation of Aristotle's *Poetics* (1448b27, 32–34), which derives epic from praise poetry, I have argued elsewhere that the form and content of a Greek poetic tradition that calls itself *aînos* or 'praise', as represented by the victory odes of Pindar, can be reconstructed as a basis for the development of what we know as epic.[149] In line with my intent to avoid monogenetic theories for the origins of Greek epic,[150] it is important to stress that praise poetry can be reconstructed as *a* basis, not *the* basis, for the development of epic.[151] Still, the internal testimony of ancient Greek epic itself implies the outright derivation of epic from praise. We may note references made by Greek epic to primal scenes of praise and blame poetry, as we see in the brief retelling of the Judgment of Paris scene in *Iliad* 24.29–30, where the Homeric tradition itself represents the genesis of epic in terms of a primal opposition of praise poetry to blame poetry.[152]

As we look more closely at the comparative evidence concerning the relationship of praise poetry and epic, we can find further justification for deriving Greek epic, at least in part, from praise poetry.

---

149. N 1990a:146–198, an expanded version of N 1986a. Cf. Lord 1991:36–37.

150. N 1990a:459–464.

151. Following J. W. Johnson 1980:321, Sienkewicz (1991:200) notes that the existing combination of the narrative with praise song in the *Sunjata* epic tradition demonstrates "the multigeneric nature of African epic." Besides praise poetry, other kinds of songmaking that shape the development of epic include lament, especially women's lament. See N 1979:94–117 on the affinities of epic with the song traditions of lamentation; see also Martin 1989:86–87, 131, 144. Moreover, as Martin shows at p. 144, "praise and lament are intertwined." In Pindar *Isthmian* 8.56–60, the song of lament performed by the Muses at the funeral pyre of Achilles is represented as the germ for a song of praise glorifying the heroic deeds of Achilles; this song becomes, implicitly, the epic tradition of Achilles. See N 1979:177: "Pindar's words are . . . implying that the epic of Achilles amounts to an eternal outflow of the *thrênos* [lament] performed for Achilles by the Muses themselves." On the idea, as expressed in Greek songmaking traditions, that the sung glories of men are ultimately controlled through the laments that their female kinsfolk will sing about them after they are dead, see Sultan 1993.

152. See N 1990b:16–17. Cf. Martin 1989:102–103, 108, 110 on praise poetics embedded in Homeric narrative, especially with reference to the poetics inherent in the discourse of Nestor. Martin (p. 102) remarks that "Nestor resembles the perfect praise-poet" (at p. 103 he refutes the stereotype of Nestor as "a caricature of geriatric loquacity"). For a particularly acute set of observations on the functional opposition of praise and blame, as played out in *Iliad* 10.249–250, see Martin 1989:94–95, extending the arguments developed about the same passage in N 1979:34–35.

62   In my earlier work, I studied in great detail the *occasional* nature of
the ancient Greek praise-poem or *aînos*.[153] Here I simply compare
this feature of occasionality in ancient Greek praise-poetry with the
occasionality of epic in the oral traditions of India, especially on the
more local levels. In India, we find clear instances where plot variation is radically conditioned by the nature of the audience.[154] Such
conditioning reveals the dependence of the performers on their audiences. Let us take as an example of such performers the Nayaks, a
caste of hereditary singers of the Pābūjī epic tradition found primarily in central and south Rajasthan, who "circulate from village to village on a yearly beat seeking patrons."[155] The musical instruments of
the professional performers tend to be chordophonic, requiring rigorous training.[156] In the commissioning of a Nayak performance of
the Pābūjī epic, "the patron's devotion is the most important measure
of the performance."[157] The patronage can occur on the level of festivals, but most often occur on the level of the village; "patrons may
sponsor a performance for one night or a series of nights."[158] One
motivation for a sponsor's undertaking of a sponsorship is to fulfill a
vow.[159] Such a relationship between patron and poet offers a wide
spectrum of comparative insights into the sociology, as it were, of
praise poetry in ancient Greece.

The ad hoc orientation of the ancient Greek praise-poem or *aînos*,
with its persistent internal references to the occasion of its performance and to the expectations of its audience, stands in marked contrast to the stance taken in the Homeric tradition of epic, which
programmatically shades over any reference to any specific occasion
of performance and thus implies that it is worthy of universal accep-

---

153. N 1990a: 146–338.

154. E.g., Flueckiger 1989: 50 n. 17.

155. Kothari 1989: 103.

156. Ibid.

157. Ibid., 104.

158. Ibid.

159. Ibid.

tance, that is, of unconditional reception.[160] It is as if the epic of Homer had outgrown the need for occasionality of performance. Similarly in the praise poetry of the Xhosa, the phenomenon of diffusion entails the widening of perspective in the content of praise:

> The elliptical Xhosa *isibongo* [praise-songs] consist of short-hand allusions that are normally understood by the poet's local audience, familiar as they are with the subjects of the poetry and the context of historical narrative and anecdote current in the community. But if the poet is conscious that his audience is suddenly wider, expanded beyond the local limits of his usual performances, then he might wish to gloss the potentially puzzling allusions, to incorporate the footnotes into his text, as it were.[161]

The wording here, with emphasis on *text* as a metaphor for *composition* in oral poetics, is apt, in the sense that the authoritativeness of such a composition is made analogous to the potential authoritativeness of a written text. And so we come back full circle to our point of departure, which is the historical reality of the Homeric text. We have yet to consider the text as text, but by now we can see, at least in its broad outlines, the process of evolution that led to this reality.

---

160. Extensive discussion, with examples from both epic and praise poetry, is found in N 1990a: 146–214. Opland (1989:139) offers an interesting application of Xhosa evidence as a parallel to my model of pan-Hellenization.

161. Opland 1989:139.

 CHAPTER 3

Homer and the Evolution of a Homeric Text

In searching for a historical context for the writing down of the Homeric text, the most obvious strategy is to look for a stage in ancient Greek history when the technology of writing could produce a text, *in manuscript form,* that conferred a level of authority distinct from but equivalent to the authority conferred by an actual performance. As we have seen in the previous chapter, the opportunity for a text to become the equivalent of a performance already exists in the case of early poetic inscriptions from the eighth century B.C.E. onward. But manuscripts as distinct from inscriptions are another matter. It is only at a later period, after 550 B.C.E. or so, that we begin to see actual examples of the use of writing in the form of manuscripts. As we shall now see, some of these examples involve the use of a manuscript for purposes of a transcript, that is, in order to record any given *composition* and to control the circumstances of any given *performance.*[1]

One such example comes from the era of Peisistratos and his sons, tyrants at Athens in the second half of the sixth century B.C.E.: from various reports, we see that this dynasty of the Peisistratidai maintained political power at least in part by way of controlling poetry.[2] One report in particular is worthy of mention here: according to Herodotus, the Peisistratidai possessed manuscripts of oracular poetry, which they stored on the acropolis of Athens (5.90.2).[3] I draw attention to a word used by Herodotus in this context, *kéktēmai*

---

1. Cf. N 1990a: 158–162, 168–174.

2. Ibid., 158–162; also pp. 75–76 n. 114, with reference to Aloni 1986: 120–123; cf. Catenacci 1993: 8 n. 2; and Shapiro 1990, 1992, 1993.

3. See more on Herodotus 5.90.2 in N 1990a: 158–159.

66 'possess', in referring to the tyrants' possession of poetry. As I have argued elsewhere, "The possession of poetry was a primary sign of the tyrant's wealth, power, and prestige."[4] We may recall in this context the claim in Athenaeus 3a that the first Hellenes to possess "libraries" were the tyrants Polykrates of Samos and Peisistratos of Athens.

For Herodotus, the control of poetry by tyrants was a matter of *private* possession, a perversion of what should be the *public* possession of the city-state or polis.[5] An example of public possession is evident in Herodotus's description of a consultation of the Oracle at Delphi that took place *after* the era of the tyrants, at a time when the Athenian state was already a democracy. We see from Herodotus's account of the consultation that there was a conventional procedure for the use of oracular poetry, and this procedure can be divided into three stages: (1) the poetry could be transcribed by delegates that had been sent to Delphi in order to hear the actual delivery of the oracular poetic message; (2) these delegates were to bring home the transcript, from Delphi to the people of the polis of Athens; and (3) these same delegates would proclaim to the people, on the basis of the transcript, the poetic message of the oracle (*apéngellon es tòn dêmon* 7.142.1).[6] This procedure, which Herodotus describes as if it were a regular practice in Athens during the era that followed the fall of the tyrants, stands in marked contrast to the earlier practice of the Peisistratidai, which he describes as if it were a usurpation of the public possession of poetry: to have private possession of poetry as a text is to control the occasion of its performance and the contents of its composition.[7]

It is, then, in this era of the tyrants, the Peisistratidai, that we may imagine a plausible historical occasion for the transcription of the

---

4. Ibid., 158.

5. Herodotus implies that the tyrants, by having control over the performance of poetry, have the power to withhold poetry from the public, and in that sense they *begrudge* the public their opportunities to hear poetry. In the propaganda of the tyrants themselves, however, they presented themselves not as stinting or *begrudging* but rather as lavish and *generous* to the public in providing them with opportunities to hear poetry. See N 1990a:160–161, including a discussion of "Plato" *Hipparchus* 228d, on which more at note 50 below.

6. N 1990a:168.

7. Ibid.

Homeric poems in manuscript form. As we shall see further below, the plausibility seems enhanced by various reports from the ancient world about an event that some classicists have described as the "Peisistratean recension" of the Homeric poems. Before we can take up the whole question of such a "recension," however, we must first examine further what exactly it means to speak of a *transcript* in the era of the Peisistratidai and thereafter.

It is easiest to start with a negative consideration: a transcript is not the equivalent of a performance, though it may be an aid to performance. In other words, a transcript need not be a speech-act. Aside from the testimony that I have already considered from sources like Herodotus, there is also the evidence of pictures, in vase paintings, representing the use of manuscripts. As we examine the representations of people using manuscripts—that is, books or papyrus rolls in these vase paintings—we can see that "books seem to have a mainly mnemonic role supplementing oral recitation."[8]

By the fifth century, however, there are cases where something that was written in a manuscript form could indeed become the equivalent of a performance. In other words, we now start seeing clear traces of an impulse to reenact the performative dimension by way of a manuscript's written word. For example, in the case of Herodotus's own large-scale composition, the *Histories,* it is clear that the *writing down* of this composition in manuscript form was meant to be the equivalent of a performance, a genuine speech-act.[9] For Herodotus, to say "I write something" is deliberately made equivalent to saying "I say something" in solemn, public situations (e.g., 2.123.3, 4.195.2, 6.14.1, 7.214.3)—because whatever he is saying in this solemn way at the moment that the reader reads it *has already been written down.*[10] In other words, whatever is staged as being said by the speaker of the *Histories* of Herodotus is predicated on the fact that it has already been framed by the medium of writing, as if the staging itself were a creation of the writing.[11] "I am saying this now in what I have written, therefore I am writing this now."

---

8. Thomas 1989:21 n. 22, following Immerwahr 1964.

9. See further discussion in N 1990a:169, 217, 219.

10. Ibid., 219.

11. It is for this reason that *apodekhthénta* 'made public', applied in the very first sentence of Herodotus to the deeds of Hellenes and barbarians that are to be highlighted by history,

68   The main difference between this kind of stance in early literature and similar effects in modern literature is that, for someone like Herodotus, the situations in the text where it is written "I write this now" instead of "I say this now" still match conventional situations in public life where one would normally say "I say this now." Thus, even as late as the second half of the fifth century, the era of Herodotus, the actual writing down of any given text could still be viewed as tantamount to the production of yet another performance, to the extent that the technology of writing could produce a text that conferred a level of authority parallel to that conferred by an actual performance.[12] In the *Histories* of Herodotus, the written text is not only an equivalent to performance: it is considered the *authoritative* equivalent.

By contrast, a transcript is not an equivalent to performance but merely a potential means to achieve performance. To that extent, a transcript in the era of the Peisistratidai may be viewed as a prototypical "script." In what follows, I shall argue that whatever poetry might have been transcribed in this era still has to be defined in terms of oral poetics, that is, it has to be viewed as resulting from a fundamental interplay between the dimensions of composition and performance. Further, I shall continue to argue that there is no evidence for assuming that the *Iliad* and the *Odyssey*, as compositions, *resulted* from the writing down of a text. The point remains that the writing down of a composition as text does not mean that writing was a prerequisite for the text's composition—*so long as the oral tradition that produced it continued to stay alive.* Moreover, the writing down of any kind of composition that could otherwise be produced in performance will not necessarily freeze the process of recomposition-in-performance.[13] There are numerous parallels in European medieval literature, as we see, for example, in the following description, with

---

can be translated as 'performed'. N 1990a:219: "The obvious explanation for these usages of *apo-deîk-numai* in the sense of *performing* rather than *publicly presenting* or *demonstrating* or *displaying* a deed is that the actual medium for publicly presenting the given deed is in all these cases none other than the language of Herodotus."

12. From an insider's point of view, writing can become a "technology toy": witness the last words in the *Helen* of Gorgias (DK 82 B 11.21): Ἑλένης μὲν ἐγκώμιον, ἐμὸν δὲ παίγνιον 'Helen's encomium, my plaything'.

13. N 1990a:19 and the cross-references given at n. 9 there.

reference to fifteenth-century English manuscript production: "The surviving manuscripts of a poem like *Beves of Hamptoun* make it clear that each act of copying was to a large extent an act of recomposition, and not an episode in a process of decomposition from an ideal form."[14] Paul Zumthor describes as *mouvance* the process whereby the act of composition, so long as this composition belongs to a living tradition of composition-in-performance, is regenerated in each act of copying.[15]

So the question is: if indeed a transcript could have been made of the Homeric poems in the era of the Peisistratidai, how exactly are we to imagine the use of such a transcript? As a parallel to the pattern that we have seen reflected in the account of Herodotus, where he describes the Peisistratidai as establishing control over oracular poetry, we may suppose that this dynasty sought to control epic poetry as well. We shall return later to this aspect of the parallelism. The problem for now is that the parallelism cannot be extended in other respects. Oracular poetry is visibly occasional, responsive to the ad hoc requirements of time and place.[16] The epic poetry of the *Iliad* and the *Odyssey,* on the other hand, is distinctly nonoccasional and at least *notionally* unchanging, to be performed again and again on a seasonally recurring basis at formal occasions like the Feast of the Panathenaia. As I have already suggested, the Homeric poems reveal a high degree of text-fixation or textualization, and again I am using the concept of *text* without the implication that writing is a prerequisite.[17] So the question still remains: what use is there for a transcript of such a text?

Another way to approach the question is to consider the textuality of the Homeric poems. Although I shall continue to argue that no writing had been required to bring about this textuality, I propose now to rethink the question in terms of a later era when written texts were indeed the norm. Even in this later era, I insist, any written text

---

14. See Pearsall 1984:126–127. For medieval Irish parallels, see the discussion of J. F. Nagy 1986, esp. p. 289.

15. Zumthor 1972:507. For an application of this principle in the editing of medieval lyric texts, see the exemplary work of Pickens 1977 (also 1978), as discussed in N 1996: Ch. 1.

16. N 1990a:158–160.

17. See p. 40 above.

70 that derives from an oral tradition can continue to enjoy the status of a recomposition-in-performance—so long as the oral tradition retains its performative authority.[18] In such a later era, where written text and oral tradition coexist, the idea of a written text can even become a primary metaphor for the authority of recomposition-in-performance. As I shall now argue, the very concept of a "Peisistratean recension" can be derived from such a metaphor.

The intrinsic applicability of *text* as metaphor for *recomposition-in-performance* helps explain a type of myth, attested in a wide variety of cultural contexts, where the evolution of a poetic tradition, moving slowly ahead in time until it reaches a relatively static phase, is reinterpreted by the myth as if it resulted from a single incident, pictured as the instantaneous recovery or even regeneration of a lost text, an archetype. In other words, myth can make its own "big bang" theory for the origins of epic, and it can even feature in its scenario the concept of writing.

A particularly striking example is a myth about the making of the Book of Kings in the classical Persian epic tradition:

> According to Ferdowsi's *Shāhnāma* I 21.126–136, a noble vizier assembles *mōbad-s*, wise men who are experts in the Law of Zoroaster, from all over the Empire, and each of these *mōbad-s* brings with him a "fragment" of a long-lost Book of Kings that had been scattered to the winds; each of the experts is called upon to recite, in turn, his respective "fragment," and the vizier composes a book out of these recitations. . . . The vizier reassembles the old book that had been disassembled, which in turn becomes the model for the *Shāhnāma* "Book of Kings" of Ferdowsi (*Shāhnāma* I 21.156–161). We see here paradoxically a myth about the synthesis of oral traditions that is articulated in terms of written traditions.[19]

There is a comparable myth in Old Irish traditions, concerning the recovery of the "lost" *Cattle Raid of Cúailnge*.[20] There are also similar themes in Old French traditions. The work known as *Guiron le cour-*

---

18. See p. 67 above.

19. N 1990a:74 n. 110, following Davidson 1985:111–127; cf. Davidson 1994:29–53.

20. N 1990a:74 n. 110, following J. F. Nagy 1985:292–293; cf. J. F. Nagy 1983 and 1986 (esp. pp. 284 and 289 in the latter article).

tois, for example, composed around 1235 C.E., lays the foundation
for its authority by telling of the many French books that were produced from what is pictured as an archetypal translation of a mythical Latin book of the Holy Grail.[21]

We can find further examples in the living oral traditions of India. In Telugu society, there is an aetiological myth explaining why
the Palnāḍu epic is now sung by untouchable Malas: "The epic, it is
claimed, was first written by a Brahmin poet, torn into shreds, dis-
carded, and then picked up by the present performers."[22] Another
example comes from the Pābūji oral epic tradition of Rajasthan: "A
bhopo [*bhopā* or medium, folk-priest] of Pābūji like Parbū will insist
that the epic he performs 'really' derives from a big book composed
by high-caste Cāraṇ poets and kept in Pābūji's native village of Koḷū:
for him it is the *written* word that carries authority."[23]

I have saved till now two examples from ancient Greece. Both involve myths, but in the second case the myth in question seems at
first to be a report based on historical events. This is not the place to
explore at length the role of myth as a reflex of institutional history
in ancient Greece.[24] For the moment, it is enough to say that both
myths about to be examined concern the institutions of the respective communities to which they belong, and that the two communities in question are Sparta and Athens. Since the myths may not seem
like myths at first sight, I will for the moment refer to both of them by
way of the more neutral term "story."

The first story is from Sparta, centering on the topic of a dis-
assembled text, scattered here and there throughout the Greek-
speaking world, and then reassembled in a single incident, at one

---

21. Lathuillère 1966:176–177. For an indispensable discussion, see Huot 1991:218–221.

22. Blackburn 1989:32 n. 25.

23. J. D. Smith (1990:18), who also observes (pp. 17–18): "It may be that the orality of
these traditions is a strength rather than a weakness, for Hindu worship—including Vedic
ritual—has always emphasized oral skills: books may be used for learning from, but they
are not for use in ritual performance, and there is no 'holy book' in Hinduism to compare
with the Bible, the Koran, or the *Gurū granth sāhib.* The Vedas are holy of course, but they
are holy in performance, not as a manuscript or printed volume." Contrasting the "primary" orality of the Rajasthani epic traditions with the "secondary oral ability of the literate Brahmin who learns texts from a book," Smith concludes (p. 18): "It is an intriguing
paradox that the two widely-separated worlds of orality and literacy should each seek legitimacy by claiming characteristics belonging to the other."

24. For some detailed examples, see N 1985:36–41; also N 1990a:170, 368.

72   particular time and place, by a wise man credited with the juridical framework of his society, Lycurgus the lawgiver. According to this story, as reported by Plutarch (*Life of Lycurgus* 4.4), Lycurgus brought to Sparta the Homeric poems, which he acquired from a lineage of epic performers called the Kreophyleioi, descended from Kreophylos of Samos.[25] In archaic Sparta, it appears that the Kreophyleioi of Samos were more authoritative than the epic performers elsewhere credited with the transmission of Homeric poetry, the Homeridai of Chios: as Aristotle reports (F 611.10 Rose), the Homeric poems were introduced to Sparta by Lycurgus, who got them from the Kreophyleioi when he visited Samos.[26] With reference to the Homeric poems, Plutarch reports that Lycurgus, having received them from the Kreophyleioi, 'had them written down', *egrápsato,* and that he then 'assembled' them (*Life of Lycurgus* 4.4). What follows in Plutarch's account is worth citing verbatim (ibid.):

ἦν γάρ τις ἤδη δόξα τῶν ἐπῶν ἀμαυρὰ παρὰ τοῖς Ἕλλησιν, ἐκέκτηντο δὲ οὐ πολλοὶ μέρη τινά, σποράδην τῆς ποιήσεως, ὡς ἔτυχε, διαφερομένης. γνωρίμην δὲ αὐτὴν καὶ μάλιστα πρῶτος ἐποίησε Λυκοῦργος.

For there was already a not-too-bright fame attached to these epics among the Greeks, and some of them were in possession [verb *kéktēmai*] of some portions, since the poetry had been scattered about, carried here and there by chance, and it was Lycurgus who was the first to make it [the poetry] well-known.

In this passage, I have highlighted the word *kéktēmai* 'possess', with reference to the "ownership" of Homeric poetry. The same word is used by Herodotus in referring to the "ownership" of oracular poetry on the part of the Peisistratidai, the dynasty of tyrants at Athens (5.90.2).[27] Elsewhere, Herodotus refers to the manipulation, by the

25. In another version, which goes back to Ephorus of Cyme (FGH 70 F 129 by way of Strabo 10.4.19), Lycurgus acquired the Homeric poems directly from Homer at Chios; cf. Davison 1955a:15 n. 22. For more on the mythological relationship between Homer, "ancestor" of the Homeridai of Chios, and Kreophylos, "ancestor" of the Kreophyleioi of Samos, and the rivalry between the two groups, see N 1990a:23, 74, with special reference to Strabo 14.1.18 and Callimachus *Epigram* 6. Cf. Burkert 1972.

26. Cf. Davison 1955a:15 n. 22; also Janko (1992:30 n. 45), who (at p. 31 n. 50) considers the possibility that the Aristotle story about Lycurgus in Samos goes back to the late sixth century.

27. See pp. 65–67 above. See further details in N 1990a:159, 168–169, 220.

Peisistratidai, of oracular poetry with the help of one Onomakritos, described in this context as *diathétēs* 'arranger' of this poetry (7.6.3).[28]

This detail about a *diathétēs* 'arranger' of poetry brings us to the second of the two ancient Greek examples of the kind of myth that we are presently considering. This second story is from Athens. Even more than the first story, it seems at first to be not a myth but a straightforward account of a historical *event*. As I shall argue presently, however, it can be explained as a myth that happens to account for a historical *process*. This myth, like others we have already examined, reinterprets the evolution of a poetic tradition as if it resulted from a single incident, pictured as the dramatic recovery of a lost text. Again, myth is offering a "big bang" theory for the origins of epic. As I shall argue, what makes the Athenian version of this type of myth more distinct than other versions is that we know more about the historical circumstances of its ultimate political appropriation.

For now, a summary of the Athenian story will suffice. According to Tzetzes (*Anecdota Graeca* 1.6 ed. Cramer), a certain Onomakritos, the same person whom we have just seen described by Herodotus as a *diathétēs* 'arranger' of oracular poetry (7.6.3), was the member of a group of four men commissioned in the reign of Peisistratos to supervise the 'arranging' of the Homeric poems, which were before then 'scattered about': διέθηκαν οὑτωσὶ σποράδην οὔσας τὸ πρίν.[29] There is a convergent report in Aelian *Varia historia* 13.14, where the introduction of Homeric poetry to Sparta by Lycurgus the lawgiver is explicitly compared to a subsequent introduction of the *Iliad* and the *Odyssey* to Athens by Peisistratos. The most explicit version of the story can be found in Cicero *De oratore* 3.137: Peisistratos, as one of the Seven Sages (*septem fuisse dicuntur uno tempore, qui sapientes et haberentur et vocarentur*),[30] was supposedly so learned and eloquent that "he is said to be the first person ever to arrange the books of Homer, previously *scattered* about, in the order that we have today": *qui primus*

---

28. Further details can be found in ibid., 174.

29. Ibid. T. W. Allen (1924:233) thinks that the source of Tzetzes here was Athenodorus, head of the Library at Pergamum. Note the parallel wording in the *Greek Anthology* 11.442: ὃς τὸν Ὅμηρον ἤθροισα, σποράδην τὸ πρὶν ἀειδόμενον 'I who gathered together Homer, who was previously being sung here and there, scattered all over the place'. See also Pausanias 7.26.13.

30. There is emphasis on the idea that each of the Seven Sages except Thales had been head of state (Cicero *De oratore* 3.137: *hi omnes praeter Milesium Thalen civitatibus suis praefuerunt*). For more on the Seven Sages tradition, see Martin 1993.

74 *Homeri libros confusos antea sic disposuisse dicitur, ut nunc habemus.*[31] In these accounts of the supposedly original Athenian reception of Homeric poetry, reinforced by the story in "Plato" *Hipparchus* 228b claiming that it was Hipparkhos, the son of Peisistratos, who introduced the Homeric poems to Athens, we confront the germ of the construct that has come to be known among classicists as the "Peisistratean recension."[32]

On the basis of the other narrative traditions that we have examined concerning the topic of an archetypal text that disintegrates in the distant past only to become reintegrated at a later point by a sage who then gives it as a gift to his community, the story of a "Peisistratean recension" can be explained as a myth that bears clear signs of political appropriation by the Peisistratidai. Particularly striking is the parallelism in the accounts of Plutarch and Cicero between Lycurgus, lawgiver of Sparta who gives his community the Homeric poems, and Peisistratos, described as one of the Seven Sages, who likewise gives his community of Athens the Homeric poems. I repeat an observation made earlier: Greek myths about lawgivers, whether they are historical figures or not, tend to reconstruct these figures as the originators of the sum total of customary law.[33] Traditions about the Seven Sages, the most prominent of whom is Solon the lawgiver of Athens, are closely linked to those about lawgivers in general.[34]

The distinction between historical tyrants on the one hand and mythical lawgivers or sages on the other is oftentimes blurred.[35] In

---

31. On Cicero's own reinterpretation of this myth, see Boyd 1996.

32. For a brief restatement and survey of primary information pertinent to the concept of a "Peisistratean recension," see Allen 1924:225–238. See also N 1990a:21–22 n. 20. For a most useful bibliography on the concept, see Janko (1992:29), whose own position is that "the text existed *before* [Peisistratos'] time." At p. 32, with bibliography, Janko brings up the suggestion of earlier scholars that the Peisistratean recension was a "theory" invented by the scholars of Pergamum. For a compelling defense of the reliability of the actual information provided by "Plato" *Hipparchus* 228b, see Davison 1955a:10–13.

33. See p. 21 above. Cf. N 1985:33 and N 1990a:170, 368 (with special reference to Lycurgus, as portrayed in Plutarch *Life of Lycurgus* 4.2–3).

34. See especially N 1990a:185–186, 226 n. 61, 243 n. 122, 333–334.

35. See especially ibid., 185–186.

the account of Aelian, the parallelism between the lawgiver par excellence and the tyrant Peisistratos is explicit: just as Lycurgus gives the Homeric poems to Sparta, so also Peisistratos gives the Homeric poems to Athens. The parallelism may possibly be extended: just as Lycurgus is reputed to have brought the Homer performed by the Kreophyleioi of Samos to Sparta (Plutarch *Life of Lycurgus* 4), so also the Peisistratidai seem to have taken credit for bringing the Homer performed by the Homeridai of Chios to Athens.[36]

The Homeric poems took shape, according to Athenian versions of the story, in the context of what is now called the "Panathenaic rule," where the performance of the *Iliad* and the *Odyssey* by *rhapsōidoí* 'rhapsodes' was not allowed to favor some parts of the epic narrative over others, in that the narrative had to be performed by one rhapsode after another *in sequence* ("Plato" Hipparchus 228b and Diogenes Laertius 1.57).[37] I shall have more to say at a later point about this story and about its pertinence to the question of rhapsodes. For now I simply draw attention to the fact that this "Panathenaic rule" is attributed by the sources *either* to the Peisistratidai ("Plato" *Hipparchus* 228b) *or* to Solon himself (Diogenes Laertius 1.57). The parallelism linking the Peisistratidai with Solon, lawgiver of Athens, can be compared to the parallelism linking Peisistratos with Lycurgus, lawgiver of Sparta. Again we see indications of the appropriation of a myth by the Peisistratidai.

The politics involved in the attribution of this Homeric institution to the Peisistratidai are to be expected. Also to be expected, I suggest, is that this attribution to the tyrants would in time be ousted by an attribution to Solon, once the tyrants themselves were ousted: it makes sense for the credit that they once could claim as would-be lawgivers to be retrojected to an earlier figure, Solon, whose status as primary culture hero of the State, originator of a wide variety of institutions, makes him the ideal recipient of any credit taken away from others who came after him.

---

36. For more on the parallelisms between the Kreophyleioi and Homeridai, see ibid., 23, 74.

37. Davison 1955a:7; cf. Sealey 1957:342–351. Besides "Plato" *Hipparchus* 228b and Diogenes Laertius 1.57, the following passages are pertinent: Isocrates *Panegyricus* 159; Lycurgus *Against Leokrates* 102; Plutarch *Pericles* 13.6; cf. Davison (1955a:7–15), with whom I agree that the Panathenaia, as reshaped by Pericles in 442 (cf. Plutarch *Pericles* 13.6), in-

These stories about the fixation of Homeric performance traditions will help provide an answer to a basic question about the dimensions of Homeric composition: how, after all, are we to account
for the sheer length of these epics? How was it possible for the *Iliad*
and the *Odyssey* to reach the monumental proportions of over 15,000
and 12,000 verses respectively?[38]

In order to appreciate the mythological answer to such questions,
let us first consider a common feature of oral poetic traditions, which
is the potential for either expansion or compression of a given topic.
Analysis of this phenomenon in living oral epic traditions makes it
clear that neither the relatively more expanded nor the relatively
more compressed versions need necessarily be considered basic from
the internal standpoint of the given tradition.[39] Such an absence of
standardization in length is of great importance for coming to terms
with the Homeric tradition, where we find a great variety of compression as well as expansion of themes. Of these two features, expansion
and compression, the more noticeable is of course expansion, in that
the impact of an overall composition may keep being augmented
with the expansion of size, whereas any instances of compression,
even if they happen to be miniature feats of artistic skill, will have to
be contained within an expanding composition. In the aesthetics of
Homeric poetry, multiple marvels of compression are fated to be
contained by the singular marvel of ultimate expansion, such as the
monumental composition of the *Iliad*.[40] It is much harder for us to
appreciate compression, enclosed as it is within the expansive monumentality of the whole *Iliad*, the whole *Odyssey*.

---

cluded competitive performances by *rhapsōidoí* 'rhapsodes' of consecutive parts of the *Iliad*
and the *Odyssey;* but I disagree with the idea (Davison p. 8) that Pericles originated these
competitive performances. I also agree with the argument (p. 8) that Isocrates' reference
to "musical" contests (τοῖς μουσικοῖς ἄθλοις, *Panegyricus* 159) includes the institution of
rhapsodic contests.

38. On the notion of an eighth-century Homer's "monumental" *Iliad* and *Odyssey,* see Kirk
1985:10. For an important redefinition of Homeric monumentality, see Martin 1989, esp.
p. 223.

39. N 1990b:55, following Lord 1960:25–27, 68–98, 99–123. Cf. Svenbro 1988a:80 n. 20
(= 1993:70 n. 18).

40. See Martin 1989:196, 205, 206–230 (esp. p. 215 n. 11) on the "expansion aesthetic"
of the *Iliad*. Martin refers to instances of compression in terms of "telescoping": see

Aside from instances of bravura in compression and expansion, however, we should also expect to find in living oral traditions the more ordinary levels of these phenomena, where the context of a given occasion leads to shortening or lengthening by default. Even in such default situations, however, it appears that relatively longer versions of a given epic performance have more to say about their given occasion than do shorter versions. We have considerable evidence about the potential monumentality of Indian epic performance, in both size and scope, and how that monumentality is managed in terms of actual performance. A key element is the subdivision of monumental epic performance into performance segments—which may be called "episodes":

> Immensely long epic stories, which would take hundreds of hours
> to sing if performed in one sitting, are commonly divided into
> more manageable segments. The Palnāḍu epic, for example,
> contains thirty *kathalu* (stories), each of which may take one or
> more nights to perform. The Pābūjī epic is similarly divided into
> twelve *parvāṛo* (episodes), and the Ālhā into various *laṛāī* (battles)
> which organize the performance of these epics. These perfor-
> mance segments are not, however, *evenly weighted,* like chapters.
> Certain *episodes* are more popular than others and are repeatedly
> performed; others are rarely heard and may even be unknown
> to certain singers. Furthermore, even when an epic story is well
> known to the audience, the complete story, from beginning
> to end, is rarely presented in performance—or even in a series
> of performances. The full story is sometimes found in written
> and published texts, but we prefer to speak of an epic tradition
> that encompasses not only text and performance but also what
> is unwritten and unperformed.[41]

Drawing attention to the principle of *unevenly weighted episodes* in this description, I propose that the evolution of ancient Greek epic involved a progression from *uneven weighting* toward *even weighting.* Let us take as our point of departure the example of uneven weighting

---

pp. 213, 215. For instances of contrasting expansion and compression, see Martin p. 34, 213, 215 (with n. 11), 216–219, 225.

41. Blackburn and Flueckiger 1989:11. Highlighting mine.

78 that we have just considered in the Indian evidence. We find a striking analogy in the following description of Homeric poetry at an early stage when it was supposedly divided into separate narrative portions, which have actually been described by one commentator as "episodes": [42]

> ὅτι τὰ Ὁμήρου ἔπη πρότερον διῃρημένα ᾖδον οἱ παλαιοί. οἷον
> ἔλεγον Τὴν ἐπὶ ναυσὶ μάχην καὶ Δολώνειάν τινα καὶ Ἀριστείαν
> Ἀγαμέμνονος καὶ Νεῶν κατάλογον καὶ Πατρόκλειαν καὶ Λύτρα
> καὶ Ἐπὶ Πατρόκλῳ ἆθλα καὶ Ὁρκίων ἀφάνισιν. ταῦτα ὑπὲρ τῆς
> Ἰλιάδος. ὑπὲρ δὲ τῆς ἑτέρας Τὰ ἐν Πύλῳ καὶ Τὰ ἐν Λακεδαίμονι
> καὶ Καλυψοῦς ἄντρον καὶ Τὰ περὶ τὴν σχεδίαν καὶ Ἀλκίνου
> ἀπολόγους καὶ Κυκλώπειαν καὶ Νέκυιαν καὶ Τὰ τῆς Κίρκης καὶ
> Νίπτρα καὶ Μνηστήρων φόνον καὶ Τὰ ἐν ἀγρῷ καὶ Τὰ ἐν Λαέρτου.
> ὀψὲ δὲ Λυκοῦργος ὁ Λακεδαιμόνιος ἀθρόαν πρῶτος ἐς τὴν Ἑλλάδα
> ἐκόμισε τὴν Ὁμήρου ποίησιν· τὸ δὲ ἀγώγιμον τοῦτο ἐξ Ἰωνίας,
> ἡνίκα ἀπεδήμησεν, ἤγαγεν. ὕστερον δὲ Πεισίστρατος συναγαγὼν
> ἀπέφηνε τὴν Ἰλιάδα καὶ Ὀδύσσειαν. (Aelian *Varia historia* 13.14)

> That the ancients used to sing the poetic utterances of Homer in separate parts: for example, they spoke of "The Battle over the Ships," "A Story of Dolon," "The Greatest Heroic Moments (*aristeía*) of Agamemnon," "The Catalogue of Ships," "The Story of Patroklos," "The Ransom," "The Funeral Games over Patroklos," and "The Breaking of the Oaths." These were in place of the *Iliad*. In place of the other poem there were "The Happenings in Pylos," "The Happenings in Sparta," "The Cave of Calypso," "The Story of the Raft," "The Stories Told to Alkinoos," "The Story of the Cyclops," "The Spirits of the Dead," "The Story of Circe," "The Bath," "The Killing of the Suitors," "The Happenings in the Countryside," and "The Happenings at Laertes' Place." At a late date, Lycurgus of Sparta was the first to bring the collected poetry of Homer to Greece. He brought this cargo from Ionia, when he traveled there. Later, Peisistratos collected it together and featured it as the *Iliad* and *Odyssey*. [43]

For earlier stages of Homeric poetry, we may link the principle of uneven weighting with the preeminence, let us say, of the Achilles theme in the narrative traditions about the Trojan War—at the expense of themes magnifying the epic deeds of other heroes at Troy.

---

42. Sealey 1957:344 and 351 n. 115.

43. Translation after Sealey 1957:344.

This preeminence or even popularity of Achilles is surely still reflected by the *Iliad* that we have. As for the later stages of Homeric
poetry, however, we see an integration of epic themes that had been
sloughed off, as it were, by the driving theme of Achilles, so that the
Iliad in the end has something to say about practically every epic
theme connected with the Trojan War: it restages, in the final year
of the war, a Catalogue of Ships—which would be more appropriate, like the Catalogue of the *Cypria,* to the very beginning of the
Trojan War; it reintroduces Helen of Troy—as if for the first time,
rematching Menelaos and Paris to fight over her as if she had just
been abducted; it even retells, toward the end of its own narrative,
the Judgment of Paris—which had ultimately started it all.[44] Such
feats of narrative integration, I suggest, exemplify an impulse of even
weighting.

I propose now to refine this notion of even weighting by considering the actual sequence as well as the content of what is being
performed. Let us start with a comparative example, taken from
the description by Keith H. Basso of a girls' puberty ritual or *na ih es*
as performed by a group of Apaches living at Cibecue on the Fort
Apache Indian Reservation in Arizona.[45] This ritual is made up of
eight distinct parts or "phases":

> Each phase has a unique meaning, name and set of ritual actions;
> each is initiated, perpetuated, and terminated by a group of songs,
> or "song set." The Apaches do not conceive of *na ih es* as an un-
> broken continuum, but rather tend to emphasize and stress its dif-
> ferent parts.[46]

I draw attention to the positioning of the songs within a preordained
sequence. There is a set of 32 or so of these songs that are sung at the
na ih es, and it is believed that the whole set, collectively called *goh
jon sin'* 'full-of-great-happiness songs', was "originally" sung by an
archetypal female known as Changing Woman.[47] The totality that is

---

44. Cf. N 1992c:x–xi.

45. Basso 1966.

46. Ibid., 153.

47. Ibid., 151. Needless to say, the notion of song is understood here not in terms of a text
but in terms of a composition that is recognized, *within the tradition,* as the "same" composition each time that it is performed.

80   realized every time its "parts" are performed in song is merely no-
tional. Moreover, there is a correlation here of meaning and sequence, where part of the meaning *is* the sequence:

> Each medicine man arranges the 32 or more *goh jon sin*' songs
> which comprise *na ih es* to fit his own stylistic scheme. This pro-
> duces great variation as to the number of songs in a given phase.
> But the sequence of phases is a stable pattern from which there is
> rarely any deviation. For example, one medicine man may sing
> 12 songs in phase I, while another may sing 8 or 16. Nevertheless,
> phase I always precedes phase II. In short, regardless of the num-
> ber of songs in a phase, the order of the phases never changes.[48]

In this case, the option of free variation, a function of meaning, is
subordinated to the nonoption of fixed order, which is also a function of meaning. Such a pattern of subordination, I suggest, is a feature of even weighting.

In light of these considerations, let us reconsider the final and
definitive stages of Homeric poetry, marked by a tightening-up of
epic conventions. My focus is on a story ("Plato" *Hipparchus* 228b–c)
that explains the institution, in Athens, of a customary law applying
to the festival of the Panathenaia, where the performance of the *Iliad*
and the *Odyssey* by *rhapsōidoí* 'rhapsodes' was not allowed to favor
some parts of the epic narrative over others, in that the narrative had
to be performed by one rhapsode after another *in sequence:*

> Ἱππάρχῳ, . . . ὃς ἄλλα τε πολλὰ καὶ καλὰ ἔργα σοφίας ἀπεδείξατο,
> καὶ τὰ Ὁμήρου ἔπη πρῶτος ἐκόμισεν εἰς τὴν γῆν ταυτηνί, καὶ
> ἠνάγκασε τοὺς ῥαψῳδοὺς Παναθηναίοις ἐξ ὑπολήψεως ἐφεξῆς
> αὐτὰ διιέναι, ὥσπερ νῦν ἔτι οἵδε ποιοῦσιν.

> Hipparkhos, . . . who publicly enacted many and beautiful things
> to manifest his expertise (*sophía*),[49] especially by being the first
> to bring over (*komízō*) to this land [Athens] the poetic utterances

---

48. Ibid., 153.

49. The archaizing phraseology of the entire passage about Hipparkhos in "Plato" *Hipparchus* 228b–229d, only a small portion of which I quote here, is strikingly consistent in
leaving unspecified the question of authorship and in emphasizing instead the fact of authority, which is expressed as *sophía* 'expertise' in the understanding of poetry; this *sophía*
is in turn implicitly equated with *sophía* in *performing* this poetry, without specification of
the process of actually *composing* the poetry. For further details, see N 1990a:161.

(*épē*) of Homer,[50] and he forced the rhapsodes (*rhapsōidoí*) at the Panathenaia to go through (*diiénai*) these utterances in sequence (*ephexês*), by relay [*ex hupolépseōs*], just as they [the rhapsodes] do even nowadays.

According to another version, this law about fixed narrative sequence in Homeric performance was introduced not by Hipparkhos of the Peisistratidai but rather by the lawmaker of Athens himself, Solon: τά τε Ὁμήρου ἐξ ὑποβολῆς γέγραφε ῥαψῳδεῖσθαι, οἷον ὅπου ὁ πρῶτος ἔληξεν, ἐκεῖθεν ἄρχεσθαι τὸν ἐχόμενον 'he [Solon the lawgiver] wrote a law that the works of Homer were to be performed rhapsodically (*rhapsōidéō*), by relay (*ex hupobolês*), so that wherever the first person left off, from that point the next person would start' (Diogenes Laertius 1.57).[51] We have already observed that the story is appropriate to either Solon or Peisistratos in the role—deserved or undeserved—of lawgiver. More important for now, in any case, is the fact that these stories attempt to explain the unity of Homeric composition as a result of sequencing in performance.

As we have seen, classicists conventionally refer to this customary law about Homeric performance as the "Panathenaic rule."[52] I sug-

---

50. Hipparkhos also 'brings over' (*komízō*), by ship, the poet Anacreon from Athens (228c), just as he 'brings over' (*komízō*) the *épē* 'poetic utterances' of Homer in the passage quoted here (228b). According to the logic of the narrative, Hipparkhos demonstrates to the people of Athens that he is not 'stinting with his *sophía*', σοφίας φθονεῖν (228c), by virtue of providing the people of Athens with the poetry and songmaking of Homer, Anacreon, and Simonides (the latter is coupled with Anacreon, 228c); by implication, his *sophía* 'expertise' is the key to the performances of these poets (N 1990a:161). We may ask why the application of *komízō* to the epic of Homer is matched by its application to the songs of Anacreon and, by implication, of Simonides. Perhaps the point of the story is that Hipparkhos did something more than simply invite these poets for a single occasion of performance: rather, he institutionalized such performances in contests of *kitharōidía* 'lyre-singing' at the festival of the Panathenaia (on which subject, see N 1990a:98, 104), parallel to contests of *rhapsōidía* at the same festival.

51. Further analysis is found in N 1990a:21, 23. It is argued by Schnapp-Gourbeillon (1988:810) that the law mentioned in these testimonia concerns not the order of performance but the idea that only "Homer" was supposed to be performed. I would counter-argue that the explicit reference in Diogenes Laertius 1.57 to Solon the *lawgiver* as the one who set the sequence of performance suggests that the specification of the sequence was indeed part of the *law*. Likewise in "Plato" *Hipparchus* 228b, the pronoun αὐτά 'these things' designating what the rhapsodes had to perform in fixed sequence surely refers to τὰ Ὁμήρου ἔπη 'the [poetic] utterances of Homer'.

52. Again, Davison 1955a:7.

82   gest that this "rule" is actually a Greek reflex of the principle of even
weighting, indicative of a communalization of repertoire. I also suggest that an even more appropriate term might be *equalized weighting*.

Once the sequencing of Homeric "episodes" becomes a tradition
in its own right, it stands to reason that any cross-referencing from
one episode of the sequence to another will also become a tradition.
It is from a diachronic perspective that I find it useful to consider the
phenomenon of Homeric cross-references, especially long-distance
ones that happen to reach for hundreds or even thousands of lines:
it is important to keep in mind that any such cross-reference that
we admire in our two-dimensional text did not just happen one time
in one performance—but presumably countless times in countless
reperformances within the three-dimensional continuum of a specialized oral tradition. The resonances of Homeric cross-referencing
must be appreciated within the larger context of a long history of repeated performances.[53]

It is also from a diachronic perspective that we can appreciate
the institution and even the concept of *rhapsōidoí* 'rhapsodes', who
are the performers associated with the pattern of equalized or even
weighting in the Homeric narrative tradition. In my earlier work on
the rhapsodes, I concluded: "It is simplistic and even misleading to
contrast, as many have done, the 'creative' *aoidós* ['singer'] with the
'reduplicating' *rhapsōidós*."[54] In terms of my evolutionary model for
the making of Homeric poetry, the figure of the rhapsode is the very
embodiment of an evolving medium that continues, in the course of
time, to put more and more limitations on the process of recomposition-in-performance. The succession of rhapsodes linking a Homer
in the remote past with Homeric performances in the "present" of
the historical period—as extrapolated from such accounts as Plato's
Ion—is a *diachronic* reality. This reality can only be distorted by any
attempt to arrive at a *synchronic* definition of rhapsodes, meant as
some kind of foil for an idealized definition of Homer.

———————

53. For more on the notion of "diachronic cross-referencing" in the Homeric tradition,
see N 1990a:53–54 n. 8. On the "immanence" of referencing, not just cross-referencing,
see Foley 1991: the referent of a reference in oral poetics is not restricted to the immediate context but extends to analogous contexts heard in previous performances.

54. N 1982 [1990b:42]; see the detailed discussion in N 1990a:21–28. This conclusion is
corroborated by Ford 1988.

The diachronic reality of the *rhapsōidoí* 'rhapsodes' is expressed indirectly by the various myths that link the fixity of Homeric composition with the fixation of rhapsodic performance. According to the myths that we have considered so far, the reintegration of a prototypical text causes both the fixity of Homeric composition and the fixation of rhapsodic performance. But there are other myth patterns that are even more radical, making the concept of a *sequence of rhapsodes* more basic than the concept of a *prototypical text*. As we have seen, the evolution of a poetic tradition, moving ahead in time until it reaches a static phase, can be pictured by myth as the result of a single incident, a "big bang," represented as the recovery or even regeneration of a lost text, an archetype. As we shall now see, the "big bang" can also be pictured as the actual sequencing of rhapsodes.

Among the explanations given by the scholia to Pindar *Nemean* 2.1d for the concept of *rhapsōidós*, one version tells of a reintegration of Homeric poetry by way of rhapsodic performance, which is equated with a process of *sewing* the disintegrated parts back together again:

οἱ δέ φασι τῆς Ὁμήρου ποιήσεως μὴ ὑφ' ἓν συνηγμένης,
σποράδην δὲ ἄλλως καὶ κατὰ μέρη διῃρημένης, ὁπότε ῥαψῳδοῖεν
αὐτήν, εἱρμῷ τινι καὶ ῥαφῇ παραπλήσιον ποιεῖν, εἰς ἓν αὐτὴν
ἄγοντες.

But some say that—since the poetry of Homer had not been brought together under one thing, but rather had been scattered about and divided into parts—when they performed it rhapsodically (*rhapsōidéō*), they would be doing something that is similar to sequencing or sewing, as they produced it into one thing.

In the scholia to Dionysius Thrax, Codex Venetus 489, it is reported that the Homeric poems were "sewn together" (συνερράφησαν) by Peisistratos himself.[55]

The scholia to Pindar *Nemean* 2.1d proceed to offer yet another version, which explicitly links the term *rhapsōidós* with the innovation of an equalized distribution of "parts" assigned to the performers of Homeric poetry:

---

55. The relevant passage is printed in Allen 1924:230.

84   *οἱ δέ, ὅτι κατὰ μέρος πρότερον τῆς ποιήσεως διαδεδομένης τῶν*
    ἀγωνιστῶν ἕκαστος ὅ τι βούλοιτο μέρος ᾖδε, τοῦ δὲ ἄθλου τοῖς
    νικῶσιν ἀρνὸς ἀποδεδειγμένου προσαγορευθῆναι τότε μὲν
    ἀρνῳδούς, αὖθις δὲ ἑκατέρας τῆς ποιήσεως εἰσενεχθείσης τοὺς
    ἀγωνιστὰς οἷον ἀκουμένους πρὸς ἄλληλα τὰ μέρη καὶ τὴν
    σύμπασαν ποίησιν ἐπιόντας, ῥαψῳδοὺς προσαγορευθῆναι,
    ταῦτά φησι Διονύσιος ὁ Ἀργεῖος.

Others say that, previously—since the poetry had been divided
part by part, with each of the competitors singing whichever part
he wanted, and since the designated prize for the winners had
been a lamb—[those competitors] were in those days called
arnōidoí [lamb-singers]—but then, later on—since the competitors, whenever each of the two poems[56] was introduced, were
mending the parts to each other, as it were, and moving toward
the whole composition—they were called *rhapsōidoí.* These things
are said by Dionysius of Argos [between the fourth and third centuries B.C.E.; FGH 308 F 2].

The metaphor inherent in the word *rhapsōidós* itself is pertinent to
these myths. The compound noun *rhapsōidós* means, etymologically,
'he who sews together [*rháptō*] the song(s) [*aoidḗ*]'.[57] This metaphor
is actually attested in the syntax of a song composed by Pindar, referring to the very beginning of a Homeric performance by the *Homērídai* 'Sons of Homer': *ὅθεν περ καὶ Ὁμηρίδαι ῥαπτῶν ἐπέων τὰ
πόλλ' ἀοιδοὶ ἄρχονται, Διὸς ἐκ προοιμίου* 'Starting from the very
point where (*hóthen*) the *Homērídai,* singers (*aoidoí*) of sewn-together
(*rhaptá*) utterances (*épē*), most often take their start [verb *árkhomai*],
from the prelude (*prooímion*) of Zeus' (Pindar *Nemean* 2.1–3).
    The point of all departures, as this song claims, is the *prooímion*
'prelude' of the ultimate god, Zeus.[58] As such, Zeus is designated as
the god of the ultimate songs, the songs of Homer. It is precisely
within the framework of this form, the *prooímion* 'prelude' (plural
prooímia), that the author of a given song conventionally identifies

---

56. The expression *ἑκατέρας τῆς ποιήσεως* 'each of the two poems' implies that the *Iliad*
and the *Odyssey* are meant.

57. Schmitt 1967:300–301 (his discussion of the morphology of *rhapsōidós* is indispensable); Durante 1976:177–179; N 1979:298 par. 10 n. 5 and 1990a:28. On the accent of
rhapsōidós, see Durante 1976:177.

58. For a more detailed discussion of Pindar *Nemean* 2.1–3, see N 1996: Ch. 3.

himself.[59] In the Homeric *Hymn to Apollo,* to which Thucydides explicitly refers as a *prooímion* (3.104.4–5), the first-person speaker identifies himself as the blind singer of Chios, whose songs will win universal approval in the future (*Hymn to Apollo* 172–173); the singer of this hymn *claims* to be none other than Homer, "author" of the universally approved Homeric poems.[60] According to this particular *prooímion,* the performer who speaks these words in the first person is not just *representing* Homer: he *is* Homer.[61]

The *prooímia* or 'preludes' are represented in Pindar's song as performances of the *Homērídai* 'Sons of Homer'; this name applies to a lineage of rhapsodes in Chios who traced themselves back to an ancestor called *Hómēros,* or Homer.[62] Pindar's representation of the Homeric *prooímion* is pertinent to the etymology of this word, which I have up to now translated conventionally as the 'prelude' of a song. It stems from *oímē* 'song', so that the *pro-oímion* is literally the *front* or, better, the *starting end* of the song.[63] Further, *pro-oímion* is the starting end of the *thread* of the song, if indeed the noun *oímē* stems from a verb-root meaning 'sew'.[64] The metaphor implicit in this etymology of *oímē,* where making songs is equated with a process of sewing together or threading songs, is explicit in Pindar's reference to the Homeric rhapsodes at the beginning of *Nemean* 2, where *rhaptá* 'sewn together' is applied to *épē* in the sense of poetic 'utterances'. The same metaphor is implicit, as we have seen, in the etymology of the

---

59. N 1990b:53–54.

60. N 1990a:22 (esp. n. 23), 376.

61. N 1979:5–6, 8–9; 1990a:375–377. On the mimesis or "re-enactment" of Homer by rhapsodes, see N 1996: Ch. 3.

62. Scholia to Pindar *Nemean* 2.1; Plato *Phaedrus* 252b; Strabo 14.1.33–35; *Contest of Homer and Hesiod* p. 226.13–15 Allen. Cf. N 1990a:23. On an alternative tradition, which attributes the final form of the Homeric *Hymn to Apollo* not to Homer but to Kynaithos of Chios, a rhapsode who supposedly could not trace himself back to Homer (scholia to Pindar *Nemean* 2.1), see ibid., 22–23, with further bibliography.

63. Ibid., 353. The genitive of *oímē* at *Odyssey* 8.74, marking the point of departure for the performance of the first song of Demodokos, is functionally a genitive of origin, parallel to the origin-marking adverb *hóthen* 'starting from the very point where' in Pindar's representation of the *prooímion* at *Nemean* 2.1.

64. Durante 1976:176–177; *pace* Chantraine (*DELG* 463 and 783). See further discussion in N 1996: Ch. 3.

86   actual word for rhapsode, *rhapsōidós,* 'he who sews together (*rháptō*) the song(s) (*aoidḗ*) '.[65]

This metaphor of *sewing together the song(s)* must be contrasted with a related metaphor in archaic Greek traditions, that of *weaving the song(s),* which is in fact so old as to be of Indo-European linguistic provenience.[66] An example is this phrase of Pindar (F 179): ὑφαίνω δ' Ἀμυθαονίδαισιν ποικίλον ἄνδημα 'I <u>weave</u> [*huphaínō*] a <u>patterned</u> [*poikílos*] <u>headband</u> [that is, of song] for the Amythaonidai'.[67] As we see from such passages, song is being visualized as a web, a fabric, a textile (Latin *textilis,* from *texō* 'weave'), or—to use only for the moment an English word that no longer retains its metaphorical heritage—even a *text* (Latin *textus,* again from *texō*).[68]

As we juxtapose these two metaphors for songmaking in archaic Greek traditions, weaving and sewing, we discover that the second of the two is more complex than the first.[69] The idea conveyed by *rhapsōidós,* 'he who sews together [*rháptō*] the song(s) [*aoidḗ*]', corresponds to an idea conveyed by the myths: that many and various fabrics of song, each one already made (that is, each one already woven), become remade into a unity, a single new continuous fabric, by being sewn together. The paradox of the metaphor is that the many and the various become the single and the uniform—and yet there is supposedly no loss in the multiplicity and variety of the constituent parts. In effect, this metaphor conveyed by the concept of *rhapsōidós* amounts to an overarching aesthetic principle, one that may even ultimately settle the ever-ongoing controversy between advocates of unitarian and analytic approaches to Homer.

Eustathius, in his *Commentary on the Iliad* (vol. 1 p. 10), quotes the Pindaric description (*Nemean* 2.1–3) of the *Homērídai* 'Sons of Ho-

---

65. Schmitt 1967:300–301; Durante 1976:177–179; N 1979:298 par. 10 n. 5 and 1990a:28.

66. Schmitt 1967:298–300. For arguments against the view that the terminus post quem of this metaphor must be set in the era of Simonides (Scheid and Svenbro 1994: 119–138), see N 1996: Ch. 3.

67. Schmitt 1967:300.

68. Ibid., 14–15; Dubuisson 1989:223; on Latin *textus,* see Scheid and Svenbro 1994: 139–162, esp. p. 160, with reference to Quintilian *Institutio oratoria* 9.4.13.

69. The arguments that follow are developed further in N 1996: Ch. 3.

mer' as ῥαπτῶν ἐπέων . . . ἀοιδοί 'singers (*aoidoí*) of sewn-together (*rhaptá*) utterances (*épē*)', interpreting these words as a periphrasis of the concept inherent in the word *rhapsōidoí* 'rhapsodes'. Eustathius goes on to offer what he considers a second interpretation (again, 1.10), claiming that this concept of *sewing together* can be taken either in the sense that we have seen made explicit in Pindar's wording or in a more complex sense—a sense that I think is actually implicit in the same Pindaric wording—which emphasizes the characteristic unity of the *Iliad* and the *Odyssey:*

> ῥάπτειν δὲ ἢ ἁπλῶς, ὡς εἴρηται, τὸ συντιθέναι ἢ τὸ κατὰ εἱρμόν
> τινα ῥαφῇ ὁμοίως εἰς ἓν ἄγειν τὰ διεστῶτα. σποράδην γάρ, φασί,
> κειμένης καὶ κατὰ μέρος διῃρημένης τῆς Ὁμηρικῆς ποιήσεως, οἱ
> ᾄδοντες αὐτὴν συνέρραπτον οἷον τὰ εἰς ἓν ὕφος ᾀδόμενα.

> Sewing together (*rháptō*) either in the simple sense, as just men-
> tioned, of putting together or, alternatively, in the sense of bring-
> ing different things, in accordance with some kind of sequencing
> (*heirmós*) in sewing, uniformly into one thing; for they say that
> Homeric poetry, after it had been scattered about and divided into
> parts, was sewn together by those who sang it, like songs sung into
> a single fabric (*húphos*).

Following up on what he considers two different interpretations of Pindar *Nemean* 2.1–3, Eustathius (again, p. 10) offers a third one as well: that the concept of sewing together songs is parallel to the concept of *rhapsōidía,* a word that he uses to designate any one of the twenty-four books of the *Iliad* or the *Odyssey.* Although this interpretation still invokes the aesthetic principle of sewing songs together into a unified whole, the songs are now visualized *textually,* as separate *rhapsōidíai* or 'books' of Homer. Eustathius contrasts this usage of *rhapsōidíai* as 'books' of Homer with what he describes in the same context as earlier conventions of "the ancients," the majority of whom had referred to the totality of Homeric poetry as *rhapsōidía* 'rhapsody,' and to those who sing it as *rhapsōidoí* 'rhapsodes' (p. 10): οἱ δὲ πλείους τῶν παλαιῶν τήν τε ὅλην Ὁμηρικὴν ποίησιν ῥαψῳδίαν λέγουσι καὶ ῥαψῳδοὺς τοὺς αὐτὴν ᾄδοντας 'But the majority of the ancients refer to the totality of Homeric poetry as *rhapsōidía* and to those singing it as *rhapsōidoí*'.

There is, to be sure, an ongoing debate about the origins of the eventual division of the *Iliad* and the *Odyssey* into twenty-four books each. Some would argue that these book divisions are derived from

88   earlier patterns of performance segmentation,[70] whereas others
think that they are merely editorial superimpositions deriving from
the era of Alexandrian scholarship.[71] What is needed to supplement
this debate, I submit, is a diachronic perspective. What may be a performance break in one stage of the performance tradition may not
be in another.[72] In other words, I hold open the possibility that the
eventual division of the *Iliad* and the *Odyssey* each into twenty-four
books results from the cumulative formation of episodes in the process of equalized or even weighting. It is from a diachronic point of
view that I emphasize the *cumulative* formation of episodes in the *process* of even weighting. The point remains, in any case, that the concepts of *rhapsōidós* and *rhapsōidía* are compatible with myths about
Homeric origins.

In fact, the concept of *rhapsōidós* can be applied by myth to Homer
himself as prototypical poet, as also to his counterpart, Hesiod. For
example, the scholia to Pindar *Nemean* 2.1 (the source is Philochorus FGH 328 F 212) quote the following verses attributed to Hesiod (F 357), who speaks of performing, in competition with Homer,
hymns to Apollo:

ἐν Δήλωι τότε πρῶτον ἐγὼ καὶ "Ομηρος ἀοιδοὶ
μέλπομεν, ἐν νεαροῖς ὕμνοις ῥάψαντες ἀοιδήν,
Φοῖβον 'Απόλλωνα.

Then it was, in Delos, that Homer and I, singers (*aoidoí*), for
    the first time
Sang, in new hymns, sewing together (*rháptō*) the song (*aoidḗ*),
[Sang] of Phoebus Apollo.

---

70. S. West (1988:39–40) accepts the possibility that the book divisions of the *Iliad* and
the *Odyssey* reflect performance units ordained by Hipparkhos, son of Peisistratos, of the
Peisistratidai; cf. Janko 1992:31 n. 47 for a summary of her views. Jensen (1980:88–89)
likewise considers the book divisions to be performance-related; she goes on to devise a
dictation theory that is meant to account for these divisions.

71. Taplin (1992:285–293) argues that the book divisions "do not go back to the formation of the poems" (p. 285) and that they are relatively recent, probably the work of
Aristarchus. Taplin's main line of argumentation is that he can find other possible episode
breaks, some that seem to him even more distinct than the breaks separating the presently
constituted books.

72. What may be a three-part division in one stage of the tradition, which is what Taplin
(1992) posits for the *Iliad,* may not necessarily be incompatible with a twenty-four-part division at another stage. See further argumentation in N 1996: Chs. 5–7.

So Homer and Hesiod are models of rhapsodes by way of performing like rhapsodes.[73] Even for Plato (*Republic* 600d), Homer and Hesiod can be visualized as performing like rhapsodes (*rhapsōidéō*). For Plato, a figure like Phemios, represented as a prototypical poet in the *Odyssey*, is likewise a *rhapsōidós* (*Ion* 533c).

The mythical view of the poet as a rhapsode does not only imply that he is a performer. The metaphor of sewing, as conveyed by the word *rhapsōidós*, refers also to the poet's powers as a composer. Moreover, this metaphor of sewing is closely related to another metaphor, that of woodworking, which refers to the process of poetic composition in a strikingly analogous way.

The key word in this metaphorical world of woodworking is the name of Homer himself, *Hómēros*. In order to understand the traditional force of the metaphor at work, let us begin by reconsidering the traditional status of Homer as a prototypical author.[74] The further back in time we reconstruct this figure, the greater the repertoire attributed to him: in the preclassical period, it seems that he is credited with all the so-called Cycle, all the Theban epics, and so on.[75] As we have already noted, the very concept of "Cycle"—that is, *kúklos*—had once served as a metaphor for all of Homer's poetry.[76] But now we discover that this same word *kúklos*, used as a metaphor for the sum total of Homeric poetry, is attested with the meaning of 'chariot wheel' in Homeric diction (*Iliad* 23.340, plural *kúkla* at 5.722). This meaning will help explain the name of Homer himself.

In the poetic traditions of Indo-European languages, we find a direct attestation of a metaphor that compares a well-composed song to a well-crafted chariot-wheel: in the oldest Indic poetic traditions, we see the verb *takṣ*- 'join, fit together', regularly used to designate

---

73. Scheid and Svenbro (1994:120) concede that the concept of *rhapsōidós* is driven by the metaphor of songmaking as *sewing together*. Still, they argue that this metaphor cannot be taken further back and applied to Homer. In their view, to repeat, the metaphors of *weaving* and *sewing together* did not exist before the era of Simonides. See N 1996: Ch. 3, where it is argued at greater length that these metaphors are at least residually attested in even the earliest evidence, and that the concept of Homer as rhapsode is basic to Homer.

74. N 1990a:52–81.

75. Ibid., 70–79.

76. See p. 38 above. Cf. Pfeiffer 1968:73.

90 the handiwork of a carpenter, combined in one passage (*Rig-Veda* 1.130.6) with the direct object *vác-* 'poetic voice' (cognate of Latin *vōx*); in the same passage, this combination is then made explicitly parallel to that of *taks-* plus the direct object *rátha-* 'wheel' (in the metonymic sense of 'chariot'; cf. the Latin cognate *rota* 'wheel').[77] The Indic root *taks-* 'join, fit together', designating the craft of a carpenter, is cognate with the root of Greek *tékton,* meaning 'carpenter', which is applied in Pindar *Pythian* 3.112–114 as a metaphor for the poet as master carpenter or "joiner" of words (*épos* plural; cf. the cognate *vácas-,* direct object of *taks-* in *Rig-Veda* 6.32.1).[78] In the Greek poetic traditions, the specific image of crafting a chariot wheel is implicit: the root *ar-* of *ararískō* 'join, fit together' (the verb refers to the activity of the carpenter in the expression ἤραρε τέκτων 'the joiner [*tékton*] joined together [*ar-*]' at *Iliad* 4.110, 23.712) is shared by the word that means 'chariot wheel' in the Linear B texts, *harmo* (Knossos tablets Sg 1811, So 0437, etc.); in another dialectal form, *hárma* (ἄρμα) becomes, metonymically, the word for 'chariot' (*Iliad* 5.231, etc.). I submit that this same root *ar-* is shared by the name of Homer, *Hómēros,* the etymology of which can be explained as 'he who joins together' (*homo-* plus *ar-*).[79] If this etymology is correct, then the making of the Cycle, the sum total of epic, by the master poet Homer is a metaphor that pictures the crafting of the ultimate chariot-wheel by the ultimate carpenter or "joiner."

To be sure, the parallelism between *aoidós* 'singer' and *tékton* 'carpenter, joiner' exists beyond the level of metaphor. Both professions belong to the category of *dēmiourgós* or 'itinerant artisan', as we see from *Odyssey* 17.381–385.[80] Moreover, the carpenter is not the only craftsman who is comparable to the poet in the poetic traditions of Indo-European languages. To pursue this point, let us consider the root **tek(s)-* in the Greek noun *tékton* 'carpenter, joiner', also attested in *tékhnē* 'craft, art'. This root, which we have already seen in Indic *taks-* 'join, fit together', does not survive as a verb in Greek, but we

---

77. N 1979:297–300, following Schmitt 1967:296–298.

78. N 1979:297–300.

79. Ibid., 300. Bader (1989:269 n. 114) offers a different etymology, the arguments against which are presented in N 1996:74 n. 45.

80. N 1979:233–234, 310–311 par. 2 n. 3.

find it in Latin, where *texō* is attested with the meaning 'join, carpenter' (as in Virgil *Aeneid* 11.326).[81] Ordinarily, however, Latin *texō* means 'weave' (as in Ovid *Metamorphoses* 6.62). The parallelism in craftsmanship between carpenter and weaver, implicit in the semantics of the Latin verb *texō,* is even more pervasive: in Indo-European languages, the metaphor of carpentry as songmaking is actually paralleled by the metaphor of weaving.[82]

Let us return to the image of *Hómēros* as a primordial *rhapsōidós*. We now see that the parallelism between carpenter and weaver as metaphors for the poet corresponds to the association of *Hómēros* and *rhapsōidós*.

The key to this parallelism, I suggest, is the idea of a specialist. In the case of woodwork, we may say that only a master carpenter will have the skills required to put together, say, a chariot wheel. Let us hereafter consistently refer to such a specialist as a "joiner," someone who joins the pieces that other woodworkers have already fashioned. In the case of textiles, on the other hand, we have already seen that the word *rhapsōidós* implies a specialist. It implies an ability to sew together, into an artistic whole, pieces that other textile workers have already woven. In other words, I propose a proportionality of metaphors: the *carpenter* of song is to the *joiner* of song as the one who *weaves* the song is to the one who *sews together* or *stitches* the song, that is, to the *rhapsōidós*.[83] Just as a joiner is a master craftsman, capable of special feats like the making of a chariot wheel out of pieces of woodwork already made by himself or by other carpenters, so also the stitcher, one who sews together pieces of fabric already woven, is a master craftsman in his own right, fashioning something altogether "new" that is tailor-made to suit a given form. Thus the metaphor of a joiner or a stitcher, as distinct from a carpenter or a weaver, conveys the idea of a master singer.[84]

---

81. Schmitt 1967:14–15; N 1979:297–300. Whereas the root of Greek *tékhnē* 'craft, art' is attested as a verb in Latin *texō*, the root of Latin *ars/artis* 'craft, art' is attested as a verb in Greek *ar-ar-ískō* 'join, fit together' (cf. Latin *artus* 'joint').

82. Schmitt 1967:298–301.

83. This point is argued at greater length in N 1996: Ch. 3.

84. Ibid. There I point out that the English word *stitcher* may be inappropriate for expressing the aesthetics of a master's handiwork, in that *stitch* implies something makeshift, as if

Whichever way myth figures the creation of Homeric poetry, whether it be a joiner's chariot wheel or a stitcher's perfect fit, the actual creation is viewed as happening at a remote point in time, not over time. From the standpoint of the myth, it is as if there had been a "big bang" that produced a fixed pattern of composition, which led to a fixed pattern of performance, or both.[85]

Moreover, as I have already argued in Chapter 1, Homer is not just the creator of heroic song: he is also the culture hero of this song. To repeat the essence of what I said earlier: ancient Greek institutions tend to be traditionally retrojected, by the Greeks themselves, each to a proto-creator, a culture hero who gets credited with the sum total of a given cultural institution; and it was a common practice to attribute any major achievement of society, even if this achievement may have been realized only through a lengthy period of social evolution, to the episodic and personal accomplishment of a culture hero who is pictured as having made his monumental contribution in an earlier era of the given society.[86] So also with Homer: he is retrojected as the original genius of heroic song, the proto-poet whose poetry is reproduced by a continuous succession of performers. Conversely, each successive performer of Homer is one step further removed from this original genius: in Plato's *Ion,* for example, Socrates envisages the rhapsode Ion as the last in a chain of magnetized metal rings connected by the force of the original poet Homer (533d–536d). In Plato's mythical image of Homer and his successors, the magnetic force of the poetic composition weakens with each successive performer. Pictured as the last, or at least the latest, replicant of Homer, Ion becomes the weakest of all replicants.[87]

From the standpoint of an evolutionary model for the fixation of Homeric poetry, by contrast, the reality is altogether different from the myth: "Even if the size of either the *Iliad* or the *Odyssey* ultimately defied performance by any one person at any one sitting, the monumental proportions of these compositions could *evolve* in a social

---

stitchwork were simply patchwork. More appropriate than *stitcher*—at least aesthetically, perhaps—is *tailor.*

85. This formulation is reapplied in N 1996: Ch. 3.

86. See p. 21 above.

87. N 1990a:55.

context where the sequence of performance, *and thereby the sequence of*
narrative, could be regulated, as in the case of the Panathenaia."[88] In
quoting this formulation, I have highlighted the idea that an evolving fixity in patterns of performance leads to a correspondingly
evolving fixity in patterns of composition, given that performance
and composition—or, better, recomposition—are aspects of the same
process in this medium.

By now we have seen a variety of myths offering "big bang" explanations for the creation of Homeric poetry, and we have noted in
each case a variety of metaphors that articulate these myths.[89] First
there is the myth of Homer's making the Homeric poems himself. A
metaphor associated with this myth is that of a master craftsman who
produces a masterpiece of craftsmanship. Then there are the myths
of a post-Homeric remaking of the poems. Among the metaphors
used in these myths is that of an integral fabric produced by the
"sewing together" of different parts of fabrics, corresponding to a total song that rhapsodes put together by singing parts of songs in sequence. But perhaps the most salient metaphor of them all comes
from later stories about a prototypical written text, disintegrated into
separate parts that are then all at once reintegrated at the initiative
of a culture hero. As I have argued, this metaphor is the germ of
the concept that we now know as the "Peisistratean recension." I see
no need, in short, to defend the concept of a "Peisistratean recension"—as a historical event.

The concept of a "Peisistratean recension" has been generally attacked or ignored by unitarians, supported by analysts.[90] Since such
an event—and the concept of a recension surely requires that it
be viewed as an event—supposedly took place sometime after the
middle of the sixth century, it is almost two centuries removed from
the era assigned to Homer by many experts. The concept is therefore
not congenial to those who see a need to recover the presence of a
"text" composed by a Homer who lived in the eighth century—I refer to them for the moment under the more general heading of "unitarians"—since there is no way of bridging the gap between this
"Homer" and a written text that supposedly first came into being

88. Ibid., 23.

89. Cf. W. C. Smith 1993:83, on "big bang" formulations in the study of religions.

90. Jensen 1980:128, following Merkelbach 1952:42–43.

94   only some 200 years later. By contrast, "analysts" who do not care about singular authorship can afford to be less concerned about the prospect of moving the date of Homeric composition forward by two centuries. After all, we would expect them to view this composition as a matter of patchwork—in a negative sense of the word. In his *Homerische Untersuchungen,* for example, Wilamowitz describes the *Odyssey* as the end product of "a not very gifted patchwork-poet" ("ein gering begabter Flickpoet").[91]

Particularly influential in questioning the concept of a "Peisistratean recension" has been an article by J. A. Davison,[92] whose negative views are restated in a widely read chapter dealing with the transmission of the Homeric text in *A Companion to Homer.*[93] Although Davison explicitly rejects the concept of a "Peisistratean recension,"[94] he speaks of a "Panathenaic text,"[95] with reference to the evidence indicating that the "text" of the *Iliad* and the *Odyssey* was regularly performed, as we have already seen, at the Athenian festival of the Panathenaia (Lycurgus *Against Leokrates* 102; "Plato" *Hipparchus* 228b; Diogenes Laertius 1.57).[96] From his point of view, such a "text" is a script, as it were, for the seasonally recurring performance of the *Iliad* and the *Odyssey* at the Panathenaia.

Presumably, such a "Panathenaic text" eventually became available for private ownership by way of the book trade at Athens, which we see already flourishing at the end of the fifth century B.C.E.[97] Davison goes on to offer this warning: "Any attempt to speak of *a single* [my emphasis] 'pre-Alexandrian vulgate,' and still more to create out of it a version of the Panathenaic text by arguing back to sixth- or

---

91. Wilamowitz 1884:228; cf. Davison 1962:249–252.

92. Davison 1955a.

93. Davison 1962.

94. See, for example, Davison 1962:220.

95. See, for example, ibid., 224.

96. See pp. 75 and 81–82 above.

97. Cf. Davison 1962:221. For a helpful bibliographical survey of the extent of literacy in the late fifth century and thereafter, see Thomas 1989:17–24. She stresses at p. 23 (slightly modifying the picture presented by Turner 1977) that books become relatively common only toward the first quarter of the fourth century.

fifth-century Athens from the conditions which existed in Egypt after
the establishment of the Alexandrian library, is doomed to failure
from the beginning."[98] Even in this context, however, we note that
he speaks of "the Panathenaic text" as if it were a given.

Although I agree with Davison to the extent that any attempted
reconstruction of such a Panathenaic text presents major difficulties,
I disagree with his argument that the story suggesting a "Peisistratean
recension," as reflected by the testimony of "Plato" *Hipparchus* 228b
and Cicero *De oratore* 3.137, was invented by a scholar from Pergamum, perhaps Asclepiades of Myrlea (around 100 B.C.E.), in order
to undermine rival scholars from Alexandria.[99] As Davison puts it,
such a scholar would have intended to discredit "the 'authentic' text
which his Alexandrian rivals were so successfully imposing on the
reading public."[100] In disagreeing here with Davison, I follow in part
the reasoning of Raphael Sealey, who argues that we have no grounds
for assuming the successful production of an Alexandrian standard-
ized text of the Homeric poems.[101] Referring to the earlier work of
T. W. Allen,[102] which antedates that of Davison, Sealey stresses that
the Alexandrian editorial adjustments made on the Homeric poems,
as we can ascertain especially from the scholia to the *Iliad,* have had
"singularly little effect" on the Homeric text as preserved in the medieval "vulgate" manuscript tradition.[103] Sealey goes even further,
paraphrasing Allen: "Either . . . there was no Alexandrian edition or,
if Alexandrian scholars did publish editions of Homer, . . . these did
not become popular with the reading public."[104]

Sealey also objects to Davison's formulation of the motive behind
the Pergamene scholar's purported "invention" of the story about a

---

98. Davison 1962:221, with specific reference (at p. 231 n. 30) to the works of Ludwich
1898 and Bolling 1925, 1944, 1950.

99. Davison 1955a:21.

100. Ibid.

101. Sealey 1957:344–346.

102. Allen 1924:302–307; as Sealey (1957:345 n. 100) points out, Allen's discussion was
"overlooked also" by Page 1955b:143.

103. Sealey 1957:345.

104. Ibid.

96 "Peisistratean recension."[105] Davison had put it this way: "Without challenging the Athenian origin of *the new text* [emphasis mine]," the "invented" story supposedly strips away the authority of this "new text" edited by the Alexandrian scholars because it lowers the date of the Homeric text's creation from about 1050 B.C.E., as conjectured by Aristarchus of Alexandria (Proclus F a 58–62 Severyns), to about 550, the era of the Peisistratidai.[106] Disputing the notion that an Alexandrian edition of Homer could assert such authority over text production, Sealey concludes: "No one ever successfully imposed an Alexandrian text on the reading public."[107]

There are other experts who stop short of such a conclusion. Let us begin with what may well be, at the time that I write this, the most widely read account of the Homeric textual tradition, a chapter by Stephanie West entitled "The Transmission of the Text," to be found in the opening pages of a new commentary on the *Odyssey*.[108] Though she concedes that the editorial work of the earlier Alexandrian scholars Zenodotus and Aristophanes "had little if any effect on the book trade," West draws a line at the next step in the succession of Alexandrian scholars, the era of Aristarchus, whose scholarly activity is dated around the middle of the second century B.C.E.:

> From about 150 [B.C.E.] a change is observable, as "wild" texts, characterized by a high proportion of variants and additions, die out; later papyri offer a text which differs little from that of the medieval manuscripts. Given the date of this development, it must surely be connected, directly or indirectly, with the activity of Aristarchus.[109]

---

105. Ibid. For further criticism of Davison's theory, see Jensen 1980:131–132.

106. Davison 1955a:21. Aristarchus not only dated the Homeric text at about 1050 B.C.E.: he also believed that Homer was an Athenian (*Life of Homer* [p. 244.13, p. 247.8 Allen]).

107. Sealey 1957:345.

108. S. West 1988:33–48.

109. Ibid., 45; cf. pp. 7–8, 283–287; and Jensen 1980:107, 109. Parry (1930 [1971:268]) considered the possibility that the "wild" or eccentric texts of papyri dated before 150 B.C.E. reflect variations typical of oral poetry. Jensen (1980:108) objects: "[Parry's] own subsequent fieldwork, however, made this improbable. The variations are small and do not alter the text essentially." And yet, the "smallness" of variation may be due to a static phase in the evolution of the Homeric tradition, on which topic see more below. See further discussion in N 1996: Ch. 5.

Even if the papyri dated after the era of Aristarchus "offer a text which differs little from that of the medieval manuscripts," we need not necessarily connect this fact with the activity of Aristarchus. No one, in my opinion, has yet been able to refute successfully the observation of T. W. Allen that Aristarchus's editorial prescriptions exerted practically no effect on the Homeric text as preserved in the medieval "vulgate" manuscript tradition.[110] What West has called the eventual "standardization" of the Homeric text after around 150 B.C.E. can be explained in other ways, without recourse to the editorial authority of Aristarchus. One factor, it seems, is the nature of the book trade during the period in question.

West herself stresses the role of the book trade and "a general rise in standards of book-production at this period."[111] Conceding that the editorial judgments of Aristarchus were ignored by the booksellers and proprietors of *scriptoria,* West nevertheless makes an exception in the case of Homeric lines deemed non-Homeric by Aristarchus, arguing that such lines were leveled out in the process of commercial copying, thanks to the authority of an Aristarchean text that featured special notations for supposedly non-Homeric lines:

> But the common reader was unlikely to be interested in the minutiae of textual criticism, particularly since the choice of one reading rather than another would seldom much affect the sense. Booksellers and proprietors of *scriptoria* could thus easily fall in with popular demand by cancelling lines omitted by Aristarchus, without needing to alter the wording of their texts extensively. Copies so corrected would become commercially fashionable, while any alternative would die out naturally.[112]

In the end, then, West's model does not differ all that much from Allen's, which rejects altogether the idea of a standard Alexandrian edition. In West's own words, "The Alexandrian scholars did not impose a single specialist's version on the tradition, but effected a

---

110. See again Allen 1924:302–307; cf. Sealey 1957:345. But see Apthorp (1980), whose important contributions to the question of "numerus versuum" I discuss at length in N 1996: Ch. 5.

111. S. West 1988:48.

112. Ibid., 47–48.

98 general purge of extraneous material and an increase in knowledge which afforded some permanent protection."[113]

Still, I do not even see any compelling reason to infer, as does West, that such a "purge" depended on the authoritativeness of a given edition promulgated by Aristarchus. The very technology of the *scriptorium*, I submit, could easily promote the kind of leveling process where additional lines found only in some manuscripts but not in others tended to be omitted. The editorial minimalism espoused by Aristarchus, whose practice was to question the authenticity of lines that were missing in those manuscripts that he specially valued, could be matched by a pragmatic minimalism in the *scriptorium*. As West concedes, even the papyri dated after 150 B.C.E. "offer too wide a range of variants to allow the hypothesis that they might all be copies of a single edition."[114]

It seems to me, then, that the new degree of textual "standardization" in the era after 150 B.C.E. reflects not the authority of Alexandrian scholarship but other factors—including the advances being made in the kind of minimalist quasi-editing techniques that would be needed for large-scale commercial copying of manuscripts.[115] In this connection, we may note Sealey's observation that "one could achieve multiple production on a small scale by setting one slave to read a text aloud while many slaves sat around him and wrote down what they heard."[116] A successful publisher in the Roman era, T. Pomponius Atticus, is said to have employed men described as *anagnostae optimi et plurimi librarii* 'the best readers and the greatest number of scribes' (Nepos *Life of Atticus* 13.3).[117] This mode of manuscript production may be appreciably different from that of earlier times, if we accept the following description of manuscript production in the era before 150 B.C.E. or so:

---

113. Ibid., 48.

114. Ibid., 47.

115. I discuss other factors in N 1996: Ch. 7.

116. Sealey 1990:129.

117. Ibid., 129 and 183 n. 17. The form *anagnostae* 'readers' is borrowed from the Greek *anagnốstēs* 'reader'. In a lecture given on Jan. 13, 1993, entitled "Démétrius et les rhapsodes," in the seminar of Françoise Létoublon at the Centre d'Études Anciennes, École Normale Supérieure, I compared *anagnốstēs* with the French stage-word *souffleur*. In N 1996:

A scribe copying the whole of Homer, having been taught in school how to read and write from the text of Homer, *living in an age where rhapsodic recitals were still common* [highlighting mine], must have had his mind crowded with epic lines and half-lines. If he found himself introducing an extra line he would hardly [worry about it]; deliberate additions cannot be excluded either. And the next scribe copying this exemplar would have no chance of noticing anything unusual.[118]

The point remains that, even for West, the textual "standardization" of the Homeric poems after 150 B.C.E. is due to developments in the book trade, and the Homeric text of this era and thereafter can hardly be described, even in terms of her argument, as an Aristarchean text, let alone an Alexandrian one. Conversely, we may infer that the greater degree of variation in the papyri attested before 150 B.C.E. is due not to the vagaries of a more old-fashioned sort of book trade but to the absence of even the limited kind of textual standardization that we see taking place after that date.

West uses the term "second standardization" in referring to the era of Homeric textual history after 150 B.C.E.[119] For her, the first standardization takes place in the era of Peisistratos, as she speaks of "this sixth-century standardization of the text."[120] She also speaks of "this sixth-century recension," which "must be regarded as the archetype of all our Homeric manuscripts and of the indirect tradition represented by ancient quotations and allusions."[121] West thus basically accepts the concept of a "Peisistratean recension," citing for support the arguments advanced in favor of this concept by Reinhold Merkelbach and Minna Skafte Jensen.[122] She is in effect also accepting the concept of a "Panathenaic text."

Ch. 6, the usage of *anagnōstēs* is connected with that of *paranagignōskō* 'read from a model', as attested in the Plutarchean *Lives of the Ten Orators* 841f, a passage that deals with Lycurgus's reform of performance traditions in Athenian tragedy.

118. Jensen 1980:108. On the topic of traditions in Homeric performance by rhapsodes in the Alexandrian era, see the brief discussion in N 1990a:29 (with n. 64).

119. S. West 1988:48.

120. Ibid., 40.

121. Ibid., 39.

122. Ibid., 36 n. 13, citing Merkelbach 1952 and Jensen 1980.

Jensen's model of a "Peisistratean recension" requires an outright dictation that was supposedly commissioned in the era of the Peisistratidai,[123] which in turn leads to a standard "Panathenaic text."[124] Her model differs from the one developed here mainly in the fact that she thinks of the hypothetical dictated text not as a transcript but as a new archetype. I can agree with the general notion of a "Panathenaic text" as the main source of the Homeric papyri in the Alexandrian era and of the later Homeric "vulgate" tradition in general.[125] But I do not go so far as to posit a single archetypal written text, preferring instead an evolutionary model that allows for the eventual textualization of the Homeric poems in the process of seasonally recurring performance at the Panathenaia.[126] As I have already argued, this *textualization* could have taken place without the intervention of writing, but it could indeed yield a transcript, or a variety of transcripts, at various possible stages of the performance tradition of Homer at the Panathenaia, starting from around 550 B.C.E. and proceeding toward the middle or even the end of the fifth century.[127]

---

123. Jensen 1980:154, 166.

124. Cf. ibid., 109.

125. N 1996: Ch. 5. Thus I find the point made by Jensen (1980:109) compelling: "Among the various texts called after cities [as cited by the Alexandrian scholars, whose comments are sporadically preserved in the Homeric scholia] one might have expected to find an Athenian one; that such a text is never mentioned indicates that this was the basic text referred to."

126. If indeed Athens is the setting for a definitive—and terminal—textualization of the Homeric poems, then we have a ready explanation for the sporadic intrusions of Attic dialect into the eventual text. The formulation of Janko (1992:37) is helpful: "The superficial Attic traits in the epic diction do prove that Athens played a major role in the transmission, and this must be related to the Pisistratids' patronage of Homeric poetry." Cf. Jensen 1980:131.

127. I agree with Jensen (1980:110) and Janko (1992:37) that such early texts were probably written in the Ionic alphabet. But I disagree with the idea that "the" Panathenaic text was imported from Ionia. For a basic statement of this idea, see Mazon 1943:269–270, 276–278; for variations on this idea, see Jensen 1980:132 ("If descendants of Homer or [Kreophylos] possessed the true, authoritative text, they would no doubt have kept a copy of it") and Janko 1992:37 ("[The Peisistratidai] probably procured the first complete set of rolls to cross the Aegean"). It is enough to say that the performance tradition of the Homeridai was imported from Ionia, probably from Chios.

We have seen that Davison, too, assumes a "Panathenaic text," though he does not go so far as to accept the concept of a "Peisistratean recension."[128] As for Sealey, his disbelief in a standard Alexandrian edition of Homer is matched by a disbelief in a standard Panathenaic edition: he goes only so far as to say that the Panathenaic version of the *Iliad* and the *Odyssey* could have been written down any time between 550 B.C.E. and 450 B.C.E.[129] He connects the possibility of a more precise dating for any writing down of the text with the need to come up with a more precise dating for the rise of the book trade in Athens.[130] By implication, then, there is for him no standard Panathenaic archetype on which the manuscripts of the incipient book trade are based. In terms of Sealey's model, I infer that any writing down of the *Iliad* and the *Odyssey* in this period between 550 B.C.E. and 450 B.C.E. would amount to a mere transcript, not some standard of reference for future performances.[131]

I find that my position is closest to that of Sealey, to the extent that I, too, see no proof for the existence of an archetypal Panathenaic manuscript of Homer, any more than there seems to be any proof for an archetypal Alexandrian manuscript. There is, however, room for positing an archetypal Panathenaic *form* for *performing* the *Iliad* and the *Odyssey*, as embodied in a Greek development that we have already compared with similar developments attested in living oral traditions. As we have seen, that development is the "Panathenaic rule," attributed either to the Peisistratidai or to Solon himself ("Plato" *Hipparchus* 228b and Diogenes Laertius 1.57, respectively).[132] It is instructive to consider the following formulation by Sealey:

> Now the work of Peisistratos and his sons amounts to this, that the *episodes* of Homeric story-telling were arranged in a constant order for rhapsodes to follow. This work could hardly be necessary, if the

128. See again Davison 1962:225 and 220 on the "Panathenaic text" and the "Peisistratean recension," respectively.

129. Sealey 1957:351.

130. Ibid.

131. Ibid., 349–350.

132. See p. 75 above.

poems had already been reduced to writing and thus it furnishes one more argument against the hypothesis of an early writing-down of the poems.[133]

I disagree with Sealey's formulation to the extent that the arrangement of the narration is viewed here as a historical *event,* corresponding to an event in the story that told about the Peisistratidai and how they produced a standard text of the Homeric poems. I propose instead an evolutionary model for both "events," that is, for both the arrangement of narration and the textualization of the poems.

I must stress again that my goal is not to revive the case for positing a "Peisistratean recension," where *recension* is obviously to be understood in the conventional sense of a critical revision that takes into account the basic available sources of a text. Rather, I have approached the problem in a different way by pointing out that the details of reports leading to the very idea of a "Peisistratean recension" happen to match the details of myths explaining the composition, performance, and diffusion of epic. The emphasis of these myths on the ultimate unity or integrity of any given epic, as we see most dramatically illustrated in the classical Persian example, corresponds to the reality of a unified and integrated text, such as the Homeric *Iliad* and *Odyssey.* It also corresponds to the narratives, already analyzed above, concerning a customary law in effect at the Athenian festival of the Panathenaia, where it was ordained that the performance of the *Iliad* and the *Odyssey* by *rhapsōidoí* 'rhapsodes' had to follow the *sequence* of composition, and that the entire composition had to be performed by one rhapsode after another, likewise *in their own sequence.* Our two clear references to this customary law, "Plato" *Hipparchus* 228b and Diogenes Laertius 1.57, disagree about the identity of the initiator of this practice, the first source indicating the Peisistratidai, and the second, Solon the lawgiver. For our purposes, the question of determining the originator of this custom is irrelevant to the more basic question of the significance of the custom itself.[134] The narratives about this customary law, I submit, serve as a clear indication that unity or integrity of composition was itself a tradition, and was venerated as such.

---

133. Sealey 1957:349. Highlighting mine.

134. See further comments in N 1990a:21, 23. See also Chapter 2, note 58 above.

If, then, the "Peisistratean recension" is a myth, whose myth is it? The answer is, surely, that the Peisistratidai owned it, or, better, appropriated it as an instrument of propaganda for their dynasty. We may note that Cicero's account, which is most explicit about the recension, portrays the tyrant Peisistratos as one of the canonical Seven Sages in the context of crediting him with the arrangement of the Homeric poems. Other narratives, as we have also seen, draw an explicit parallel between Peisistratos and a venerable lawmaker like Lycurgus of Sparta.[135] In short, the historicity of the "Peisistratean recension" is to be found not in the actual story of the recension but in the appropriation of the story, the myth, as a source of propaganda for the Peisistratidai.

Reinhold Merkelbach argues that the "Peisistratean recension" was a genuine historical event, though he treats the story itself as an extrapolated invention, probably to be dated to the fourth century.[136] The central point for him is that there was a Homeric text, in manuscript form, which took shape in the sixth century, the era of Peisistratos. He also thinks that the Lycurgus story is based on the Peisistratos story. The comparative evidence that I have already adduced suggests otherwise, that it was in fact the Peisistratos story that was based on an appropriation of earlier narrative patterns concerning sages and lawmakers. I also disagree with Merkelbach when he argues that the Homeric poems would have disintegrated through the repeated performances of "improvising" rhapsodes had it not been for the primacy of a written manuscript.[137] In positing a disintegration through reperformance, Merkelbach is appealing to the concept generally known as *zersingen,* which has been successfully challenged by folklorists.[138]

Merkelbach also argues that the relative stability of the Homeric textual transmission, in comparison with the far more pronounced manuscript variations of other epics like the *Song of Roland,* proves

---

135. See pp. 73–74 above.

136. Merkelbach 1952. He also argues that Aristarchus knew the story of a Peisistratean recension but did not believe it.

137. See especially Merkelbach 1952:34.

138. Ibid. For a reassessment of the concept of *zersingen,* see Bausinger 1980:46, 268–276.

104   the archetypal existence of a written Homeric text.[139] But I have already argued, by reapplying the comparative perspectives applied by Merkelbach, that the alternative model of a relatively static phase in the evolution of the Homeric poems can account for such textual stability. In the meantime, Merkelbach seems to leave out of consideration the fact that the Homeric poems were *performed*. I repeat what I said earlier: the fact that Homeric poetry was meant to be performed live, and that it continued to be performed live through the classical period and beyond, remains the primary historical given.[140] A Panathenaic written *text* cannot be the primary medium of the Homeric poems. I find even less plausible Merkelbach's supplementary thesis of a "reading public" for these poems.[141] In this regard, I also find it difficult to reconcile Stephanie West's acceptance of Merkelbach's overall thesis[142] with her own special emphasis on the performance traditions of Homeric rhapsodes.[143]

These objections are not meant to slight the importance of Merkelbach's contributions, especially when it comes to the actual dating of the narrative traditions about the so-called Peisistratean recension.[144] According to Merkelbach, our sources go at least as far back as the fourth century B.C.E., the era of Dieuchidas of Megara, who claimed that it was Solon, not Peisistratos, who "interpolated" into the *Iliad* verses favorable to the Athenians (FGH 485 F 6, by way of Diogenes Laertius 1.57): if Dieuchidas has to go out of his way to claim that the "interpolator" was Solon, not Peisistratos, then there must have been a preexisting version featuring Peisistratos.[145]

Clearly the act of "interpolation" is viewed as a fraud, as we see from a story about Onomakritos, who is caught red-handed in the act of inserting his own verses into a body of oracular poetry (Herodotus

---

139. Merkelbach 1952:34–35.

140. For a brief review of the arguments, see N 1990a:21–24, 28–29.

141. Merkelbach 1952:36.

142. S. West 1988:36, 39.

143. Ibid., 35–38, 40.

144. Cf. Jensen 1980:132.

145. Merkelbach 1952:24, 27–31.

7.6.3).[146] This is the same Onomakritos whom we have already seen described as a *diathétēs* 'arranger' of the oracular poetry possessed by the Peisistratidai (7.6.3),[147] and whom we see described elsewhere as actually performing oracular poems on behalf of the Peisistratidai (Herodotus 7.6.5).[148] This is also the same Onomakritos who is reputedly one of the four "arrangers" of the Homeric poems (Tzetzes in *Anecdota Graeca* 1.6 ed. Cramer).[149] I have already suggested that, once the Peisistratidai were ousted, the positive stories about their "recension" of the Homeric text could be reshaped by way of transferring the credit for achieving an Athenian version of Homer from the Peisistratidai to Solon the Lawgiver.[150] Meanwhile, the motive of Dieuchidas of Megara is to undermine *any* standard Athenian version of Homer, since the Athenians had a long history of using citations from Homer—especially from the Catalogue of Ships in *Iliad* 2— in their ongoing territorial claims against Megara.[151] It therefore suits the purposes of Dieuchidas to undermine Solon, who is viewed positively by the Athenians, instead of Peisistratos, who is now viewed negatively by them. What is a matter of "recension" in a positive version of the myth can become a matter of "interpolation" in a later negativized version—as we have just seen in the case of the Peisistratidai and their agent Onomakritos. What Dieuchidas is trying to accomplish, I suggest, is to extend such a negativized version of the myth from Peisistratos to Solon, who would be at that given moment the current culture hero of the positive version.

Let us return to the basics of what we have explored so far on the subject of Homeric textualization. We have concentrated on a relatively static phase of Homeric performance traditions extending roughly from the middle of the eighth century B.C.E. all the way to

---

146. N 1990a: 170, with commentary.

147. See pp. 72–73 above.

148. N 1990a: 159.

149. See p. 73 above.

150. See p. 75 above.

151. Merkelbach 1952:28–31, especially with reference to Plutarch *Solon* 10, Aristotle *Rhetoric* 1375b30, Apollodorus via Strabo 9.1.10, Diogenes Laertius 1.48, and Scholia B to *Iliad* 2.557.

the middle of the sixth, at which point I posit the reaching of a near-textual status for the *Iliad* and the *Odyssey* in the specific historical context of the Feast of the Panathenaia at Athens, as reorganized under the régime of the Peisistratidai.

This relatively static phase in my evolutionary model for Homeric poetry, lasting almost two centuries and culminating in a near-textual status for the *Iliad* and the *Odyssey* at Athens under the Peisistratidai, can be correlated with a relatively static phase in the iconographic representations of "Iliadic" and "Odyssean" themes in the archaic period, and the convergences linking epic and iconographic treatments of epic themes become increasingly pronounced as we approach the middle of the sixth century B.C.E.

Let us survey a few examples from the earliest attested iconographical evidence. In the case of "Odyssean" themes, we may note in particular the story of Odysseus and the Cyclops, well attested in the seventh century.[152] For "Iliadic themes," we may turn to the dossier assembled by Friis Johansen.[153] I draw attention to a bronze relief from Olympia that he dates to the second half of the seventh century B.C.E. and that represents an Embassy to Achilles that is comprised of Phoenix, Odysseus, and Ajax (corresponding to the narrative that we find in *Iliad* 9).[154] We may note also a plate from Rhodes, dated to the last quarter of the seventh century and featuring a representation of the Death of Euphorbos (corresponding to the narrative in *Iliad* 17.1–113).[155] After pointing out analogies between the style of this plate from Rhodes and the style of painting attested for archaic Argos, Friis Johansen observes other connections between Argos and Rhodes, including the Rhodian claim of descent from Argos (cf. Pindar *Olympian* 7.19).[156] In this context, I merely record the possibility of connecting a relatively early proliferation of Iliadic narrative traditions in Rhodes with the extraordinary highlighting of Rhodes in *Iliad* 2.653–670.

---

152. Kannicht 1982:78.

153. Friis Johansen 1967.

154. Ibid., 53–54, fig. 8 on p. 52.

155. Ibid., 79.

156. Ibid., 80.

The evidence of such examples adduced by Friis Johansen makes clear that we are dealing with iconographical references to Iliadic *narrative traditions,* not to the Iliadic *text* as we know it. Still, I suggest that a relatively static phase in the development of Iliadic narrative traditions is what makes it possible for us to recognize as distinctly Iliadic whatever correspondences we find in iconographical evidence that is contemporaneous with this posited phase.

If indeed we are dealing with a lengthy static phase of Iliadic narrative traditions, not with the Iliadic text as we know it, we may still expect a considerable degree of variation. If we take as an example the François vase, dated around 570 B.C.E. and of Attic provenience, we see there a representation of the Funeral Games for Patroklos, converging with the narrative of *Iliad* 23 in the following details: (1) the appearance of five chariot-teams, (2) Achilles as president of the games, and (3) the participation of Diomedes in the chariot race.[157] There are also the following narrative details in the vase painting that diverge from details in *Iliad* 23: (1) each chariot is drawn by a team of four horses, not two as in the *Iliad;* (2) besides Diomedes, the participants are Odysseus, Automedon, Damasippos, and Hippothoon rather than Eumelos, Menelaos, Antilokhos, and Meriones, as in the *Iliad;* (3) Diomedes comes in third, whereas he is the winner in the *Iliad.*[158] Still, the *relative* stability of narrative traditions in archaic Greek iconography is illustrated by the similarity between the painting on the François vase and another painting, dated almost a hundred years earlier, on a proto-Corinthian aryballos:

If we give the name of Achilles to the leader of the games on the Proto-Corinthian vase, it becomes just as good an "Iliad illustration" as that on the François vase. For his rendering of the chariot-race held by Achilles, then, Klitias [the artist of the François vase] drew upon a traditional composition that had been created by Corinthian art long before his time, and apart from bringing the number of horses in a team up to date, he did not feel himself called upon to make any major changes in the formula he had inherited.[159]

---

157. Jensen 1980:104, following Friis Johansen 1967:266.

158. Jensen 1980:104.

159. Friis Johansen 1967:90, cited also by Jensen 1980:104.

In this context, we may note in general Friis Johansen's own frequent observations of variations between the corresponding narrative details in the attested artifacts and in the attested epic of the *Iliad*. Still, if we choose to emphasize the continuity that is manifested in the phenomenon of these variations, then Friis Johansen's terminus post quem of 630 B.C.E. or so for the inception of distinctively "Iliadic" themes in iconographical representations need not be deemed too early.[160] As we turn to later developments, we see that significant variations persist until the middle of the sixth century B.C.E., or even as late as 530 B.C.E., which can serve as a terminus post quem for the textualization or quasi-textualization of the *Iliad* and the *Odyssey*.[161] It may also serve as a terminus post quem for reforms of the Homeric performance traditions during the régime of the Peisistratidai.

It is in this context that I am ready to ask the question for the last time: when was it that the *Iliad* and the *Odyssey* were recorded as written texts? On the basis of linguistic criteria, Richard Janko has proposed 750–725 B.C.E. and 743–713 B.C.E. as definitive dates for the text-fixation of the *Iliad* and the *Odyssey* respectively.[162] On the basis of historical and archaeological considerations, Ian Morris agrees, to the extent that the contents of the Homeric poems may reflect a social context datable to the eighth century before our era.[163] Both these assessments require the "dictation theory" for establishing such

---

160. For Fittschen (1969), who reassesses the early Greek iconographical representations corresponding to epic, the variations themselves serve as proof for the absence of distinctly "Iliadic" themes; on the basis of this reassessment, Kannicht (1982:85) concludes that "the *Iliad* as an artistic subject is virtually neglected by seventh-century art." (As we have already seen, however, Kannicht at p. 78 concedes that the Odyssean narrative tradition about the Cyclops is strongly represented in the seventh century.) Such conclusions presuppose a fixed text for the *Iliad*. (Cf. Jensen 1980:106: "Only from [around] 520 onwards do the Attic representations seem to reflect the *Iliad that we know*" [highlighting mine].) Also, I disagree with Kannicht's further argument, extending from these conclusions, that the *Iliad*, unlike other epics, resisted iconographic representation because it was so artistically extraordinary: see N 1990a:73 n. 105.

161. For a discussion of the evidence of vase paintings as a criterion for determining the fixation of Homeric traditions, especially in Athens, see Lowenstam 1993a, in particular p. 216; also Lowenstam 1992. Cf. Ballabriga 1990:19, referring to Brillante 1983:119. See also the remarks on the Panathenaia in N 1990a:21–23, 28, 54, 73, 75, 160, 174, 192. On the Peisistratidai and the Panathenaia, see again Shapiro 1990, 1992, 1993.

162. Janko 1982:228–231; see also the modified formulation in Janko 1992:19.

163. Morris 1986, esp. pp. 93, 104.

an early date.[164] As I have already pointed out, however, the evidence of the earliest poetic inscriptions suggests that the very concept of a poetic transcript is not likely to have evolved until around 550 B.C.E.[165] Thus I continue to resist the arguments for an early dating of Homeric poetry as a *text*.

Given the strong parallelisms between textuality and certain patterns of evolution in oral poetic traditions, I have been arguing that the fixation of Homeric poetry as a *text* can be viewed as a process, not necessarily an event. Text-fixation becomes an event only when the text finally gets written down. But there can be textuality—or better, textualization—without written text.[166] I have been arguing further that the Homeric tradition of epic provides an example of such textualization: in the process of evolution in composition, performance, and diffusion, the Homeric tradition of epic became increasingly less fluid and more stable in its patterns of recomposition, moving slowly ahead in time until it reached a relatively static phase.[167] We may refer to this static phase as an era of *rhapsōidoí* 'rhapsodes'.[168]

---

164. Ibid. I have already quoted, in another context, the observation of Janko (1982:191): "It is difficult to refuse the conclusion that the texts [*Iliad* and *Odyssey*] were fixed at the time when each one was composed, whether by rote memorisation or by oral dictated texts."

165. See pp. 35–36 above.

166. See further argumentation in N 1990a:53.

167. Cf. N 1990a:52–81. We need not postulate, however, that each performance became identical with each previous performance. Granted, there could have been an *ideology* of identical reperformance toward the end of this process of text-fixation without writing. But an ideology of fixity does not prevent recomposition-in-performance, even if the rate of recomposition has been slowing down. See further in N 1990a:52–81. On the descriptive term *crystallization*, see N 1990a:53, 60, 414 n. 4, and N 1990b:42 (with reference to N 1979:5–9), 47, 51–52, 61, 78–79 (cf. Sherratt 1990:820–821). For a similar though hardly identical use of the image, describing the formation of Kirghiz epic traditions, see Radloff 1885 [1990:78]: "Like new crystals that develop in a saturated sodium solution during evaporation and group together around a large crystal center in the fluid, or like fine iron filings that cluster around the magnetic pole, all single legends and tales, all historical memories, stories, and songs are strongly attracted to the epic centers and become, by being broken into pieces, parts of a comprehensive picture." See also Cook 1995:4: "The crystallization of the Odyssean tradition into a written text, the growth of Athenian civic ritual, and the process of state formation in Attica were simultaneous and mutually reinforcing developments."

168. Cf. Sealey 1957, and parallel argumentation in Jensen 1980:96–106 and Ballabriga 1990:28.

110   As we have seen, the static phase of Homeric performance traditions could easily have lasted about two centuries. If we were to make
cross-sections at either end of this static phase, I would picture at one
end a relatively more *formative* stage starting with the middle of the
eighth century and, at the other end, an increasingly *definitive* stage
toward the middle of the sixth century, by which time I can imagine
the achievement of a near-textual status of the Homeric poems in
the context of performance by rhapsodes at the Panathenaia.[169]

My evolutionary model differs from that of G. S. Kirk, who posits a
sequence of oral transmission starting with a monumental composer
in the eighth century B.C.E., to be defined as an individual Homer,
and proceeding from there into the historical period of sixth-century
Athens.[170] Either model takes us down to 550 B.C.E. or so.[171] Significant variations of Homeric themes in the iconographical evidence of
vase paintings—especially variations of "Iliadic" themes—persist until around 530 B.C.E.[172] In sum, the approximate date of 550 B.C.E.—

---

169. See especially N 1990a:80. In dating the definitive stage toward 550 B.C.E., I follow, at
least in part, the discussion of Sealey 1957 (see esp. p. 348), who also places at the mid-
point of the sixth century B.C.E. the following: (1) the arbitration, by Periandros of Corinth,
of the war between the Athenians and the Mytilenaeans of Lesbos over Sigeion (p. 320);
(2) the era when Pittakos, Alcaeus, and Sappho flourished (pp. 324–325); and (3) the era
when Ibycus flourished (p. 327). I should add that even the notion of a *definitive* phase
leaves room for variation in still later phases of the performance tradition. The fragments
of papyri of the Homeric poems from the third and the second centuries B.C.E. suggest, in
the opinion of Sealey (1990:128), that "there were *Iliad*s and *Odyssey*s which were a good
deal longer than the Byzantine *Iliad* and *Odyssey;* the long texts may well have exceeded the
later text by a quarter of its length or even more."

170. Kirk 1962:88–98 and 1976:130–131. For a critique of Kirk's model, see Jensen
1980:95, 113–114. I agree with Jensen's arguments against Kirk's "devolutionary" premise. Jensen's own model, as we have seen, posits a dictation that was supposedly commissioned by the Peisistratidai. Her candidate as the man who dictated the text is Kynaithos
(on whom see N 1990a:22–23, 73–75). For yet another model, see Ballabriga (1990),
who retains the idea of a "creative Homer" at one end of the chronological spectrum but
rejects Kirk's idea of decadence by positing a "creative rhapsode at the later end." His candidate as this "creative rhapsode" is Kynaithos (see esp. his pp. 21, 28). For another critique of Kirk's model, from yet another angle, see M. L. West 1990:36–37.

171. Cf. Sealey (1990:133), who argues that "the *Iliad* and *Odyssey* do not have a date of
composition. They came into being during a long period, which began well before the end
of the Bronze Age and lasted into the sixth century or later."

172. On the evidence of vase paintings as a criterion for determining the fixation of
Homeric traditions, especially in Athens, see again Lowenstam 1993a, in particular p. 216.

or perhaps a few decades later—seems to me the most plausible one as a terminus post quem for a potential transcription of the *Iliad* and the *Odyssey*.

This evolutionary model of Homeric poetry culminating in a static phase that lasts about two centuries, framed by a relatively formative stage in the middle of the eighth century and an increasingly definitive stage in the middle of the sixth, is comparable to the model that I have worked out for the body of poetry attributed to Theognis of Megara, where the external dating criteria applied to the contents suggest a span of evolution exceeding a century and a half.[173] There are also other points of comparison. With reference to Hesiod, Archilochus, and Tyrtaeus, Stephanie West has dated the compositions attributed to all three before the last third of the seventh century, adding that "their precisely worded compositions could not long have survived their authors without a written record."[174] I prefer to apply an evolutionary model to all three, noting the rhapsodic traditions explicitly attested in the case of Hesiod[175] and Archilochus;[176] similar arguments can be made in the case of Tyrtaeus.[177]

The time has come to reach conclusions. The comparative evidence of living oral epic traditions goes a long way to show that unity or integrity results from the dynamic interaction of *composition, performance,* and *diffusion* in the making of epic. Such evidence, added to the internal evidence of the *Iliad* and the *Odyssey* as texts, points to an evolutionary process in the making of Homeric poetry.

And yet, this envisioning of Homer in evolutionary terms may leave some of us with a sense of aching emptiness. It is as if we have suddenly lost a cherished author whom we could always admire for the ultimate achievement of the *Iliad* and the *Odyssey*. But surely what we have really admired all along is not the author, about whom we never did really know anything historically, but the Homeric poems themselves. To this extent, the evolutionary model may even become

---

173. See N 1985:33–34.

174. S. West 1988:34.

175. See N 1990a:29 n. 66.

176. N 1990a:25–26 and 363–364 n. 133.

177. See N 1990b:269–275, with reference to Philochorus FGH 328 F 216. On the evolutionary model in the case of elegiac traditions in general, see N 1985:46–51.

112   a source of consolation: we may have lost a historical author whom
we never knew anyway, but we have recovered in the process a mythical author who is more than just an author: he is *Hómēros,* culture
hero of Hellenism, a most cherished teacher of all Hellenes, who
will come back to life with every new performance of his *Iliad* and
Odyssey.

 CHAPTER 4

Myth as Exemplum in Homer

There are questions about the Homeric *parádeigma*, which I translate for the moment by way of Latin *exemplum* 'example', following the lead of earlier inquiries.[1] In an influential article on the subject of mythological exempla in Homer, Malcolm Willcock proposes that the contents of myths cited by Homeric characters, with reference to their own situations, are oftentimes a matter of ad hoc personal invention by the poet.[2] In a follow-up article, arguing specific cases of ad hoc inventions of myth in the *Iliad,* Willcock sums up his position this way: "Homer has a genial habit of inventing mythology for the purpose of adducing it as a parallel to the situation of his story."[3] My presentation disagrees with this position and offers an alternative formulation. The key is the idea of myth as performance.

I begin by recording my admiration of Willcock as a scholar and teacher, because my disagreement with his formulation is not hostile and in fact does not affect some of his basic findings. The frequency of my references to Willcock in the pages that follow reflects a recognition of the pervasive influence that his formulation of Homeric *parádeigma* or exemplum has achieved in classical scholarship. In this field, it could be argued, his formulation has even reached the status of a *parádeigma* in itself. Here I am thinking of the modern derivative *paradigm*—in the specific sense of Thomas Kuhn's terminology in his inquiry into the structure of scientific revolutions.[4] What I propose is not a displacement of Willcock's paradigm but rather—to borrow

---

1. For example, Öhler 1929.

2. Willcock 1964. Cf. Braswell 1971.

3. Willcock 1977:43.

4. Kuhn 1970.

114 again from Kuhn's terminology—a "paradigm shift," with some new additions as well as subtractions.[5]

A successful paradigm shift, as Kuhn observes, should make it possible to account for a wider range of phenomena or to account more precisely for some of those that are already known. Such a gain is "achieved only by discarding some previously standard beliefs or procedures and, simultaneously, by replacing those components of the previous paradigm with others."[6] It is in this spirit that I will cite, in the arguments that follow, various classicists who are recognized experts on the subject of Homeric poetry. Their names are prominent in my argumentation not for the sake of controversy but because they represent the primary authorities for the paradigms that are being challenged.[7]

Let us begin with the central challenge. I call into question the very idea that Homeric myth is a matter of personal invention. Such an idea, I will argue, leads to an attitude that divorces the study of Homeric poetry, under the control of classicists, from the study of myth, as illuminated by the discipline of anthropology.

The divorce is suggested in Willcock's own conclusion: "If Homer invents so freely, it must be dangerous for us to use the *Iliad* as if it were a handbook of mythology."[8] Implicit in this statement is the recognition, however vaguely expressed, that the study of myth is indeed founded on some form of academic discipline. Explicit is the message that such a discipline is inappropriate to the study of Homer.

A major problem lies in the instability of our own concept of *myth*, which leads to the destabilization of the concepts of creativity and invention in the contexts of myth. It is one thing for the ancient commentators to say that Homer created something for the moment, as for example when Aristarchus takes this stance about a story told by Thetis, retold by Achilles in *Iliad* 1.396–406, about a conspiracy

---

5. Cf. especially Kuhn 1970:66.

6. Ibid.

7. In the present version, I hope that I have transcended the earlier version (N 1992b) by resorting far less often to outright polemics.

8. Willcock 1977:53.

against Zeus by Hera, Poseidon, and Athena (scholia A to *Iliad* 1.400; cf. scholia to 1.399–406). After all, as Willcock observes, the ancient commentators "treat Homer as a creative poet."[9] But it is quite another thing for modern commentators who wish to defend the creativity of Homer to describe this story as "sheer invention."[10] For the poets of ancient Greece, as I shall argue, creativity is a matter of applying, to the present occasion, mythology that already exists. For modern commentators, however, creativity tends to be viewed as a matter of actively and consciously rejecting the versions of myths that already do exist. If indeed Homer is a creative poet, their reasoning goes, then whatever myths we find in Homer need not be ancient myths per se, but personal creations of new versions. Willcock puts it this way:

> Of course what [Homer] invented may in certain cases have
> become a part of mythology for later writers; but there is surely
> a qualitative difference between new poetic invention and the
> tradition from the past. Homer is very much at home in the tradi-
> tional myths, and often uses them as background for his *autosche-
> diasmata* . . . ;[11] but his invention is of a different kind and origin.
> So the neo-analytical search for external sources for assertions
> about the past in the *Iliad* (e.g., in Kullmann *Die Quellen*) is a per-
> ilous one. It is far too easy to leap to conclusions, and assume
> debts to hypothetical models.[12]

The so-called neo-analysts, as represented by Wolfgang Kullmann in this critique, point to the independent traditions of the Epic Cycle, as attested primarily in the plot summaries of Proclus's *Chrestomathy*, in arguing for the existence of external sources for the myths of Homeric poetry.[13] In the case of the Homeric passage just

---

9. Ibid., 43 n. 10.

10. Willcock 1964:143. We may note the cautious wording of Martin 1989:129 in describing the "invention" of Diomedes at *Iliad* 6.215–231.

11. Willcock is using *autoschediasmata* in the sense of "improvisations."

12. Willcock 1977:53.

13. Kullmann 1960.

116   cited, about a conspiracy against Zeus by Hera, Poseidon, and Athena (*Iliad* 1.396–406), Kullmann himself is on record as claiming an external source.[14]

This view is challenged by Jasper Griffin, who explicitly sides with Willcock in arguing, with reference to this same passage, that "the poet of the *Iliad* even invents archaic-sounding myths."[15] Griffin disagrees with Kullmann, who "believes the story is really ancient."[16] Griffin's wording here makes it clear that, for him, the myth in *Iliad* 1 about the conspiracy by Hera, Poseidon, and Athena against Zeus cannot be "really ancient" if indeed this particular constellation of three gods is ad hoc to the narrative at hand.

It is as though myth cannot be traditional if it is ad hoc. I submit that such an assumption cannot be justified. My basic challenge to the paradigm of ad hoc innovation in Homeric myth entails a call for adding the perspectives of social anthropology. Let us consider a statement about myth that has clearly benefited from such perspectives: according to Walter Burkert's working definition, myth is "a traditional narrative that is used as a designation of reality. Myth is *applied* narrative [emphasis mine]. Myth describes a meaningful and important reality that applies to the aggregate, going beyond the individual."[17]

More needs to be said, however, about the meaning and the truth-value of myth. "From the viewpoint of a social anthropologist like myself," writes Sir Edmund Leach, "myth loses all meaning when it is taken out of context."[18] As Leach argues, "Myth is 'true' for those who use it, but we cannot infer the nature of that truth simply from reading the text; we have to know the context to which the text

---

14. Kullmann 1956:14. Kullmann's position is modified as his discussion proceeds (pp. 14–16), in that he accepts a variant reading reported by Zenodotus (scholia A to *Iliad* 1.400) at the line ending of *Iliad* 1.400: Φοῖβος Ἀπόλλων 'Phoebus Apollo' instead of Παλλὰς Ἀθήνη 'Pallas Athena'. Kullmann infers that Παλλὰς Ἀθήνη was an innovative replacement of an earlier Φοῖβος Ἀπόλλων. To that extent, even for Kullmann, there is at least partial innovation, against tradition, in this line as transmitted. On the role of Hera, Poseidon, and Athena in *Iliad* 24.25–26, see especially O'Brien 1993:91–94.

15. Griffin 1980:185.

16. Ibid., 185 n. 17.

17. My translation, with slight modifications, of Burkert 1979b:16–39.

18. Leach 1982:6.

refers."[19] The empirical evidence of such a context, as ascertained by "fieldwork" in our era of recording machines, is the primary given of social anthropology.

In the case of texts like the *Iliad* and the *Odyssey,* unfortunately, we have of course no such direct evidence available. For social anthropologists like Leach, who recognize the stories of the *Iliad* and the *Odyssey* as myths, the successful analysis of these stories *as myths* is nonetheless elusive for this very reason: "We do not ignore literary evidence altogether, but we are very skeptical about the possibility of making ethnographic sense of literary texts which have been divorced from their original context of time and space."[20]

The problem can be extended even to myths gathered by the anthropologists themselves, if the contexts for those myths have been lost in translation, as it were:

> As far as anthropology is concerned, a great deal of the present vogue for the study of mythology is a response to the stimulus provided by the work of Lévi-Strauss, in particular his essays on "The Structural Study of Myth," "The Story of Asdiwal," and the four volumes of *Mythologiques.*[21] But in a technical sense, all the myth data which Lévi-Strauss uses is drastically defective. Most of it is completely divorced from its original social context, and all of it has suffered the deformations which result from transcription into a written text, ruthless abbreviation, and translation from the vernacular into a European language or even a succession of European languages. For example, most of the myths which are analyzed in *Mythologiques* take up only a few lines of printed text and have been translated by Lévi-Strauss himself from similarly abbreviated Portuguese versions recorded by Christian missionaries. It seems highly probable that, in context, each paragraph of such material corresponds to several hours of oral recitation accompanied by elaborately staged dramatic performance.[22]

---

19. Ibid., 6–7.

20. Ibid., 4.

21. Lévi-Strauss, "The Structural Study of Myth" (1967a); "The Story of Asdiwal" (1967b); and the four volumes of *Mythologiques: Le cru et le cuit* (1964); *Du miel aux cendres* (1966); *L'origine des manières de table* (1968); and *L'homme nu* (1971).

22. Leach 1982:7.

118   These observations should be of particular concern to classicists whose familiarity with anthropological approaches to myth is based mainly on the works of Lévi-Strauss, as criticized here. Worse, such familiarity is hardly a direct one for many English-speaking students of the classics, who rely on G. S. Kirk's introductory books about myth, featuring summaries of the summaries made by Lévi-Strauss, as a short-cut to an understanding of "structuralism."[23] Worse still, these books by Kirk, who is not an anthropologist, adopt an attitude of self-distancing from the very methods that he applies. As a result, readers are scared away from consulting directly the anthropological perspectives of Lévi-Strauss himself. I suggest that not enough credit is being given to the methods of Lévi-Strauss in analyzing the myths of small-scale societies like the Bororo of central Brazil, even if we may agree with Leach that not enough attention is being paid to the contexts of performance. The works of Lévi-Strauss, I maintain, remain models of "structuralist" techniques in revealing the richness and complexity of human thought in the institutions of so-called primitive societies. For many who read Kirk, however, the myths of small-scale societies like the Bororo will seem more like a foil for showing the distinctness and, in many instances, the purported superiority of the myths of the ancient Greeks. Such an attitude is criticized by Marcel Detienne in an essay bearing the ironic title, "Les Grecs ne sont pas comme les autres."[24]

Worst of all, Kirk's very use of such things as Bororo myths, for any kind of comparison with the Greeks, is attacked by some classics scholars as an act of disloyalty to classicism: with specific reference to Kirk, for example, Jasper Griffin writes of "scholars who have begun to take seriously the bizarre myths of primitive peoples," observing that "the revolt from classicism" makes these myths "seem deeper and truer than the human scale and coherent logic of the myths of Homer."[25] Again I see a need for applying the perspectives of social anthropology. Without referring to Lévi-Strauss directly,[26] Griffin pro-

---

23. Kirk, *Myth, Its Meaning and Functions* (1970); *The Nature of Greek Myths* (1974).

24. Detienne, the first chapter of *Dionysos mis à mort* (1977:17–47); see especially the remarks at pp. 24–25 concerning Kirk. At one point in his book on myth, Kirk (1970:179) says about the ancient Greek heroes: "The Greeks are *a special case* [emphasis mine]. In the mythology of most other peoples, heroes . . . are either inconspicuous or absent."

25. Griffin 1980:173.

26. See ibid., 175 n. 66.

ceeds to quote at length one of Kirk's retellings of Lévi-Strauss's retellings of selected Bororo myths, taking Kirk to task for his subjective
presentation.[27] Such is the fate of Bororo myths, and of Lévi-Strauss
himself, in this format of indirect mediation: all has been lost in the
translation. How hopeless it seems, then, this task of "making ethnographic sense of literary texts" like Homeric poetry!

All hope is not lost, however. There may yet be ways of talking
about the myths of Homeric poetry *as they are performed in context.*
Although the outermost narrative frames of the *Iliad* and the *Odyssey,* the two monumental compositions themselves, give us for all
practical purposes no information whatsoever about context of performance, let alone occasion, the stories that are *framed* by the
compositions, the myths actually spoken by Homeric characters, are
indeed contextualized. In his 1989 book, *The Language of Heroes,*
Richard Martin shows how Homeric narrative actually recovers, al-
beit in stylized form, the contexts of speech-acts such as formal
boasts, threats, laments, invectives, prophecies, prayers.[28] When Hektor is lamented by Andromache at the end of the *Iliad,* to cite just
one example for the moment, her dramatized song of lamentation is
not just a set of words spoken by a Homeric character and quoted by
Homeric narrative: it is a speech-act, brought to life by the narrative.
I shall now argue that myth itself, as spoken by Homeric characters in
ad hoc situations, is in its own right a speech-act.

There is a key word that figures in this argument. As Martin shows
in his *Language of Heroes,* a word used in Homeric diction to designate any speech-act is *mûthos,* ancestor of our word myth. In Homeric
diction, the Greek word for "myth" reveals itself in its broadest sense.

In order to grasp the special meaning of *mûthos* in Homeric
language, let us consider the distinction between *marked* and *unmarked* members of an opposition—to use the terminology of Prague
School linguistics.[29] Here is Martin's own working definition of these
terms:[30]

---

27. Ibid., 174–175. The Bororo myth is described as having an "eerie, almost poetical
quality" (Kirk 1970:63).

28. Martin 1989, esp. pp. 12–42. Cf. Létoublon 1986, following up on her earlier work,
1983:27–48. See also Muellner 1976.

29. Waugh 1982. There is an extended discussion of these terms in N 1990a:5–6.

30. Martin 1989:29.

120   The "marked" member of a pair carries greater semantic weight, but can be used across a narrower range of situations, whereas the unmarked member—the more colorless member of the opposition—can be used to denote a broader range, *even that range covered by the marked member:* it is the more general term.[31]

In terms of Prague School linguistics, then, a speech-act is "marked" speech, whereas ordinary or everyday speech is "unmarked" speech.[32] With reference to Homeric language, Martin shows that *mûthos* is a marked way to designate 'speech', whereas *épos* is the unmarked way—at least with reference to an opposition with *mûthos*.[33] The Homeric sense of *mûthos*, in Martin's working definition, is "a speech-act indicating authority, performed at length, *usually in public*, with a focus on full attention to every detail."[34] The counterpart *épos*, on the other hand, is "an utterance, ideally short, accompanying a physical act, and focusing on message, as perceived by the addressee, rather than on performance as enacted by the speaker."[35]

As the unmarked member of the opposition, *épos* or its plural *épea* can be expected to occur even in contexts where *mûthos* would be appropriate.[36] The reverse situation, however, is not to be found: in Homeric diction, it appears that "one can never simply substitute the semantically restricted term *mûthos*—meaning authoritative speech-

---

31. Highlighting mine.

32. See the extended discussion in N 1990a:8–9, 31 and following.

33. Martin 1989:10–26.

34. Ibid., 12.

35. Ibid.

36. Ibid., 26–30. With reference to the six types of dramatized speech-act that I have listed earlier as examples to be found in the Homeric poems—that is, boasts, threats, invectives, laments, prophecies, and prayers (see note 28 above)—we may note the observation of Martin (p. 38) that prayer is never explicitly designated as *mûthos* in Homeric diction. In my earlier discussion of dramatized Homeric speech-acts (N 1990a:38), I have nevertheless listed prayer as belonging implicitly to the Homeric category of *mûthos*. One reason for making this connection is that the Homeric verb *eúkhomai* means not only 'boast' in a martial context or 'declare' in a juridical context but also 'pray' in a sacral context (see Muellner 1976). Cf. the discussion of *apeiléō* 'make a promise, boastful promise, threat' in N 1994c.

act, or 'performance'—for the ordinary term *épos*."[37] Also, whereas *épos* can be found in place of *mûthos* in Homeric diction, the reverse does not happen: "In Homer, a speech explicitly said to be an *épos*, and not also represented as *épea* (the plural), is never called a *mûthos*."[38] The irreversibility extends even further: "*Épea* can co-occur to refer to a *mûthos*, but *mûthoi* in the plural is never correlated with the singular form *épos*, to describe a speech."[39]

With reference to the "ordinary" or "everyday" aspect of speech as designated by *épos*, I should stress in general that the unmarked category of "ordinary" or "everyday" speech is a default category: in other words, "ordinary" is a variable concept, depending on whatever is being perceived as "special" in a given comparison or set of comparisons. In an earlier work, with reference to the general question of unmarked and marked speech, I had put it this way: "The perception of plain or everyday speech is a variable abstraction that depends on the concrete realization of whatever special speech . . . is set apart for a special context."[40]

Let us reexamine in this light the wording of Martin's useful working definition of *épos*: "an utterance, ideally short, accompanying a physical act, and focusing on message, as perceived by the addressee, rather than on performance as enacted by the speaker." In line with the argument that unmarked speech is "ordinary" speech only inasmuch as it serves as a default category in opposition to a special category of marked speech, we could say that Homeric *épos* is "ideally short" precisely because Homeric *mûthos* is ideally long. Or again, we could describe Homeric *épos* as "focusing on message, as perceived by the addressee" precisely because Homeric *mûthos* focuses not only on message but also "on performance as enacted by the speaker." If it were not for the opposition to unmarked *épos* by way of marked *mûthos*, the word *épos* would not need to designate speech that is "ideally short," nor would it need to be perceived as merely "focusing on message."

---

37. Martin 1989:30.

38. Ibid.

39. Ibid.

40. N 1990a:30 and again at p. 31.

There are, of course, other Homeric forms besides *mûthos* that can mark speech as special, set apart from "ordinary" *épos* or *épea*. Even an adjective added to the plural of unmarked *épos* can achieve a marked opposite in Homeric diction: as Martin shows, *épea pteróenta* 'winged words' is a functional synonym of *mûthos* in denoting certain kinds of marked speech.[41]

As we look beyond Homeric diction, however, at later stages in the history of Greek poetics, we can find evidence for the emergence of yet another word that marks speech as special—so special that it is set apart even from *mûthos,* which in such contexts then becomes in its own turn "ordinary." I mean "ordinary" only to the extent that the given opposing word becomes even more special. The word in question is *alēthḗs* 'true' or *alḗtheia* 'truth'. In the diction of a fifth-century poet like Pindar, for example, this word is used in explicit opposition to the word *mûthos* in contexts where true speech is being contrasted to other forms of speech that are discredited, that cannot be trusted (ἀλαθῆ λόγον versus μῦθοι at *Olympian* 1.29–30, μύθοις versus ἀλά-θειαν at *Nemean* 7.23–25).[42]

There is, to be sure, nothing post-Homeric about the actual word *alēthḗs* 'true' or *alḗtheia* 'truth', or even about the concept inherent in the formation of the word, which expresses an explicit denial, by way of the negative element *a-*, of forgetting, *lēth-*, and thereby an implicit affirmation of remembering, *mnē-*.[43] As Martin has shown convincingly, the Homeric word *mûthos* is associated with *narrating from memory,*[44] which he describes as the rhetorical act of *recollection.*[45] This speech-act of recollection, which qualifies explicitly as a *mûthos* (as at

---

41. Martin 1989:30–37; "Every speech called 'winged words' is meant to make the listener do something" (p. 31).

42. See extensive discussion of the relevant passages in N 1990a:65–68, 134, 203 n. 17, 423–424.

43. There is a detailed discussion at N 1990a:58–61.

44. Martin 1989:44.

45. Ibid., 80. Martin adds: "As a general rule, characters in the *Iliad* do not remember anything simply for the pleasure of memory. Recall has an exterior goal." Martin (p. 81 n. 60) cites Moran 1975:204 "on the introduction of non-Homeric poetry with the verb *mémnē-mai.*" We may note with interest the idea of "non-Homeric" here.

Iliad 1.273), is the act of *mnē-* 'remembering'. An ideal example is the wording of Phoenix in *Iliad* 9.527 as he introduces the story of the hero Meleagros to Achilles and the rest of the audience: μέμνη-μαι 'I remember [*mnē-*]'.[46] The failure of any such speech-act is marked by the act of *lēth-* 'forgetting' (as with λήθεαι at *Iliad* 9.259).[47] The very concept of *alēthḗs* 'true' or *alḗtheia* 'truth' expresses the need to avoid such failure in the speech-act, the *mûthos*, of recollection or narrating from memory, and Homeric diction can actually combine *alēthḗs* 'true' with a derivative of *mûthos*, the verb *muthéomai* 'make a *mûthos*', as in the expression *alēthéa muthḗsasthai* 'speak true things' at *Iliad* 6.382 (the whole speech in question is introduced as a *mûthos* at 6.381). The Homeric meaning of *muthéomai* 'make a *mûthos*' has all the force of *mûthos* itself, as we see from this description by Martin: "When this word for speech occurs, the accompanying discourse has a formal nature, often religious or legal; full detail is laid out for the audience, or is expected by the interlocutor in the poem; at times, a character comments on the formal qualities of the discourse labelled with this verb."[48]

Granted, then, that there is nothing post-Homeric about the actual word *alēthḗs* 'true' or *alḗtheia* 'truth'; also, that this word does not enter into opposition with *mûthos* in Homeric diction. In post-Homeric traditions, however, as we have seen, for example, in the diction of Pindar, *mûthos* has indeed become an opposite of *alēthḗs* 'true' or *alḗtheia* 'truth', which is now marked as being distinct from *mûthos*. In the Pindaric examples that we have already considered, the word *mûthos* has defaulted into a vague plural (μῦθοι at *Olympian* 1.30, μύθοις at *Nemean* 7.23), representing a murky multiplicity of discredited versions against which backdrop the singular truth of *alḗtheia* is being highlighted in shining contrast.[49] In brief, as I have argued at length in my earlier work on such post-Homeric

---

46. On the function of the myth of Meleagros as retold by Phoenix to Achilles and the rest of the audience, see N 1990a:196–197, 205, 253, 310 n. 164, following up on N 1979: 105–111.

47. See the extensive discussion in Martin 1989:77–88; of special interest is p. 78.

48. Ibid., 40.

49. N 1990a:65–66.

124   contexts, the meaning of *mûthos* as a speech-act has thus become marginalized.⁵⁰

There are traces of this marginalization at even earlier stages. Let us consider the expression *alēthéa gērúsasthai* 'announce true things' in Hesiod *Theogony* 28, which is a formulaic variant of *alēthéa muthḗsasthai* 'speak true things', as attested at *Iliad* 6.382.⁵¹ It appears from such variations that *gērúomai* 'announce' has become the marked member in opposition to *muthéomai* 'speak', which then becomes unmarked.⁵² Similarly with *alēthéa muthḗsasthai* 'speak true things', as attested at *Homeric Hymn to Demeter* 121, as also at *Iliad* 6.382: this formula is in turn a variant of *etḗtuma muthḗsasthai* 'speak genuine things', as attested at *Homeric Hymn to Demeter* 44. Just as *gērúomai* 'announce' has become the marked member in opposition to *muthéomai* 'speak', so also *alēthéa* 'true things' has become the marked member in opposition to *etḗtuma* or *étuma* 'genuine things'.⁵³ The latter opposition is made explicit in the quoted words of the Muses themselves in Hesiod *Theogony* 27–28, where the unique truth-value of the *Theogony* itself is heralded by the goddesses as *alēthéa* 'true things' (28) in opposition to a multiplicity of versions that *look* like *étuma* 'genuine things' but are in reality *pseúdea* 'fallacies' (ψεύδεα πολλὰ . . . ἐτύμοισιν ὁμοῖα 'many fallacies that look like genuine things' 27).⁵⁴

In my earlier work, I have argued at length that such variations result from a chain of differentiations setting off a single marked pan-Hellenic version from a multiplicity of unmarked versions that are perceived as local or at least more local.⁵⁵ For now I need only emphasize that this newer concept is marked as distinct from earlier

---

50. Ibid., 66–68.

51. In fact, *alēthéa muthḗsasthai* 'speak true things' is attested as a *textual* variant of *alēthéa gērúsasthai* 'announce true things' in Hesiod *Theogony* 28: see N 1990a:68 n. 84.

52. Ibid.

53. Ibid.

54. Ibid.

55. Ibid., 52–81. On the equivalence of what I describe as pan-Hellenic and what is explicitly described as Olympian in archaic Greek poetics, see N 1990b [1982]:46 (also pp. 10, 37); also Clay 1989:9–10. For more on pan-Hellenism as a hermeneutic construct,

concepts that thereby default into an unmarked category. As the word *alēthḗs* 'true' or *alḗtheia* 'truth' becomes marked in opposition to *mûthos,* which in turn becomes unmarked in the context of such opposition, the meaning of *mûthos* becomes marginalized to mean something like 'myth' in the popular sense of the word as it is used today in referring to the opposite of 'truth'. In the poetic diction of Pindar, for example, *mûthos* can practically be translated as 'myth' in this modern sense of the word. In terms of Pindar's poetics, as I have argued elsewhere, "*mûthoi* 'myths' stand for an undifferentiated outer core consisting of local myths, where various versions from various locales may potentially contradict each other, while *alḗtheia* 'truth' stands for a differentiated inner core of exclusive pan-Hellenic myths that tend to avoid the conflicts of the local versions."[56]

In short, the expression *alēthéa gērúsasthai* 'to herald true things' in *Theogony* 28 designates not just the process of speaking something that is privileged: it explicitly marks a speech-act, an utterance with special authority. It seems to me not enough to establish that the adjective *alēthḗs* can be interpreted as 'verifiable', in the etymological sense that it negates the idea of "escape one's consciousness," as implicit in the root from which it is derived, *lēth-* as in *lḗthē* 'oblivion' and *lanthánō* 'escape the consciousness of'.[57] Yes, *alēthḗs* conveys the

---

see pp. 39–40 above. For a critique, with bibliography, of various solutions that posit a distinction between the local Helikonian Muses and what I call the pan-Hellenic Olympian Muses, see Thalmann 1984:134–135. My own formulation differs from the earlier solutions in allowing for a preconceived overlap, in terms of the *Theogony* itself, between the Helikonian and Olympian Muses. The specialized category of Olympian, as a pan-Hellenic construct, is to be viewed as potentially *included* by the category of Helikonian: "Hesiod's relationship with the Helikonian Muses represents an older and broader poetic realm that the poet then streamlines into the newer and narrower one of a pan-Hellenic theogony by way of synthesizing the Helikonian with the Olympian Muses" (N 1990b:60). The operating principle, it seems, is that local versions may include pan-Hellenic aspects, whereas pan-Hellenic versions exclude distinctly local aspects (ibid.). Thus the objection mentioned by Thalmann (1984:134–135), to the effect that the Muses are named as Olympian already at *Theogony* 25, before their formal transfer to Olympus, is not an obstacle to my formulation. The Muses of Helikon are already potentially Olympian; once they become explicitly Olympian, however, they are exclusively Olympian.

56. N 1990b:66.

57. There is an admirable survey of the semantics of *alēthḗs,* and of various interpretations, in Cole (1983), who resists Heidegger's formulation of an "objective" truth-value inherent in the word (the truth not "hidden" in what is perceived). Cole's own interpretation is a reformulation of earlier solutions insisting on a "subjective" truth-value (the truth not

126 idea of seeing something "for real," but there is more to it: the nega-
tion of *lēth-* serves as the equivalent of the positive concept *mnē-*,
which as we have seen means not just 'remember' but something like
'narrate from memory'. We may recall the intuitive formulation of
Jean-Pierre Vernant, who defines *mnē-* as 'recover the essence of being'.[58] In ancient Greek mythical thought, such an essence is beyond
sensible reality, beyond time.[59] Even more important, as Marcel Detienne has shown, ancient Greek tradition claims that this essence is
controlled by the poet, master of "truth" or *alḗtheia*.[60]

A problem remains: *alēthéa* in *Theogony* 28 is opposed not to *lḗthē*
but to *pseúdea* 'fallacies' in the previous line. It has been argued that
such an antithesis represents "a later, more rational way of thinking,
where *alḗtheia* means 'truth'."[61] It is as if a new rationalistic opposition of *alēthéa* 'true things' versus *pseúdea* 'fallacies' were superim-
posed on an older myth-centered opposition of *alḗtheia* in the sense
of 'no lapse of consciousness' versus *lḗthē* 'lapse of consciousness',
with the result that the two oppositions overlap and in fact coexist.[62]
Further, it has been argued that there is overlap even between *alḗtheia* and *lḗthē*, as also between *alēthéa* and *pseúdea*, to the extent that
no act of remembering is free of some kind of forgetting, no telling of the truth is free of some deception.[63] I agree that there is a

---

"forgotten" by the one who perceives). He suggests (p. 12) that "the forgetting excluded
by *alḗtheia* involves primarily the process of transmission—not the mental apprehension
on which the transmission is based." Thus *alḗtheia* refers "not simply to non-omission of
pieces of information through forgetting or failure to take notice or ignoring, but also to
not forgetting from one minute to the next what was said a few minutes before, and not
letting anything, said or unsaid, slip by without being mindful of its consequences and
implications" (ibid.).

58. Vernant 1985:108–136 (from a chapter first published in 1965).

59. Cf. Thalmann 1984:147, paraphrasing Vernant. I have adopted his translation of Vernant's "le fond de l'être" as "the essence of being," described as "the reality that lies beyond the sensible world" (ibid.).

60. Detienne 1973:9–27.

61. Thalmann 1984:148 (also p. 230 n. 31), following Detienne 1973:75–79.

62. Thalmann 1984:148.

63. Ibid., following Detienne 1973 and Pucci 1977.

thought-pattern where *mnē-* in the sense of 'remember' includes an aspect of *lēth-* 'forget'.[64] I disagree, however, with the notion that the adjective *alēthḗs* and the noun *alḗtheia* are similarly inclusive; rather, as I have argued at length elsewhere, *alēthḗs* and *alḗtheia* explicitly *exclude* a lapse of the mind.[65] The nonambiguity or even absolutism of the words *alēthḗs* and *alḗtheia* is a key to their denotation of a speech-act endowed with a distinctly authoritative and authorizing force.

Such absolutism is inherent also in the earlier usages of *mûthos*, before it becomes destabilized in the process of being replaced by newer terms for the absolute. Myth becomes relative, not to be trusted, as we see even in our own everyday usage of the word. This popular sense of the word *myth* in our everyday usage must be juxtaposed with the academic sense of the word in the usage of anthropologists who observe that the *myth* of a given society can be tantamount to the *truth* for that society. As we have already seen, the anthropologist Edmund Leach offers a particularly useful discussion of *myth* perceived as *truth* in small-scale societies.[66] This academic sense of *myth* matches the earlier meaning of *mûthos* as reflected in Homeric diction: in this early phase, as we have seen, the word can refer to the speech-act of actually *narrating from memory* an authoritative myth from the past. In sum, the differences between the earlier and later meanings of the Greek word *mûthos* happen to match closely the differences between the academic and popular meanings of the modern borrowing *myth*.

The marginalization of *mûthos* in the wake of a new opposition with *alēthḗs* 'true' or *alḗtheia* 'truth' may be pertinent to the earlier opposition of marked *mûthos* and unmarked *épos*. I had put it this way in my earlier work: "At each stage of differentiation, we must allow for the probability that the unmarked member of the opposition had once been the marked member in earlier sets of opposition."[67] Martin notes the eventual differentiation of the word *épos*, which becomes specialized in the sense of 'poetic utterance' and even 'hexameter

---

64. N 1990a:58, following Detienne 1973:22–27.

65. N 1990a:59–61.

66. Leach 1982:5–7.

67. N 1990a:68 n. 84.

verse'.[68] Such semantic specialization suggests to me that *épos* itself had once been a marked word in opposition to some other unmarked word for 'speech', and that it had served as an unmarked word in Homeric diction only within the framework of an opposition with *mûthos*. The semantic specialization of *épos*, and the later semantic specialization of *mûthos*, are reflected indirectly in the modern borrowings *epic* and *myth*. We may compare Aristotle's use of *épē* in the sense of *epic* and of *mûthos* in the sense of *myth* as "plot."

As for the later semantic specialization of *mûthos*, in the context of an opposition to *alēthéa* 'true things', it remains to ask why *mûthos* eventually became marginalized to designate unreliable speech, parallel to the popular usage of the modern word that is borrowed from it, *myth*. The answer, as I have argued elsewhere, has to do with a tendency to avoid, in pan-Hellenic traditions of poetry, any explicit reference to details of local traditional *myth* as it relates to local traditional *ritual*.[69] For the moment, suffice it to stress that the semantics of the word *mûthos* bring to life, in microcosm, the relationship between myth and ritual, word and action, in ancient Greek society. Let us consider again the distinction between marked and unmarked speech.[70] We find that marked speech occurs as a rule in ritual contexts, as we can observe most clearly in the least complex or smallest-scale societies.[71] It is also in such societies that we can observe most clearly the symbiosis of ritual and myth, and how the language of ritual and myth is marked, while "everyday" language is unmarked.[72] So also with *mûthos*, ancestor of our word *myth:* this word, I have argued extensively elsewhere, had at an earlier stage meant the 'special speech' of myth and ritual as opposed to "everyday" speech.[73]

---

68. Martin 1989:13. See also N 1979:236 and 272, building on the arguments of Koller 1972; and N 1979:270–274 (cf. Martin 1989:16) on *épea* in *Iliad* 20.200, 204, 249, 250, and 256 as designating poetic utterances.

69. N 1990a:52–81.

70. See pp. 119–120 above.

71. N 1990a:31–32.

72. Ibid.; cf. Ben-Amos 1976.

73. N 1982 (review of Detienne 1981). See further details in N 1990a:31–32, 66–67.

This argument about *mûthos* has been criticized with reference to the most abbreviated available version of what I have had to say on the subject, in my foreword to Martin's book on *mûthos*.[74] Here is a summary:

> Nagy argues that the word *mûthos* has a special meaning in early Greek, is what in linguistics is called a "marked" term, meaning 'special' as against 'everyday' speech. It is akin to *múō* and to *mústēs* and *mustérion*, terms which have a special meaning in ritual.[75]

Not quite. I was discussing "the relationship between myth and ritual in ancient Greek society."[76] With reference to this relationship, I argued that "the language of ritual and myth is marked whereas 'everyday' language is unmarked."[77] Then, "as an example of these semantics," I cited *múō*, meaning 'I have my eyes closed' or 'I have my mouth closed' in everyday situations, but 'I see in a special way' or 'I say in a special way' in ritual.[78] The idea of special visualization and verbalization is further conveyed by two derivatives of *múō*, namely *mústēs* 'one who is initiated' and *mustérion* 'that into which one is initiated'; similarly with *mûthos*, I argued that this word, apparently related to *múō*, has a history of designating a special way of seeing and saying things.[79] Then I gave a contextual example of this idea of special visualization and verbalization:

> A striking example occurs in Sophocles, *Oedipus at Colonus* 1641 – 1644: the visualization and the verbalization of what happened to Oedipus in the precinct of the Eumenides at Colonus are restricted, in that the precise location of his corpse is a sacred secret (1545 – 1546, 1761 – 1763). Only Theseus, by virtue of being the

---

74. N 1989b.

75. Griffin 1991:1.

76. N 1989b:x.

77. Ibid.

78. Ibid. Perhaps the "onomatopoeia" implicit in the *mu* of *múō* has to do with the mechanics of closure, not with the sound itself.

79. Ibid.

proto-priest for the Athenians of the here-and-now, is to witness what happened, which is called the *drómena* (1644). This word is what Jane Harrison used to designate "ritual" in her formulation "myth is the plot of the *drómenon*." Thus the visualization and the verbalization of the myth, what happened to Oedipus, are restricted to the sacred context of ritual, controlled by the heritage of priestly authority from Theseus, culture-hero of the Athenian democracy.[80]

The "striking example" refers not to the specific word *múō* and other related words but to the general idea reflected by such words.[81]

My point remains that *mûthos* conveys the dimensions of ritual as well as myth and that it can refer specifically in Homeric diction to the telling of myth in the anthropological sense. In Homeric diction, this word *mûthos* reveals "myth" in its fullest meaning—not narrowly, in the sense of made-up stories that are the opposite of empirical truth, but broadly, in the sense of traditional narratives that convey a given society's truth-values.[82]

From an anthropological point of view, "myth" is indeed "special speech" in that it is a given society's way of affirming its own reality. Leach offers a particularly useful synthesis:

> The various stories [i.e., the myths of a given society] form a *corpus*. They lock in together to form a single theological-cosmological-[juridical] whole. Stories from one part of the corpus presuppose a knowledge of stories from all other parts. There is implicit cross-reference from one part to another. It is an unavoidable feature of

---

80. Ibid., quoted by Griffin 1991:1.

81. The reference is made clear in a less abbreviated version of my argument, which is cited along with this comment: "The same argument, with identical illustration, appears again, more unexpectedly, in Nagy's opening chapter to *The Cambridge History of Literary Criticism* . . . p. 3" (Griffin 1991:1). This longer version introduced the argument, as quoted above, with this explicit wording: "For an illustration of the semantics underlying the usage of these Greek words, let us consider Sophocles. . . ." (N 1989a:3; cf. also N 1982, cited by Martin [1989:13 n. 42]. I was speaking of the general concept of marked speech as reflected in the *Oedipus at Colonus* (1545–1546, 1641–1644, 1761–1763), not of the specific word *múō* and other related forms (cf. N 1990a:32). It can be argued that Theseus acts like a chief priest, an *árkhōn basileús*, when he grants (line 67) to Oedipus the right to dwell in Attica (*katoikiô*, 637); cf. Edmunds 1996:141; also Calame 1990 and the preface by P. Vidal-Naquet (pp. 9–13, esp. 10).

82. Cf. N 1990a:31–32.

storytelling that events are made to happen one after another, but in cross-reference, such sequence is ignored. It is as if the whole corpus referred to a single instant of time, namely, the present moment.[83]

Such a description of myth fits ideally the case of the myth told by Thetis, retold by Achilles in *Iliad* 1.396–406, about a conspiracy against Zeus by Hera, Poseidon, and Athena. In an important article that demands far more recognition than it has so far received, Mabel Lang has shown convincingly that this myth fits into a whole corpus—if I may apply Leach's term—of interconnected myths, spread throughout the *Iliad*, concerning conflicts of the Olympian gods.[84] Lang sums it up this way:

> This story is presented in seven different passages [of the *Iliad*]; they make up four complementary pairs, appearing in six widely-spaced books (1, 5, 14, 15, 20, and 21). Therefore it is highly unlikely that all these references were invented separately to illuminate particular situations in the *Iliad*.[85]

Arguing against Willcock's notion of ad hoc personal invention, Lang shows in detail how a complex and consistent set of *paradeígmata* or exempla concerning conflicts of the gods, as attested *within* the *Iliad*, has "priority" over the narrative points where the *paradeígmata* are cited by the characters of the *Iliad*.[86] The myth is already there, ready to be applied. "If the myth which is presented as a *parádeigma* has suffered very much in the way of innovation," Lang argues, "it will have lost its persuasive power as a precedent to be respected."[87] We may compare Martin's general description of the

---

83. Leach 1982:5.

84. Lang 1983. See further insights in Slatkin 1986:1–24; cf. Slatkin 1987, esp. pp. 261–262. Slatkin's work can be used as a counterweight to the assertion of Willcock 1977:50 that "the poet . . . needed a reason why Zeus should be under obligation to Thetis, and he therefore *invented* one" [emphasis mine].

85. Lang 1983:149.

86. See especially ibid., 151.

87. Ibid., 147. On the eventual marginalization of *mûthos* in the classical period, see pp. 123–124 above; see also the discussion in N 1990a:57 and following.

132   speech-acts embedded in Homeric narrative: "The diction . . . is most likely inherited and traditional; the rhetoric, on the other hand, is the locus of spontaneous composition in performance."[88] He goes on to say that "the way in which heroes speak to one another foregrounds for us this phenomenon of performing to fit the audience."[89]

Just as the characters in Homeric narrative are represented as making myths and any other speech-acts ad hoc, so also in "real life" situations of small-scale societies, as described by social anthropologists like Leach, the tellers of myths apply these myths to their own situations: "The principal use to which these stories are put is to justify whatever is now being done."[90] Following Bronislaw Malinowski, Leach asserts that myths "provide charters (i.e., legal precedents) for social action."[91] Moreover, this formula can be reversed: "It is not just that the myth provides a model for social reality but that social behavior is conducted as if the myth referred to a presently existing real world in which human beings attempt to participate."[92]

The idea that myth is special speech, a given society's way of affirming its own reality, can be connected with Barbara Johnson's application of J. L. Austin's notion of speech-act to *poetry*—an application that Austin himself resisted.[93] Such a line of thinking is taken further in Richard Martin's *The Language of Heroes*,[94] which applies the notion of speech-act to the oral performance of oral poetry as studied in the pathfinding works of Milman Parry and Albert Lord.[95] As Martin shows, the *mûthos* is not just any speech-act reported by

---

88. Martin 1989:85.

89. Ibid.

90. Leach 1982:5.

91. Ibid. Cf. Malinowski 1926.

92. Leach 1982:5, following Jacopin 1981.

93. B. Johnson 1980:56, in response to Austin 1962.

94. Martin 1989.

95. Parry 1971 [especially 1928a, 1928b, 1930, 1932] and Lord 1960.

poetry: it is also the speech-act of poetry itself. In this light, myth implies ritual in the very performance of myth.[96] By quoting *mûthos,* as in a mythological exemplum, Homeric poetry shows how the *mûthos* of poetry itself can be applied.

I advocate, then, an approach to the use of mythological exempla in Homer that differs from the paradigm of Willcock on the matter of ad hoc invention. It also differs, however, from that of the neo-analysts, who believe that the myths of Homer are drawn generally from earlier "sources." This difference is summed up in the following formulation:

> Even if we were to accept for the moment the dubious notion that parts of the Homeric Cycle are drawn from some text that predates our *Iliad* and *Odyssey,* the fundamental objection remains the same: when we are dealing with the traditional poetry of the Homeric (and Hesiodic) compositions, it is not justifiable to claim that a passage in any text can refer to another passage in another text. Such a restriction of approaches in Homeric (and Hesiodic) criticism is one of the most important lessons to be learned from the findings of Milman Parry and Albert Lord on the nature of traditional "oral" poetry. I will confine myself, then, to examining whether a poem that is composed in a given *tradition* may refer to other *traditions* of composition. Thus, for example, our *Odyssey* may theoretically refer to traditional themes that are central to the stories of the *Cypria*—or even to stories of the *Iliad,* for that matter. But even in that case, such traditional themes would have varied from composition to composition. There may theoretically be as many variations on a theme as there are compositions. Any theme is but a multiform [that is, a variant], and not one of the multiforms may be considered a functional "Urform." Only by hindsight can we consider the themes of our *Iliad* to be the best of possible themes.[97]

---

96. In this light, then, we may consider the semantics of *mímēsis* in the sense of 'reenacting' or 'acting' a given myth: see the discussion in N 1990a:42–44, 346, 349, 373–375, 381, 387. Cf. Martin 1989:7 n. 25 quoting Herington 1985:13: "Homeric poetry . . . seems to have been designed from the first to be *acted.*"

97. Taken from N 1979:42–43. The notion of "cross-reference," to which I allude in this statement, is indeed workable in the study of oral poetics provided we understand that any references to other stories in any given story would have to be diachronic in nature. On such diachronic cross-referencing between the *Iliad* and the *Odyssey* traditions, see N 1990a:53–54 n. 8; see also Pucci 1987:240–242.

Such a stance, relying on techniques of investigating oral poetry, differs both with the neo-analysts and with those neo-unitarians for whom Milman Parry's application of "oral theory" to the *Iliad* and the *Odyssey* has led to feelings of "disappointment at the amount of light it has shed on the poems themselves."[98]

For some neo-unitarian classicists such as Jasper Griffin, the "oral theory" is of little use for an aesthetic understanding of Homer.[99] Conceding that the *Iliad* and the *Odyssey* are heirs to an oral tradition, in that they at least "represent the end of a tradition of oral poetry,"[100] Griffin nonetheless insists that it suffices to approach Homer "with aesthetic methods not essentially or radically new, observing caution and avoiding arguments which are ruled out by an oral origin for the work."[101] At least for the moment, we have here a concession to "oral origin." But this concession is short-lived: it happens in the context of Griffin's citing at this point,[102] while bypassing the work of Parry and Lord, Ruth Finnegan's *Oral Poetry*.[103] This book is cited with approval because it claims that "there *is* no clear-cut line between 'oral' and 'written' literature."[104] Moreover, in the same context where it makes this claim, I think that Finnegan's book misreads Parry's concept of the formula in oral poetry in the very process of attempting to undermine the validity of the concept.[105]

To cite Finnegan's work instead of Parry's and Lord's is to provide a rationale, in undertaking one's own assessment of Homer, not to address directly any issues raised by differences between oral and written poetry. Such issues do indeed emerge, however, in many works

---

98. Griffin 1980:xiii.

99. Ibid., pp. xiii–xiv.

100. Ibid., p. xiii. For a more extreme argument in opposition to the oral heritage of Homeric poetry, see Shive 1987, reviewed in N 1988.

101. Griffin 1980:xiv.

102. Ibid.

103. Finnegan 1977.

104. Ibid., 2.

105. See pp. 23–25 above.

that choose at first to ignore them. At later stages of Griffin's own work, he begins to draw a sharp contrast between myths, associated indirectly with the "oral origin" of Homeric poetry, and the classicism associated directly with Homer himself. According to the paradigm that emerges, Homer becomes divorced from myth.[106] Homer becomes the hermeneutic model for classicism, while myth is left behind as the threatening outsider, the "other." In one case, Griffin retells a Sumerian myth, again taken from Kirk's book, alongside some Bororo myths; then, putting them together as a counterweight to the classicism of the ancient Greeks, he describes these myths as "this exuberant and grotesque play of fantasy."[107] The question of how to distinguish between these myths and the myths of the ancient Greeks is then addressed as follows:

> The answer is not hard to find. Greek mythology is distinguished from others above all by the dominant position within it of myths about heroes. Heroes do not, in general, turn into anteaters, or make themselves buttocks out of mashed potatoes, or impregnate three generations of their own female descendants; nor are they half-animals. They illuminate, by their actions and by their nature, not the Lévi-Straussian problems of the relationship between nature and culture, but the position, the potential, and the limitations of man in the world.[108]

To achieve this vision of the Greek hero, one would be forced to take out of consideration not only the comparative evidence supplied by such disciplines as social anthropology but also much of the internal Greek evidence. The many-sidedness of Greek heroes in particular and Greek myth in general can be illustrated with a wealth of

---

106. This line of thought is developed further in Griffin 1977, where it is argued that the Homeric epics have screened out most of "the fantastic, the miraculous, and the romantic" (p. 40) elements characteristic of the Epic Cycle because Homer was a superior or "unique" poet. For a different explanation of such "screening," see N 1979:8, par. 14 n. 1. Cf. Kullmann 1985:1–23, esp. pp. 15–18.

107. Griffin 1977:177.

108. Ibid.

136 testimony from both nonliterary and literary sources,[109] including such traditional forms as the fables of Aesop."[110]

All this is not to say that we should not expect Homeric myths to have distinctive features. But whatever distinctness we may find in Homer cannot be formulated, let alone explained, without the rigorous application of a comparative perspective.

The comparative method vindicates the efficacy and communicative power of myth in oral tradition, with reference to the here-and-now of the occasion for which the myth is being performed. If we do indeed find comparable levels of communicativeness in Homeric poetry, in situations where a character adduces a myth with reference to a given occasion in the narrative, I maintain that there is in such situations no justification for explaining the dovetailing of myth with occasion as a matter of personal invention, of Homer's veering away from the myths of the past. I agree with Willcock that the key to changes in myth is the *occasion* (he uses that word) in which people find themselves.[111] But I disagree with the inference that such changes in Homeric narrative are a sign of arbitrary personal invention predicated on an immediate context, which is purportedly likewise a matter of arbitrary personal invention. I suggest instead that such "changes" are a matter of selection *within* tradition.[112] I suggest further that there is for us a danger of grossly underestimating the extent of variation in the Homeric tradition of mythmaking. I suggest, finally, that variation in myth is itself a built-in tradition, compatible with patterns of variation in the "real life" situations of traditional society.

What goes for the myths cited by the characters quoted by Homeric narrative goes also for the myths that shape the outer narrative that frames the quoted myths. What is demonstrably applicable to characters in Homeric narrative is indirectly applicable also to people in "real life," in the spectrum of situations framed by the

---

109. A model survey, with emphasis on the hero, is Brelich 1958. Cf. Snodgrass 1987, esp. pp. 160, 165.

110. For a comparative study of the status of Aesop as hero, in terms of ancient Greek mythmaking traditions, see N 1979:279–308.

111. Willcock 1977:45.

112. Cf. the wording "selection of detail" in the discussion of Martin 1989:130 n. 78.

same traditional social system that frames Homeric poetry itself. In other words, *the outer narrative that frames mythological exempla is itself a mythological exemplum, on a large scale.*[113]

The problem is, Homeric poetry makes no overt reference to its own social context, the occasions of its own potential performability. We recall the words of Leach: "Myth is 'true' for those who use it, but we cannot infer the nature of that truth simply from reading the text; we have to know the context to which the text refers."[114] Still, if Homeric narrative itself gives us "texts" within its own "text," with appropriate contexts to which these "texts" refer, then the outer context, out there in the "real world," is at least indirectly recoverable.

Just as the myths that are cited by characters in Homeric poetry are part of a complex system of mythmaking, not a disintegrated mass of raw material that is arbitrarily reshaped by the framing narrative, so also the framing narrative itself is constituted by myths that are part of that same complex system of mythmaking. The organizing myths that constitute our *Iliad* and *Odyssey,* the framing narrative of Homeric poetry, share in the formal characteristics of myth as described by social anthropologists. By way of applying both comparative and internal analysis, the theory can be advanced that the contents of the *Iliad* and the *Odyssey* are controlled by the principles of mythmaking, the building-blocks of which can be described as *themes:* "My theory . . . has it that theme is the overarching principle in the creation of traditional poetry like the *Iliad* and the *Odyssey;* also, that the formulaic heritage of these compositions is an accurate expression of their thematic heritage."[115] Such a view of Homeric poetry, as built from myths that organize it, can become a hermeneutic model for addressing the vexed question of the unity of Homeric composition:

> The positing of a unitary *Iliad* and a unitary *Odyssey* has been for
> me not an end in itself, one that is continually threatened by con-

---

113. Only with such a premise, that Homeric poetry is itself a mythological exemplum, can I appreciate the following formulation in Andersen 1987:3: "Mythological paradigms inserted into the *Iliad* effect the transformation of single events into variants of a timeless pattern."

114. Leach 1982:6–7.

115. N 1979:3. The word *theme* (and *thematic*) is used here as a shorthand reference to a basic unit in the traditional subject patterns of myth. A model for a sensible deployment of this word is Lord 1960:68–98.

138   textual inconsistencies in this Homeric passage or that. Rather, it
has been a means for solving the problems presented by these inconsistencies. Whatever Homeric passages seem at first to be in-
consistent in the short range may in the long range be the key to
various central themes of the overall *Iliad* or *Odyssey*—central messages that are hidden away from those of us, such as we are, who
have not been raised by Hellenic society as the appreciative audience of Epos.[116]

This formulation takes into account the factor of change over time in
the traditions of mythmaking, and how any current phase of a myth,
as a system, is responsive to changes in the here-and-now of the latest
retelling of myth. But the point is, the changes themselves are responsive to the traditional variants that are available. Changes can be
symptomatic of traditional variation.

For an illustration, let us consider the celebrated problem concerning the use of dual forms, where we would have expected plural
ones, at key points in the narrative of the so-called Embassy Scene of
Iliad 9; it seems as if the duals refer to three emissaries, not two, sent
by Agamemnon in an effort to persuade Achilles to renounce his
anger and return to the company of his fellow warriors.[117] Most of
the solutions offered to the problem posit an earlier version of the
Embassy Scene, with only two emissaries instead of the three featured
in the *Iliad* as we have it, so that the sporadic use of the duals is purportedly a reflex of the earlier version; the three emissaries are Phoenix, Ajax, and Odysseus in our *Iliad,* and it is commonly assumed that
Phoenix is the intrusive element in the construct, so that the duals
can be reconstructed as referring, at an earlier stage, to Ajax and
Odysseus alone.[118] Such attempted solutions, however, imply a layer-
ing of *texts*. Instead, it can be argued that this so-called Embassy
Scene as we have it "is not a clumsy patchwork of mutually irreconcil-

---

116. N 1979:4–5.

117. See a summary of the context in N 1979:42–58.

118. Cf. Page 1959:298. A survey of the full range of proposed solutions to this problem is
given by M. W. Edwards (1987:219), who concludes that "it seems unlikely that anyone
will ever be convinced by anyone else's explanation." For solutions that explore the possibility that the duals refer to two distinct groups, not individuals, see de Jong 1987:117–
118, with reference to Gordesiani 1980. At p. 118, de Jong cites *Iliad* 17.387, a reference
to Achaeans and Trojans by way of the dual.

able texts but rather an artistic orchestration of *variant* narrative traditions [highlighting supplied]."[119]

The Embassy Scene draws upon a wealth of possible traditional variants, all of which are exempla in the making, much as we see the characters of Homeric narrative drawing upon variants in constructing their own messages.

Nestor's advice to Agamemnon, which becomes the adopted course of action, is that Phoenix, Ajax, and Odysseus be sent as emissaries to Achilles (9.168–170); Phoenix is to take the lead, as conveyed by the verb *hēgéomai* 'lead the way' (ἡγησάσθω, 9.168). The two heralds Odios and Eurybates are also sent along (9.170). So there are in fact five emissaries in all.

As the ensemble makes its way toward the tent of Achilles, we see the following description (9.182):

τὼ δὲ βάτην παρὰ θῖνα πολυφλοίσβοιο θαλάσσης.
And the two went along the shore of the much-roaring sea.

Who are the two, if five emissaries have already been mentioned? A sense of precedent—or let us say exemplum—would first suggest the two heralds, Odios and Eurybates. We may note another narrative combination, the two heralds Talthybios and Eurybates, as mentioned in Book 1 of the *Iliad* (320–321), whom we see described in the same sort of way at an earlier point in the narrative, where they are being sent by Agamemnon to take Briseis away from Achilles (1.327):

τὼ δ' ἀέκοντε βάτην παρὰ θῖν' ἁλὸς ἀτρυγέτοιο.
And the two went, unwilling, along the shore of the barren
    sea.[120]

When the two heralds arrived at the tent of Achilles, the hero greeted them thus (1.334):

---

119. N 1979:49. Cf. Schein 1984:125–126 n. 35. The whole problem can be linked with the intent built into the speech of Phoenix to Achilles, on which see Schein pp. 112–116, 126 n. 37.

120. Lynn-George (1988:54) notes the nonspecificity of the duals at *Iliad* 9.182 and thereafter, adding that they "seem to signal relation rather than nomination, referring back to the passage in book I in which Briseis was taken from Achilles (I 327)"; in this context he cites the acute observations of Segal (1968). I offer one qualification: the duals of

140   χαίρετε, κήρυκες, Διὸς ἄγγελοι ἠδὲ καὶ ἀνδρῶν.
      Hail, heralds, messengers of Zeus and of men!

So also now in Book 9, as the emissaries arrive at the tent of Achilles, the hero greets them (9.196–198):

τὼ καὶ δεικνύμενος προσέφη πόδας ὠκὺς ᾿Αχιλλεύς·
"χαίρετον· ἦ φίλοι ἄνδρες ἱκάνετον· ἦ τι μάλα χρεώ,
οἵ μοι σκυζομένῳ περ ᾿Αχαιῶν φίλτατοί ἐστον."

And he, gesturing toward the two of them, addressed them:
"Hail, the two of you! You two have come as near-and-dear
    men. Truly you have a great need for me,
You who are to me, angry though I am, the most near-and-dear
    of the Achaeans."

Just as Achilles talks of the great need for him in the present situation (χρεώ, 9.197), so also he had predicted a great need in Book 1 of the *Iliad,* when he had called on the two heralds to be witnesses (1.338) to the fact that there would yet come a time when there would be a great need for him (χρειώ, 1.341).[121]

In Book 1 the two heralds were the only emissaries. In Book 9, however, there are five. Still, Achilles' greeting in Book 9 seems appropriate to two emissaries, not five. He addresses the five emissaries as if they were two heralds, but he goes on to describe them as his nearest and dearest friends. Such a description is appropriate to Phoenix and Ajax, but not to Odysseus. As Achilles himself says, whoever says one thing and hides something else in his thoughts is as *ekhthrós* 'hateful' to him as the gates of Hades (9.312–313). Such a

---

Iliad 9.182 and thereabouts do not refer to the duals of *Iliad* 1.327 so much as they refer to the precedent of duals as attested in *Iliad* 1.327. When Odysseus reports to Agamemnon the negative answer of Achilles, he calls upon Ajax and the two heralds as witnesses (9.688–689). I agree with the observation made by de Jong (1987:118) about this detail: "The function of these two silent characters [the heralds] is, therefore, to authorize the embassy: vis-à-vis Achilles they give an official cachet to the delegation coming from Agamemnon; vis-à-vis Agamemnon they guarantee that Odysseus faithfully reports Achilles' answer."

121. On the theme of Achilles' need to be needed, see Rabel 1991:285; see also Lynn-George 1988:123–131.

description is appropriate to Odysseus.[122] The word *ekhthrós* 'hateful, enemy', as used by Achilles here in the Embassy Scene (9.312), is the opposite of *phílos* 'near-and-dear, friend', a description that he applies when he greets the emissaries in the dual (9.198).

It is as if the narrative were following traditional etiquette in talking of two emissaries, at the earlier point of the narrative where the ensemble sent to Achilles is getting under way (9.182):

τὼ δὲ βάτην παρὰ θῖνα πολυφλοίσβοιο θαλάσσης.
And the two went along the shore of the much-roaring sea.

Two is the norm, the exemplum by default. But three others come along; in fact, the three others take precedence over the heralds. Moreover, as the ensemble moves onward, the etiquette is violated (9.192):

τὼ δὲ βάτην προτέρω, ἡγεῖτο δὲ δῖος Ὀδυσσεύς.
And the two went ahead, but Odysseus took the lead.[123]

For Odysseus to take the lead *en passant* is a violation of the etiquette set forth by Nestor, whose plan explicitly called for Phoenix to lead (9.168–170):

Φοῖνιξ μὲν πρώτιστα Διὶ φίλος ἡγησάσθω,
αὐτὰρ ἔπειτ' Αἴας τε μέγας καὶ δῖος Ὀδυσσεύς·
κηρύκων δ' Ὀδίος τε καὶ Εὐρυβάτης ἅμ' ἑπέσθων.

---

122. N 1979:52–53. See also N 1979:22–25 on the *neîkos* 'quarrel' between Achilles and Odysseus as recollected in *Odyssey* 8.75, matching the quarrel between Achilles and Agamemnon in *Iliad* 1 (recollected in terms of *neîkos* 'quarrel' at 2.376: see ibid., 131). I argue at length (ibid., 42–58) that the grievances of the quarrel between Achilles and Odysseus mentioned in *Odyssey* 8.75 resurface throughout the *Iliad*, especially in Book 9. The internal evidence that I adduce comes not only from *Odyssey* 8.73–82 and the scholia but also from *Iliad* 9. For valuable arguments in addition to those that I have offered, see Martin (1989:97–98, 121, 123, 211–212), who also examines some convergences in the motives of Agamemnon and Odysseus as heroic rivals of Achilles.

123. There is no reason to assume that "the two" here include Odysseus, *pace* Wyatt 1985, esp. p. 403. This verse can just as easily be interpreted as concerning two persons plus Odysseus, who now leads the way: see N 1979:53 par. 16 n. 3. Also, I disagree with Wyatt's assertion (p. 406) that the words of Phoenix at 9.520–523 refer only to Ajax and Odysseus, not to Phoenix as well.

142
    Let Phoenix, dear to Zeus, first of all take the lead;
    Then great Ajax and brilliant Odysseus;
    And of the heralds let Odios and Eurybates follow along.

And yet, for Odysseus to violate the etiquette is not to violate the tradition of myth, in that *it is traditional for the figure of Odysseus to violate rules of etiquette.*[124] When the time comes for the speechmaking to start in the Embassy Scene, Ajax makes the gesture of nodding to Phoenix (9.223), whom we may have expected to be the first speaker, but it is Odysseus who takes note of the gesture (223), fills a cup with wine, gesturing to Achilles (224),[125] and begins to speak, thus becoming the first of the three speakers to address Achilles (225–306). The wording that describes the intervention of Odysseus is suggestive (9.223):

νεῦσ' Αἴας Φοίνικι· νόησε δὲ δῖος 'Οδυσσεύς.
Ajax nodded to Phoenix. But brilliant Odysseus took note
    (*noéō*).

The verb *noéō* 'take note, notice, perceive', as I have argued elsewhere, is a special word used in archaic Greek poetic diction in contexts where a special interpretation, a special "reading," as it were, is signaled.[126] In passages like *Odyssey* 17.281 and *Iliad* 23.305, it is clear that the verb *noéō* designates a complex level of understanding that entails two levels of meaning, one of which is overt while the other, the more important one, is latent.[127]

When Odysseus 'took note', νόησε (*noéō*), at *Iliad* 9.223, he was in effect taking an initiative with an ulterior motive, a latent purpose, in mind. As Cedric Whitman argues, the offer to Achilles by Agamemnon, as reformulated by Odysseus in his quoted speech from the Embassy Scene, endangers the very status of Achilles in epic.[128] It may be argued further that the potential ulterior motive of Odysseus, to un-

---

124. N 1979:51–52. Cf. *Odyssey* 8.475–476, where Odysseus seems to be behaving like a host in a situation where he is the guest. It is traditional for Odysseus even to speak out of turn, as we see from the formulaic analysis of *Odyssey* 14.439 by Muellner (1976:21).

125. Why does Odysseus fill his own cup, rather than wait for Achilles to do so? Perhaps here, too, we have a violation of etiquette.

126. N 1990b:202–222, a rewritten version of N 1983.

127. See N 1990b:208 and 217–219, on *Odyssey* 17.281 and *Iliad* 23.305, respectively.

dermine the heroic stature of Achilles, is "understood" by Achilles.[129]
We recall what Achilles says: whoever says one thing and hides something else in his thoughts is as *ekhthrós* 'hateful' to him as the gates of
Hades (9.312–313).[130] It may be that such a subtle "understanding"
on the part of Achilles justifies the formalistic use of the dual in
Achilles' greeting of the emissaries: this greeting in effect snubs Odysseus by excluding him from the ranks of those who are *phíloi,* near
and dear, to Achilles. We may compare the subtle snubbing of Achilles by Ajax, just a few lines later on in the Embassy Scene: Ajax sus-
tains a series of third-person constructions in order to avoid as long
as possible his having to address Achilles directly in the second person (*Iliad* 9.624–636).[131]

If indeed Achilles' use of the dual greeting at *Iliad* 9.197–198
has the subtle effect of suggesting that Achilles is actually snubbing
Odysseus, it remains to ask why the characters who are about to be
greeted are designated in the dual *by the framing narrative itself,* at
9.196, corresponding to the duals of the narrative at the earlier points
already mentioned, 9.182–183 and 192. An answer comes from the
demonstration of Richard Martin that the perspective of the narrator
of the *Iliad* becomes dramatically identified with the perspective of
the main hero of the narration, Achilles.[132] Martin's demonstration

---

128. Whitman 1958:191–192. Cf. Martin 1989:116–117, 123. Cf. also Lynn-George
1988:90–92.

129. N 1990a:52–53. Cf. Martin 1989:197 n. 82, 210–212.

130. On the rhetorical switch made by Achilles from second-person address (as still at *Iliad*
9.311) "to a third-person description of an ambiguous foil-figure" to whom he refers simply as *keînos* 'that one' at 9.312, see Martin (1989:210), who goes on to cite a parallel to
this technique in Pindar *Parthenia* 2.16 (p. 210 n. 4). Martin's observation about *keînos*
'that one' as the ultimate *ekhthrós* 'hateful one' provides valuable support for my interpretation at N 1979:255 of Pindar *Nemean* 8.23, where I take the anonymous *keînos* 'that one'
as a reference to Odysseus as the deceitful rival who is responsible for the death of Ajax.

131. Cf. M. W. Edwards 1987:229: "At last Ajax puts in a word. Addressing Odysseus, he
refers to Achilles as if he were not there." When Ajax refers to himself and Odysseus as *phíl-
tatoi* 'most dear' to Achilles (9.642), I would argue that this hero, unlike Achilles, at this
point fails to perceive the motives of Odysseus.

132. Martin 1989:233–239 (cf. Reynolds 1995). In these pages, Martin adduces a wealth
of comparative evidence, gathered from a variety of living oral traditions, for the pattern
of assimilating the narrator's perspective to the dramatized perspective of a given character in the narration.

144   helps motivate not just the use of the duals in the third-person narrative of *Iliad* 9,[133] but even such other phenomena as the Homeric convention of apostrophe.[134] To argue, however, that the narrative of *Iliad* 9 takes on the perspective of its main speaker is not to argue that the duals at 9.182–183 and 192 have to be interpreted as a snub: they would only be a narrative "set-up" for the potential of a later snub, which becomes activated only at the moment of Achilles' greeting at 9.197–198.

Such interpretations, however, attributing qualities of subtlety to the character and speech-acts of Achilles, turn out to be far too subtle for the tastes of some experts in Homer.[135] One scholar, finding fault with the use of the word *theme*,[136] reacts with the following comment to the positing of a traditional theme of rivalry between Achilles and Odysseus:

> In the first sentence to his Introduction (p. 1) poetic form is equated to 'diction', and content to 'theme'. A 'theme' is a mysterious kind of being: it belongs to "a *latent* dimension that keeps *surfacing*" (p. 136; my italics), in other words it is visible only to those seers who feel themselves at home in the sphere of ambiguities and paradoxes.[137]

I submit that complexities of meaning are visible not only to "seers" but also to anyone who takes the time to examine empirically the workings of tradition in mythmaking, as evidenced in the Homeric deployment of mythological exempla.

Another scholar, who also takes exception to the present line of analysis concerning the duals in the Embassy Scene, observes that "so sophisticated a technique of allusions is quite alien to the early epic

---

133. Martin 1989:236–237 (*pace* Griffin 1995:52). He leaves room for the possibility that the duals amount to an exclusion, without any insult being intended, of Phoenix rather than Odysseus (p. 236).

134. Ibid., 235–236.

135. Cf. Verdenius 1985 (review of N 1979).

136. On which see pp. 18, 22–23, 137 above.

137. Verdenius 1985:181.

and would hardly be found even in Hellenistic poetry."[138] Even some
defenders of Homer's "classicism," whom we would expect to be re-
ceptive to the idea of Homeric sophistication, have been known to
take a similar view: Jasper Griffin refers to "some scholars" who "are
now finding in the epics meanings of great subtlety which have been
undetected for three millennia."[139]

Such subtlety, however, becomes imaginable and even compre-
hensible once we begin to appreciate the vast array of variants, potential mythological exempla, available to Homeric tradition at any
given point of narrative. One last example will suffice. We know that
archaic Greek narratives about hostile encounters between heroes
and divine rivers can traditionally picture the river as taking the
shape of a ferocious beast: a prime example is Archilochus F 286–
287 West, where the hero Herakles fights with the divine river Ache-
loos, which has taken on the shape of a raging bull. We may contrast
the treatment of the fight between the hero Achilles and the divine
river Xanthos in *Iliad* 21, where Xanthos does not take the shape of a
bull and is not even theriomorphic: rather, the narrative opts for a
variant tradition highlighting the elemental aspect of the river, as
water personified, struggling with a hero whose ally here is Hephais-
tos, fire personified.[140] It has been argued, partly on the authority of
the scholia to *Iliad* 21.237, that the version inherited by Archilochus
is pre-Homeric.[141] It is enough for now to say that the Archilochean
representation stems from a tradition that is independent of Homer.
But the wonder of it all is this: the Homeric narrative goes out of
its way to make an indirect reference to the other tradition. The river
Xanthos, in the heat of battle with the hero Achilles, is described as

---

138. Solmsen 1981:83 (review of N 1979). Solmsen argues (p. 82) that the dual constructions of *Iliad* 9.182 and 183 "cannot be a snub since Achilles is not present," and
therefore that the duals in the greeting of Achilles at 9.197–198 cannot be a snub either.
As I have already argued, however, nobody would claim that the duals at 9.182 and 183
have to be interpreted as a snub: to repeat, they would only be a narrative "set-up" for the
potential of a later snub, which becomes activated only at the moment of Achilles' greeting
(*pace* Griffin 1995:52). I also disagree with the reasoning of Wyatt 1985:401 n. 5, 403 n. 8.

139. Griffin 1984:134 (review of Clay 1984).

140. Cf. Whitman 1958:139–142, and N 1979:321–322.

141. Scheibner 1939:120–121.

146 μεμυκὼς ἠΰτε ταῦρος 'bellowing like a bull' (*Iliad* 21.237).[142] The simile amounts to a conscious acknowledgment of a variant tradition.

In seeking to persuade those who are as yet not quite convinced by the argument that mythological *exempla* in Homer stem from a rich, complex, and, yes, subtle tradition, I close by inviting them to consider the meaning of the Latin word *exemplum,* as revealed through its own contexts. This meaning has been summed up admirably in the Latin etymological dictionary of Alfred Ernout and Antoine Meillet, who define *exemplum* as an object set apart from among other objects like it, for the sake of serving as a model.[143] For something to be set apart, to be "taken" (verb *emō*), it has to be outstanding, exceptional (adjective *eximius*). Exceptional as it is, the model as model is traditional. The model is a precedent, and that precedent would lose its rhetoric, its very power, if it were to be changed for the sake of change. It is one thing for us to recognize changes in the development of myth over time. It is quite another to assume that changes are arbitrarily being made by those who use myth as *exemplum* within their own society. As precedent, mythological *exempla* demand a mentality of the unchanging, of adherence to the model, even if myth is changeable over time.[144] The *exemplum* is there so that society may follow it or shun it, and that in itself is an exercise of the mind and spirit. The Roman lexicographical tradition says it well in contrasting *exemplum* and *exemplar* (Paulus ex Festo 72.5):

> *exemplum est quod sequamus aut uitemus. exemplar ex quo simile faciamus. illud animo aestimatur, istud oculis conspicitur.*

> An *exemplum* is something that attracts us or repels us, whereas an *exemplar* is something that we make something else resemble. The *exemplar* is visible to the eye. The *exemplum* is sensed in the spirit.

I speak of Homeric *exemplum,* not Homeric *exemplar.*

---

142. Ibid.

143. Ernout and Meillet 1959: "Exemplum est proprement l'objet distingué des autres et mis à part pour servir de modèle."

144. Cf. N 1985:32–36.

Epilogue

Throughout this work, the central aim was to reintroduce the vitality of performance, of oral tradition in general, to the conceptual framework of the classics. This aim addresses the need to be vigilant over tradition itself, all tradition. Earlier, I had argued that the field of classics, which lends itself to the empirical study of tradition, seems ideally suited to articulate the value of tradition in other societies, whether or not these societies are closely comparable to those of ancient Greece and Rome, given that we live in an era when the living traditions of traditional societies are rapidly becoming extinct, when many thousands of years of cumulative human experience are becoming obliterated by less than a century or so of modern technological progress. The rapid extinguishing of old living traditions by the same technological progress that points toward the less rapid but equally certain extinction of nature itself is forcefully expressed in the poem of a Native American:

Self-portrait: microcosm, or, song of mixed-blood
By Robert Conley[1]

1.
In me the Cherokee
wars against *yoneg* (white)
I have college degrees (2)
all major credit cards
pay my bills on time each month
on my wall is a photograph
of the Great Spirit

---

1. Printed in Hobson [1979] 1981:69.

2.
Because the meat I eat
comes wrapped in cellophane
I do not understand
the first facts of life

I have never drunk blood
and I hunt
with the channel selector
in front of my tv

3.
When I go to the supermarket
and buy some meat
pre-cut and wrapped
how do I apologize
to the spirit of the animal
whose meat I eat
and where shall I build my fires?

4.
My poems are my fires.
oh gods forgive me all
the things I've failed
to do. the things I should
have done. forgive the meat
I've used without a prayer
without apology forgive
the other prayers I haven't
said those times I should
but oh ye gods both great
and small I do not know
the ancient forms. my poems
are my fires and my prayers.

I see in this poem a legacy for American classicists, a legacy emanating from a Native American outcry that carries a special meaning
to all Americans. This poem is particularly apt because it is about
principles, in the literal sense of first elements. It explores the value
of going back in time in order to recover fundamental truths, even
when it may not any longer be clear what it is that one is recovering.
The key anxiety in the poem seems to be: *I do not know the ancient*

forms. The forms are the ritual, the ritual is the performance, the performance is the song. So what can compensate for the ancient forms? The answer is to be found in the very use of tradition, or in what is somehow linked to tradition, which is the essence of poetry as the off-shoot of performance. The ritual aspect of performance can best be symbolized in a primary form of ritual, sacrifice; and the essence of sacrifice can best be symbolized in the fires of sacrifice.[2] The key solution to the anxiety is: *My poems are my fires.*

I link the quest of going back in time through the human experience, rescuing values in societies about to be extinguished, with the quest of rescuing nature from the onslaught of technology and ideology. Or let us talk about nature as it connects with the human condition, calling it the environment.

I avoid using the word "primitive," especially with reference to small-scale societies that have in recent times been pushed to the brink of extinction by the advances of technology. A word like that implies that the given society has failed to keep up with progress, as if there were just one direction in which all societies, all humanity, must be headed. As the anthropologist Claude Lévi-Strauss has remarked, the endangered societies of our world seem to us to be at a standstill "not necessarily because they are so in fact, but because the line of their development has no meaning for us, and cannot be measured in terms of the criteria we employ."[3] He gives a striking analogy, an intuitive observation generalized from the experience of life:

> People of advanced years generally consider that history during their old age is stationary, in contrast to the cumulative history they saw being made when they were young. A period in which they are no longer actively concerned, when they have no part to play, has no real meaning for them; nothing happens, or what does happen seems to them to be unproductive of good; while their grandchildren throw themselves into the life of that same period with all the passionate enthusiasm which their elders have forgotten.[4]

---

2. I have explored at length the ritual aspects of performing song or poetry in N 1990a: 29–46; for variations on the theme of fire as a symbol of sacrifice and ritual in general, see N 1990b: 143–180.

3. Lévi-Strauss 1958:23.

4. Ibid.

Today the environment itself is in danger, but the elders presiding over what they call "Western Civilization" may seem to be indifferent to the damage caused by the technology of this civilization. If we follow for a moment the line of thought suggested just now by Lévi-Strauss, we could say that the ancient world, the world of myth, is in fact still a young world when it comes to the experiencing of nature. The Ancients, along with what is left of the so-called Primitives of today, see the world in a way that may yet rekindle our own passion for that experience.

This talk of passion brings us back to the assertion, *My poems are my fires.* Here is where the diachronic perspective is needed, with regard to cultures on the verge of becoming extinguished. Here is where philology is needed, with regard to the poems. I mean philology in the broadest sense of the ancient term, as forcefully restated by Rudolf Pfeiffer:

> The Sophists had a predilection for compounds with *phílo-*, and it may be due to them that we find *philólogos* first in Plato . . . and once in a comedy of Alexis in the later fourth century . . . ; it means [someone] fond of talk, dispute, dialectic in a wide and rather vague or ironical sense. But when Eratosthenes used it, or when the new Diegesis . . . to the first *Iambus* of Callimachus says that Hipponax coming from the dead calls *toùs philológous eis to Parmeníōnos kaloúmenon Sarapideîon,* the compound refers (according to Suetonius) to persons who are familiar with various branches of knowledge or even the whole of the *logos.*[5]

We come back to the report of Suetonius that Eratosthenes was the first scholar to formalize this term *philologos* in referring to his identity as a scholar,[6] and that in doing so he was drawing attention to a *doctrina* that is *multiplex variaque,* a course of studies that is many-sided and composed of many different elements. This ideal is built into the name of the American Philological Association, into its very identity as a group of scholars that is *multiplex variaque.* It is an ideal that is built into the city where it met for its 1991 annual convention. More than that, it is an ideal that is built into the very country whose name is part of the name, the American Philological Association. In

---

5. Pfeiffer 1968:159.

6. Suetonius *De grammaticis et rhetoribus* c. 10 (see Pfeiffer 1968:158 n. 8).

this particular moment in the history of the organization, this ideal of a *doctrina* that is many-sided and composed of many different elements needs to be reaffirmed. It is an ideal that we can reaffirm in the lingua franca of America, the English language, if we use the Anglo-Saxon word *love* to recapture our shared longing for the *logos*. I am thinking here of the way in which Gilbert Murray happened to use this word in his own musings about philology:

> "Wind, wind of the deep sea," begins a chorus in the *Hecuba*. . . . How slight the words are! Yet there is in them just that inexplicable beauty, that quick shiver of joy and longing, which as it was fresh then in a world whose very bone and iron have long since passed into dust, is fresh still and alive still; only harder to reach; more easy to forget, to disregard, to smother with irrelevancies; far more in danger of death. For, like certain other of the things of the spirit, *it will die if it is not loved.*[7]

As we ponder this idea of death, a sort of death of words, we may recollect the undying words of Phoenix in *Iliad* 9.527–528 as he introduces the story of the hero Meleagros to Achilles and the rest of the audience: μέμνημαι 'I remember (*mnē-*)'.[8]

> μέμνημαι τόδε ἔργον ἐγὼ πάλαι οὔ τι νέον γε
> ὡς ἦν· ἐν δ' ὑμῖν ἐρέω πάντεσσι φίλοισι.

> I remember, I do, this thing that happened a long time ago,
>   not recently,
> I remember how it was, and I will tell you, <u>loved ones</u> (*phíloi*)
>   that you all are.

As Martin argues, the Homeric notion of *speech-act* or *performance* is associated with such *narrating from memory*,[9] which he equates with the rhetorical act of *recollection*.[10] We have seen that this speech-act of

---

7. G. Murray 1909:19. Italics mine.

8. On the function of the myth of Meleagros as retold by Phoenix to Achilles and the rest of the audience, see N 1990a:196–197, 205, 253, 310 n. 164, following up on N 1979: 105–111.

9. Martin 1989:44. See pp. 122–123 above.

10. Martin 1989:80.

recollection, which qualifies explicitly as a *mûthos* (as at *Iliad* 1.273), is the act of *mémnēmai* 'I remember'.[11] The failure of any such speech-act is marked by the act of *lēth-* 'forgetting' (as with λήθεαι at *Iliad* 9.259),[12] which reminds us of the anxiety of *forgetting the forms* in the poem by the Native American.

In our passage from the *Iliad*, the accusative object *tóde érgon* 'this thing that happened' following *mémnēmai*, 'I remember', makes clear that the act of remembering is not just perceptual.[13] It is an active conjuring up, by the words themselves, of what is felt to be real. And the words in this passage from the *Iliad* take on their authority because those who do listen are presumed to be, all of them, *phíloi* 'near and dear', or 'loved ones': ἐν δ' ὑμῖν ἐρέω πάντεσσι φίλοισι. Here we see the essence of reception, of performer-audience interaction. The listeners are bound to the speaker of the word by their presumed love for him, presumably reciprocating his love for them. For us to be able to listen as well, to listen in, there has to be love of the word—in a word, philology.

When Achilles predicts in *Iliad* 9 that the song about him will last for all time, unwilting forever, we may marvel at the fact that his prediction holds true—up till now. If we follow Gilbert Murray's reasoning, the word did not die, has not yet died, and will not die if it is indeed loved. Philology lives. Long live philology!

---

11. See again pp. 122–123 above.

12. Martin 1989:77–88.

13. The accusative case of an object of a verb of remembering seems to denote an exterior goal, as opposed to the genitive case, denoting an interior goal. The genitive, as a partitive, implies the remembering of a part of something. The accusative implies *total recall*.

Bibliography

CEG   P. A. Hansen, ed., *Carmina epigraphica Graeca saeculorum viii–v a.Chr.n.* (Berlin and New York, 1983).

DELG   P. Chantraine, *Dictionnaire étymologique de la langue grecque,* vols. I, II, III, IV-1, IV-2 (Paris, 1968, 1970, 1975, 1977, 1980).

EG   D. L. Page, ed., *Epigrammata graeca* (Oxford, 1975).

LSJ   H. G. Liddell, R. Scott, and H. Stuart Jones, eds., *Greek-English Lexicon,* 9th ed. (Oxford, 1940).

N   G. Nagy

OEI   S. H. Blackburn, P. J. Claus, J. B. Flueckiger, and S. S. Wadley, eds., *Oral Epics in India* (Berkeley and Los Angeles, 1989).

PMG   D. L. Page, ed., *Poetae melici graeci* (Oxford, 1962).

Adams, D. Q. 1987. "Ἥρως and Ἥρα: Of Men and Heroes in Greek and Indo-European." *Glotta* 65:171–178.

Allen, T. W., ed. 1912. *Homeri Opera.* Vol. 5: Hymns, Cycle, fragments, etc. Oxford.

———. 1924. *Homer: The Origins and the Transmission.* Oxford.

Allen, W. S. 1987. *Vox Graeca: The Pronunciation of Classical Greek.* 3d ed. Cambridge.

Aloni, A. 1984. "L'intelligenza di Ipparco: Osservazioni sulla politica dei Pisistratidi." *Quaderni di storia* 19:109–148.

———. 1986. *Tradizioni arcaiche della Troade e composizione dell' Iliade.* Milan.

Andersen, Ø. 1976. "Some Thoughts on the Shield of Achilles." *Symbolae Osloenses* 51:5–18.

———. 1977. "Odysseus and the Wooden Horse." *Symbolae Osloenses* 52:5–18.

———. 1987. "Myth, Paradigm, and 'Spatial Form' in the *Iliad.*" In Bremer, de Jong, and Kalff 1987:1–13.

154   Apthorp, M. J. 1980. *The Manuscript Evidence for Interpolation in Homer.* Heidelberg.

Austin, J. L. 1962. *How to Do Things with Words.* Oxford.

Austin, N. 1975. *Archery at the Dark of the Moon: Poetic Problems in Homer's Odyssey.* Berkeley and Los Angeles.

———. 1991. "The Wedding Text in Homer's *Odyssey.*" Review of Heubeck, West, and Hainsworth 1988. *Arion* 1, no. 2:227–243.

Bader, F. 1989. *La langue des dieux, ou l'hermétisme des poètes indo-européens. Testi linguistici* 14. Pisa.

Bakker, E. 1993. "Activation and Preservation: The Interdependence of Text and Performance in an Oral Tradition." *Oral Tradition* 8:5–20.

Ballabriga, A. 1990. "La Question Homérique: Pour une réouverture du débat." *Revue des études grecques* 103:16–29.

Bass, G. F. 1990. "A Bronze-Age Writing-Diptych from the Sea off Lycia." *Kadmos* 29:169, with plate I.

Basso, K. H. 1966. "The Gift of Changing Woman." *Smithsonian Institution, Bureau of American Ethnology Bulletin* 196:113–173. Anthropological Papers no. 76. Washington, D.C.

Batchelder, A. G. 1994. *The Seal of Orestes: Self-Reference and Authority in Sophocles' "Electra."* Lanham, Md.

Bauman, R. 1977. *Verbal Art as Performance.* Rowley, Mass.

———. 1986. *Story, Performance, and Event: Contextual Studies of Oral Narrative.* Cambridge.

Bausinger, H. 1980. *Formen der "Volkspoesie."* 2d ed. Berlin.

Beaton, R. 1980. *Folk Poetry of Modern Greece.* Cambridge.

Ben-Amos, D. 1976. "Analytical Categories and Ethnic Genres." In *Folklore Genres,* ed. D. Ben-Amos, 215–242. Austin.

Benveniste, E. 1969. *Le vocabulaire des institutions indo-européennes.* Vol. 1: *Economie, parenté, société.* Vol. 2: *Pouvoir, droit, religion.* Paris. Eng. translation: *Indo-European Language and Society,* trans. E. Palmer. London, 1973.

Bergren, A. L. T. 1975. *The Etymology and Usage of ΠΕΙΡΑΡ in Early Greek Poetry.* New York.

Bers, V. 1974. *Enallage and Greek Style.* Leiden.

Bertolini, F. 1992. "Il palazzo: L'epica." *Lo spazio letterario della Grecia antica.* Vol. 1: *La produzione e la circolazione del testo,* ed. G. Cambiano, L. Canfora, D. Lanza, 109–141.

Beye, C. R. 1987. *Ancient Greek Literature and Society.* 2d ed. Ithaca, N.Y.

Biebuyck, D. 1976. "The African Heroic Epic." *Journal of the Folklore Institute* 13:5–36.

———. 1978. *Hero and Chief: Epic Literature from the Banyanga, Zaïre Republic.* Berkeley and Los Angeles.

Biebuyck, D., and K. Mateene. 1969. *The Mwindo Epic from the Banyanga.* Berkeley and Los Angeles.

Bird, C. S. 1976. "Poetry in the Mande: Its Form and Meaning." *Poetics* 5: 89–100.

Blackburn, S. H. 1988. *Singing of Birth and Death: Texts in Performance.* Philadelphia.

———. 1989. "Patterns of Development for Indian Oral Epics." In *OEI* 15–32.

Blackburn, S. H., P. J. Claus, J. B. Flueckiger, and S. S. Wadley, eds. 1989. *Oral Epics in India.* Berkeley and Los Angeles. [Abbreviated as *OEI.*]

Blackburn, S. H., and J. B. Flueckiger. 1989. "Introduction." In *OEI* 1–11.

Bloom, H., ed. 1986. *Modern Critical Views: Homer.* New York.

Bohannan, L. A. 1952. "A Genealogical Charter." *Africa* 22:301–315.

Bolling, G. M. 1925. *The External Evidence for Interpolation in Homer.* Oxford.

———. 1944. *The Athetized Lines in the Iliad.* Baltimore.

———. 1950. *Ilias Atheniensium.* Lancaster, Pa.

Bowra, C. M. 1952. *Heroic Poetry.* London.

Boyd, T. W. 1994. "Where Ion Stood, What Ion Sang." *Harvard Studies in Classical Philology* 96:109–121.

———. 1996. "Libri Confusi." *Classical Journal* 91:1–11.

Braswell, B. K. 1971. "Mythological Innovation in the *Iliad.*" *Classical Quarterly* 21:16–26.

Brelich, A. 1958. *Gli eroi greci.* Rome.

Bremer, J. M., I. J. F. de Jong, and J. Kalff, eds. 1987. *Homer: Beyond Oral Poetry. Recent Trends in Homeric Interpretation.* Amsterdam.

Brillante, C. 1983. "Episodi iliadici nell'arte figurata e conoscenza dell'*Iliade* nella Grecia arcaica." *Rheinisches Museum* 126:97–125.

Burkert, W. 1972. "Die Leistung eines Kreophylos: Kreophyleer, Homeriden und die archaische Heraklesepik." *Museum Helveticum* 29:74–85.

———. 1979a. "Kynaithos, Polycrates, and the Homeric Hymn to Apollo." In *Arktouros: Hellenic Studies Presented to B. M. W. Knox,* ed. G. W. Bowersock, W. Burkert, and M. C. J. Putnam, 53–62. Berlin.

———. 1979b. "Mythisches Denken." In *Philosophie und Mythos,* ed. H. Poser, 16–39. Berlin and New York.

———. 1983. *Homo Necans: The Anthropology of Ancient Greek Sacrificial Ritual and Myth.* Translated by P. Bing. Berkeley and Los Angeles. [Originally published in German under the title *Homo Necans* (Berlin, 1972).]

———. 1984. *Die Orientalisierende Epoche in der griechischen Religion und Literatur.* Heidelberg.

———. 1985. *Greek Religion.* Translated by J. Raffan. Cambridge, Mass. [Originally published in German under the title *Griechische Religion der archaischen und klassischen Epoche* (Stuttgart, 1977).]

———. 1987. "The Making of Homer in the Sixth Century B.C.: Rhapsodes versus Stesichorus." In *Papers on the Amasis Painter and His World,* ed. M. True, C. Hudson, A. P. A. Belloli, B. Gilman, et al., 43–62. The J. Paul Getty Museum. Malibu.

156 ———. 1992. *The Orientalizing Revolution: Near Eastern Influence on Greek Culture in the Early Archaic Age*. Translated from Burkert 1984 by M. E. Pinder and W. Burkert. Cambridge, Mass.

Calame, C. 1983. "Entre oralité et écriture." *Semiotica* 43:245–273.

———. 1986. *Le récit en Grèce ancienne*. Paris.

———. 1990. *Thésée et l'imaginaire athénien: Légende et culte en Grèce antique*. With a preface by P. Vidal-Naquet. Lausanne.

———. 1995. *The Craft of Poetic Speech in Ancient Greece*. Ithaca, N.Y.

Cantilena, M. 1982. *Ricerche sulla dizione epica*. Vol. 1: *Per uno studio della formularità degli Inni Omerici*. Rome.

Carey, C. 1992. Review of Nagy 1990. *American Journal of Philology* 113:283–286.

Caswell, C. P. 1990. *A Study of Thumos in Early Greek Epic*. Leiden.

Catenacci, C. 1993. "Il finale dell'*Odissea* e la *recensio* pisistratide dei poemi omerici." *Quaderni urbinati di cultura classica* 44:7–22.

Chadwick, J. 1976. *The Mycenaean World*. Cambridge.

Chantraine, P. 1968, 1970, 1975, 1977, 1980. *Dictionnaire étymologique de la langue grecque*. Vols. I, II, III, IV-1, IV-2. Paris. [Abbreviated as *DELG*.]

Chenu, M.-D. 1927. "Auctor, Actor, Autor." *Bulletin du Cange: Archivum latinitatis medii aevi* 2:81–86.

Clader, L. L. 1976. *Helen: The Evolution from Divine to Heroic in Greek Epic Tradition*. Leiden.

Clark, M. 1994. "Enjambment and Binding in Homeric Hexameter." *Phoenix* 48:95–114.

Claus, P. J. 1989. "Behind the Text: Performance and Ideology in a Tulu Oral Tradition." In *OEI* 55–74.

Clay, J. S. 1984. *The Wrath of Athena: Gods and Men in the Odyssey*. Princeton.

———. 1989. *The Politics of Olympus: Form and Meaning in the Major Homeric Hymns*. Princeton.

Cole, T. 1983. "Archaic Truth." *Quaderni urbinati di cultura classica* 13:7–28.

Cook, E. F. 1995. *The Odyssey at Athens: Myths of Cultural Origin*. Ithaca, N.Y.

Cramer, J. A., ed. 1839. *Anecdota Graeca e codicibus manuscriptis Bibliothecae Regiae Parisiensis*. Vol. 1. Oxford.

Crane, G. 1988. *Calypso: Backgrounds and Conventions of the Odyssey*. Frankfurt.

Davidson, O. M. 1980. "Indo-European Dimensions of Herakles in *Iliad* 19.95–133." *Arethusa* 13:197–202.

———. 1985. "The Crown-Bestower in the Iranian Book of Kings." *Acta Iranica*, Hommages et Opera Minora 10: *Papers in Honour of Professor Mary Boyce*, 61–148. Leiden.

———. 1988. "A Formulaic Analysis of Samples Taken from the *Shāhnāma* of Ferdowsi." *Oral Tradition* 3:88–105.

———. 1994. *Poet and Hero in the Persian Book of Kings*. Ithaca, N.Y.

Davies, M. 1981. "The Judgement of Paris and *Iliad* Book XXIV." *Journal of Hellenic Studies* 101:56–62.

Davison, J. A. 1955a. "Peisistratus and Homer." *Transactions of the American Philological Association* 86:1–21.

———. 1955b. "Quotations and Allusions in Early Greek Poetry." *Eranos* 53: 125–140 (= 1968:70–85).

———. 1958. "Notes on the Panathenaia." *Journal of Hellenic Studies* 78:23–41 (= 1968:28–69).

———. 1962. "The Transmission of the Text" and "The Homeric Question." *A Companion to Homer*, ed. A. J. B. Wace and F. H. Stubbings, 215–233 and 234–265. London.

———. 1968. *From Archilochus to Pindar: Papers on Greek Literature of the Archaic Period*. London.

Day, J. W. 1989. "Rituals in Stone: Early Greek Grave Epigrams and Monuments." *Journal of Hellenic Studies* 109:16–28.

Delrieu, A., D. Hilt, and F. Létoublon. 1984. "Homère à plusieurs voix: Les techniques narratives dans l'épopée grecque archaïque." *LALIES* 4:177–194.

Denniston, J. D. 1954. *The Greek Particles*. 2d ed., rev. by K. J. Dover. Oxford.

Detienne, M. 1973. *Les maîtres de vérité dans la Grèce archaïque*. 2d ed. Paris.

———. 1977. *Dionysos mis à mort*. Paris. [Eng. translation: *Dionysos Slain*, trans. M. Muellner and L. Muellner (Baltimore, 1979).]

———. 1981. *L'invention de la mythologie*. Paris.

———, ed. 1988. *Les savoirs de l'écriture. En Grèce ancienne*. Lille.

Dixon, K. 1990. "A Typology of Mediation in Homer." *Oral Tradition* 5:37–71.

Doane, A. N., and C. B. Pasternack, eds. 1991. *Vox intexta: Orality and Textuality in the Middle Ages*. Madison, Wis.

Dougherty, C., and L. Kurke, eds. 1993. *Cultural Poetics in Archaic Greece: Cult, Performance, Politics*. Cambridge.

Dubuisson, D. 1989. "Anthropologie poétique: Prolégomènes à une anthropologie du texte." *L'Homme* 111–112:222–236.

Ducrot, O., and T. Todorov. 1979. *Encyclopedic Dictionary of the Sciences of Language*. Translated by C. Porter. Baltimore. [Translation of *Dictionnaire encyclopédique des sciences du langage* (Paris, 1972).]

Durante, M. 1976. *Sulla preistoria della tradizione poetica greca*. Vol. 2: *Risultanze della comparazione indoeuropea*. Incunabula Graeca 64. Rome.

Eagleton, T. 1983. *Literary Theory: An Introduction*. Minneapolis.

Ebert, J., ed. 1972. *Griechische Epigramme auf Sieger an gymnischen und hippischen Agonen*. Berlin.

Edmunds, L. 1996. *Theatrical Space and Historical Place in Sophocles' "Oedipus at Colonus."* Lanham, Md.

Edmunds, S. T. 1990. *Homeric Nēpios*. New York.

Edwards, A. T. 1985a. *Odysseus against Achilles: The Role of Allusion in the Homeric Epic*. Beiträge zur klassischen Philologie 171. Königstein/Ts.

———. 1985b. "Achilles in the Underworld: *Iliad*, *Odyssey*, and *Aithiopis*." *Greek, Roman, and Byzantine Studies* 26:215–227.

158   ———. 1988. "ΚΛΕΟΣ ΑΦΘΙΤΟΝ and Oral Theory." *Classical Quarterly* 38:
    25–30.

Edwards, G. P. 1971. *The Language of Hesiod in Its Traditional Context.* Oxford.

Edwards, M. W. 1987. *Homer, Poet of the Iliad.* Baltimore.

Edwards, V., and T. J. Sienkewicz. 1990. *Oral Cultures Past and Present: Rappin' and Homer.* Oxford.

Elwell-Sutton, L. P. 1976. *The Persian Metres.* Cambridge.

Ernout, A., and A. Meillet. 1959. *Dictionnaire étymologique de la langue latine: Histoire des mots.* 4th ed. Paris.

Figueira, T. J. 1985. "The Theognidea and Megarian Society." Figueira and Nagy 1985:112–158.

Figueira, T. J., and G. Nagy, eds. 1985. *Theognis of Megara: Poetry and the Polis.* Baltimore.

Finkelberg, M. 1986. "Is ΚΛΕΟΣ ΑΦΘΙΤΟΝ a Homeric Formula?" *Classical Quarterly* 36:1–5.

———. 1988. "Ajax's Entry in the Hesiodic *Catalogue of Women.*" *Classical Quarterly* 38:31–41.

Finley, M. I. 1977. *The World of Odysseus.* 2d ed. London.

Finnegan, R. 1970. *Oral Literature in Africa.* Oxford.

———. 1976. "What Is Oral Literature Anyway? Comments in the Light of Some African and Other Comparative Material." Stolz and Shannon 1976: 127–166. [Reprinted in Foley 1990:243–282.]

———. 1977. *Oral Poetry: Its Nature, Significance, and Social Context.* Cambridge.

———. 1991. "Tradition, But What Tradition and For Whom?" *Oral Tradition* 6:104–124.

Fittschen, K. 1969. *Untersuchungen zum Beginn der Sagendarstellung bei den Griechen.* Berlin.

Flueckiger, J. B. 1989. "Caste and Regional Variants in an Oral Epic Tradition." In *OEI* 33–54.

Foley, J. M., ed. 1981. *Oral Traditional Literature: A Festschrift for Albert Bates Lord.* Columbus, Ohio.

———. 1985. *Oral-Formulaic Theory and Research: An Introduction and Annotated Bibliography.* New York.

———, ed. 1986. *Oral Tradition in Literature: Interpretation in Context.* Columbia, Mo.

———, ed. 1990. *Oral-Formulaic Theory: A Folklore Casebook.* New York and London.

———. 1991. *Immanent Art: From Structure to Meaning in Traditional Oral Epic.* Bloomington and Indianapolis, Ind.

Ford, A. 1988. "The Classical Definition of ΡΑΨΩΙΔΙΑ." *Classical Philology* 83:300–307.

Foucault, M. 1969. "Qu'est-ce qu'un auteur?" *Bulletin de la Société Française de Philosophie* 63:73–104. [Eng. translation: "What Is an Author?" in *Textual*

Strategies: Perspectives in Post-Structuralist Criticism, ed. J. V. Harari, 141–160   **159**
(Ithaca, N.Y., 1979); also in *Language, Countermemory, Practice,* ed. D. F.
Bouchard, 113–138 (Ithaca, N.Y., 1977).

Fowler, R. 1983. Review of Nagy 1979. *Echos du Monde Classique/Classical Views*
27:117–129.

Fraenkel, E. 1920. "Zur Form der AINOI." *Rheinisches Museum für Philologie*
73:366–370. Reprinted in his *Kleine Schriften* 1:235–239 (Rome, 1964).

Frame, D. 1978. *The Myth of Return in Early Greek Epic.* New Haven, Conn.

Francis, E. D. 1983. "Virtue, Folly, and Greek Etymology." In Rubino and
Shelmerdine 1983:74–121.

Friis Johansen, K. 1967. *The Iliad in Early Greek Art.* Copenhagen.

Frontisi-Ducroux, F. 1986. *La cithare d'Achille: Essai sur la poétique de l'Iliade.*
Rome.

Gagarin, M. 1983. "Antilochus' Strategy: The Chariot Race in *Iliad* 23." *Classical
Philology* 78:35–39.

Gentili, B. 1985. *Poesia e pubblico nella grecia antica: Da Omero al V secolo.* Rome
and Bari. [Eng. translation: *Poetry and Its Public in Ancient Greece: From Homer
to the Fifth Century,* trans. A. T. Cole (Baltimore, 1988).]

Gentili, B., and P. Giannini. 1977. "Preistoria e formazione dell'esametro."
Quaderni urbinati di cultura classica 26:7–37.

Goldhill, S. 1991. *The Poet's Voice: Essays on Poetics and Greek Literature.* Cambridge.

Goody, J. R. 1972. *The Myth of the Bagre.* Oxford.

——. 1977. *The Domestication of the Savage Mind.* Cambridge.

Goody, J., and I. Watt. 1968. "The Consequences of Literacy." In *Literacy in Traditional Societies,* ed. J. Goody, 27–68. Cambridge.

Goold, G. P. 1977. "The Nature of Homeric Composition." *Illinois Classical
Studies* 2:1–34.

Gordesiani, R. 1980. "Zur Interpretation der Duale im 9. Buch der Ilias." *Philologus* 124:163–174.

Griffin, J. 1977. "The Epic Cycle and the Uniqueness of Homer." *Journal of Hellenic Studies* 97:39–53.

——. 1980. *Homer on Life and Death.* Oxford.

——. 1984. Review of Clay 1984. *Times Literary Supplement* (10 February), 134.

——. 1987. "Homer and Excess." In Bremer, de Jong, and Kalff 1987:
85–104.

——. 1991. "Speech in the *Iliad*." Review of Martin 1989. *Classical Review*
41:1–5.

——. 1995. *Homer: Iliad IX.* Oxford.

Griffith, M. 1983. "Personality in Hesiod." In *Studies in Classical Lyric: A Homage
to Elroy Bundy,* ed. T. D'Evelyn, P. Psoinos, and T. R. Walsh. *Classical Antiquity*
2:37–65.

——. 1990. "Contest and Contradiction in Early Greek Poetry." In *Cabinet of*

160   *the Muses: Essays on Classical and Comparative Literature in Honor of Thomas R. Rosenmeyer,* ed. M. Griffith and D. J. Mastronarde, 185–207. Atlanta.

Grottanelli, C., and N. F. Parise, eds. 1988. *Sacrificio e società nel mondo antico.* Rome and Bari.

Haft, A. J. "The City-Sacker Odysseus." *Transactions of the American Philological Association* 120:37–56.

Hainsworth, J. B., and A. T. Hatto, eds. 1989. *Traditions of Heroic and Epic Poetry.* Vol. 2: *Characteristics and Techniques.* London.

Hansen, P. A., ed. 1983. *Carmina epigraphica Graeca saeculorum viii–v a.Chr.n.* Berlin and New York. [Abbreviated as *CEG*.]

Harris, W. V. 1989. *Ancient Literacy.* Cambridge, Mass.

Harrison, J. E. 1927. *Themis: A Study of the Social Origins of Greek Religion.* 2d rev. ed. Cambridge.

Hatto, A. T. 1980. "Kirghiz: Mid-Nineteenth Century." In *Traditions of Heroic and Epic Poetry,* ed. A. T. Hatto, 300–327. London.

Havelock, E. A. 1963. *Preface to Plato.* Cambridge, Mass.

———. 1982. *The Literate Revolution in Greece and Its Cultural Consequences.* Princeton.

Heath, M. 1990. "The Ancient Grasp." *Times Literary Supplement* (15–21 June), 645–646.

Held, D. t. D. 1991. "Why 'Individuals' Didn't Exist in Classical Antiquity." *New England Classical Newsletter and Journal* 18:26–29.

Hendel, R. S. 1987. "Of Demigods and the Deluge: Toward an Interpretation of *Genesis* 6:1–4." *Journal of Biblical Literature* 106:13–26.

Herington, J. 1985. *Poetry into Drama: Early Tragedy and the Greek Poetic Tradition.* Berkeley and Los Angeles.

Herzfeld, M. 1985a. *The Poetics of Manhood.* Princeton.

———. 1985b. "Interpretation from Within: Metatext for a Cretan Quarrel." In *The Text and Its Margins,* ed. M. Alexiou and V. Lambropoulos, 197–218. New York.

Heubeck, A., S. West, and J. B. Hainsworth, eds. 1988. *A Commentary on Homer's Odyssey.* Vol. 1: *Introduction and Books i–viii.* Oxford.

Hillers, D. R., and M. H. McCall. 1976. "Homeric Dictated Texts: A Reexamination of Some Near Eastern Evidence." *Harvard Studies in Classical Philology* 80:19–23.

Hintenlang, H. 1961. "Untersuchungen zu den Homer-Aporien des Aristoteles." Diss., Heidelberg.

Hobson, G., ed. [1979] 1981. *The Remembered Earth: An Anthology of Contemporary Native American Literature.* Albuquerque.

Holoka, James P. 1991. "Homer, Oral Poetry Theory, and Comparative Literature: Major Trends and Controversies in Twentieth-Century Criticism." In *Zweihundert Jahre Homer-Forschung,* ed. Joachim Latacz, 456–481. Colloquium Rauricum II. Stuttgart and Leipzig.

Hooker, J. T. 1977. *The Language and Text of the Lesbian Poets.* Innsbrucker **161**
Beiträge zur Sprachwissenschaft 26. Innsbruck.

Horrocks, G. C. 1981. *Space and Time in Homer: Prepositional and Adverbial Par-*
ticles in the Greek Epic. New York.

Householder, F. W., and G. Nagy. 1972a. "Greek." In *Current Trends in Linguis-*
tics, Vol. 9, ed. T. A. Sebeok, 735–816. The Hague.

———. 1972b. *Greek: A Survey of Recent Work.* The Hague.

Huot, S. 1987. *From Song to Book: The Poetics of Writing in Old French Lyric and Lyri-*
cal Narrative Poetry. Ithaca, N.Y.

———. 1991. "Chronicle, Lai, and Romance: Orality and Writing in the *Roman*
de Perceforest." In Doane and Pasternack 1991 : 203–223.

Immerwahr, H. R. 1964. "Book Rolls on Attic Vases." *Classical, Mediaeval and Re-*
naissance Studies in Honour of B. L. Ullman, 1 : 17–48. Rome.

Innes, G. 1974. *Sunjata: Three Mandinka Versions.* London.

Ivanov, V. V. 1993a. "On the Etymology of Latin *Elementa.*" *Elementa: Journal of*
Slavic Studies and Comparative Cultural Semiotics 1 : 1–5.

———. 1993b. "Origin, History and Meaning of the Term 'Semiotics'." *Ele-*
menta: Journal of Slavic Studies and Comparative Cultural Semiotics 1 : 115–143.

Jacoby, F., ed. 1923–. *Die Fragmente der griechischen Historiker.* Leiden.

Jacopin, P.-Y. 1981. "La parole générative de la mythologie des Indiens Yukuna." Doctoral diss., University of Neuchâtel.

———. 1988. "On the Syntactic Structure of Myth, or the Yukuna Invention of
Speech." *Cultural Anthropology* 3 : 131–159.

Janko, R. 1982. *Homer, Hesiod and the Hymns: Diachronic Development in Epic Dic-*
tion. Cambridge.

———. 1990. "The *Iliad* and Its Editors: Dictation and Redaction." *Classical An-*
tiquity 9 : 326–334.

———. 1992. *The Iliad: A Commentary.* Vol. 4: *Books 13–16.* Cambridge.

Jensen, M. Skafte. 1980. *The Homeric Question and the Oral-Formulaic Theory.*
Copenhagen.

Johnson, B. 1980. *The Critical Difference: Essays in the Contemporary Rhetoric of*
Reading. Baltimore.

Johnson, J. W. 1980. "Yes, Virginia, There Is an Epic in Africa." *Research in*
African Literatures 11 : 308–326.

———. 1986. *The Epic of Son-Jara: A West African Tradition.* Bloomington and Indianapolis, Ind.

Jong, I. J. F. de. 1987. "Silent Characters in the *Iliad.*" In Bremer, de Jong, and
Kalff 1987 : 105–121.

Kannicht, R. 1982. "Poetry and Art: Homer and the Monuments Afresh." *Classi-*
cal Antiquity 1 : 70–86, with plates.

Kaster, R. A., ed. 1995. *De grammaticis et rhetoribus/C. Suetonius Tranquillus.* Oxford.

Kazansky, N. N. 1989. "K etimologii teonima GERA." In *Paleobalkanistika i antich-*
nost', ed. V. P. Neroznak, et al., 54–58. Moscow.

162   Kelly, S. T. 1990. *Homeric Correption and the Metrical Distinctions between Speeches and Narrative*. New York.

Kiparsky, P. 1976. "Oral Poetry: Some Linguistic and Typological Considerations." In Stolz and Shannon 1976:73–106.

Kirk, G. S. 1962. *The Songs of Homer*. Cambridge.

———. 1970. *Myth, Its Meaning and Functions*. Berkeley.

———. 1974. *The Nature of Greek Myths*. Harmondsworth.

———. 1976. *Homer and the Oral Tradition*. Cambridge.

———, ed. 1985. *The Iliad: A Commentary*. Vol. 1: *Books 1–4*. Cambridge.

Kleingünther, A. 1933. *ΠΡΩΤΟΣ ΕΥΡΕΤΗΣ: Untersuchungen zur Geschichte einer Fragestellung*. Philologus Supplementband 26. Leipzig.

Koller, H. 1972. "Epos." *Glotta* 50:16–24.

Kothari, K. 1989. "Performers, Gods, and Heroes in the Oral Epics of Rajasthan." In *OEI* 102–117.

Kraft, W. B. 1989. "Improvisation in Hungarian Ethnic Dancing: An Analog to Oral Verse Composition." *Oral Tradition* 4:273–315.

Kuhn, T. S. 1970. *The Structure of Scientific Revolutions*. 2d (enlarged) ed. Chicago.

Kullmann, W. 1956. *Das Wirken der Götter in der Ilias: Untersuchungen zur Frage der Entstehung des homerischen "Götterapparats."* Berlin.

———. 1960. *Die Quellen der Ilias*. Hermes Einzelschriften 14. Wiesbaden.

———. 1985. "Gods and Men in the *Iliad* and *Odyssey*." *Harvard Studies in Classical Philology* 89:1–23.

Kurke, L. 1991. *The Traffic in Praise: Pindar and the Poetics of Social Economy*. Ithaca, N.Y.

Lachterman, D. R. 1987. "*Noos* and *Nostos:* The *Odyssey* and the Origins of Greek Philosophy." *La naissance de la raison en Grèce*, Actes du Congrès de Nice, May 1987, 33–39.

Lamberton, R. 1988. *Hesiod*. New Haven, Conn.

Lang, M. L. 1983. "Reverberation and Mythology in the *Iliad*." In Rubino and Shelmerdine 1983:140–164.

Lathuillère, R. 1966. *Giron le courtois: Étude de la tradition manuscrite et analyse critique*. Geneva.

Leach, E. R. 1982. Critical Introduction. In M. I. Steblin-Kamenskij, *Myth*, 1–20. Ann Arbor.

Lehrs, K. 1882. *De Aristarchi studiis Homericis*. 3d ed. Leipzig.

Létoublon, F. 1983. "Défi et combat dans l'*Iliade*." *Revue des études grecques* 96:27–48.

———. 1986. "Comment faire des choses avec des mots grecs." *Philosophie du langage et grammaire dans l'antiquité, Cahiers du Groupe de Recherches sur la Philosophie et le Langage* 6–7:67–90.

Lévi-Strauss, C. 1958. *Race and History*. Paris.

———. 1964. *Le cru et le cuit*. Paris.

———. 1966. *Du miel aux cendres.* Paris.

———. 1967a. "The Structural Study of Myth." In *Structural Anthropology,* 202–228. New York.

———. 1967b. "The Story of Asdiwal." In *The Structural Study of Myth and Totemism,* ed. E. Leach, 1–48. London.

———. 1968. *L'origine des manières de table.* Paris.

———. 1971. *L'homme nu.* Paris.

———. 1979. *La voie des masques.* Paris.

———. 1982. *The Way of the Masks.* Translated from Lévi-Strauss 1979 by S. Modelski. Seattle.

———. 1984. "La visite des âmes." In *Paroles données,* 245–248. Paris.

Liddell, H. G., R. Scott, and H. Stuart Jones, eds. 1940. *Greek-English Lexicon.* 9th ed. Oxford. [Abbreviated as LSJ.]

Lloyd-Jones, H. 1992. "Becoming Homer." *New York Review of Books* 39, 5:52–57. Review of Lord 1991, *inter alia.*

Lohmann, D. 1970. *Die Komposition der Reden in der Ilias.* Berlin.

Lohse, G. 1964, 1965, 1967. "Untersuchungen über Homerzitate bei Platon" I, II, III. *Helikon* 4:3–28; 5:248–325; 7:223–231.

Loraux, N. 1988. *"Poluneikēs epōnumos:* Le nom des fils d'Oedipe, entre épopée et tragédie." In *Métamorphoses du mythe en Grèce ancienne,* ed. C. Calame, 151–166. Geneva.

Lord, A. B. 1938. "Homer and Huso II: Narrative Inconsistencies in Homer and Oral Poetry." *Transactions of the American Philological Association* 69:439–445.

———. 1951. "Composition by Theme in Homer and Southslavic Epos." *Transactions of the American Philological Association* 82:71–80.

———. 1953. "Homer's Originality: Oral Dictated Texts," *Transactions of the American Philological Association* 84:124–134. Rewritten, with minimal changes, in Lord 1991:38–48 (with an "Addendum 1990" at pp. 47–48).

———. 1960. *The Singer of Tales.* Cambridge, Mass.

———. 1990a. "Perspectives on Recent Work on Oral Literature." In Foley 1990:31–51. [Excerpted from *Forum for Modern Language Studies* 10 (1974): 1–21.]

———. 1990b. "Perspectives on Recent Work on the Oral Traditional Formula." In Foley 1990:379–405. [Excerpted from *Oral Tradition* 1 (1986): 467–503.]

———. 1991. *Epic Singers and Oral Tradition.* Ithaca, N.Y.

———. 1995. *The Singer Resumes the Tale.* Edited by M. L. Lord. Ithaca, N.Y.

Lowenstam, S. 1981. *The Death of Patroklos: A Study in Typology.* Beiträge zur Klassischen Philologie 133. Königstein/Ts.

———. 1992. "The Uses of Vase-Depictions in Homeric Studies." *Transactions of the American Philological Association* 122:165–198.

———. 1993a. "The Arming of Achilleus on Early Greek Vases." *Classical Antiquity* 12:199–218.

164　———. 1993b. *The Scepter and the Spear: Studies on Forms of Repetition in the Homeric Poems*. Lanham, Md.

Lowry, E. R. 1991. *Thersites: A Study in Comic Shame*. New York.

Ludwich, A. 1898. *Die Homervulgata als voralexandrinisch erwiesen*. Leipzig.

Lynn-George, M. 1982. Review of Griffin 1980. *Journal of Hellenic Studies* 102:239–245.

———. 1988. *Epos: Word, Narrative and the Iliad*. Atlantic Highlands, N.J.

McClary, S. 1989. "Terminal Prestige: The Case of Avant-Garde Music Composition." *Cultural Critique* 12:57–81.

Maillard, J. 1959. "Coutumes musicales au moyen âge d'après le *Tristan* en prose." *Cahiers de civilisation médiévale* 2:341–353.

Malinowski, B. 1926. *Myth in Primitive Psychology*. London.

Marquardt, P. 1985. "Penelope 'polytropos'." *American Journal of Philology* 106:32–48.

Martin, R. P. 1983. *Healing, Sacrifice and Battle: Amēchania and Related Concepts in Early Greek Poetry*. Innsbrucker Beiträge zur Sprachwissenschaft 41. Innsbruck.

———. 1984a. "Hesiod, Odysseus, and the Instruction of Princes." *Transactions of the American Philological Association* 114:29–48.

———. 1984b. "The Oral Tradition." *Critical Survey of Poetry*, ed. F. Magill, 1746–1768. Foreign Language Series. LaCanada, Calif.

———. 1989. *The Language of Heroes: Speech and Performance in the Iliad*. Ithaca, N.Y.

———. 1993. "The Seven Sages as Performers of Wisdom." In Dougherty and Kurke 1993:108–128.

Mazon, P. 1943. *Introduction à l'Iliade*. With the collaboration of P. Chantraine, P. Collart, and R. Langumier. Paris.

Meillet, A. 1925. *La méthode comparative en linguistique historique*. Paris.

Merkelbach, R. 1952. "Die pisistratische Redaktion der homerischen Gedichte." *Rheinisches Museum* 95:23–47.

Merkelbach, R., and M. L. West, eds. 1967. *Fragmenta Hesiodea*. Oxford.

Miller, A. M. 1986. *From Delos to Delphi: A Literary Study of the Homeric Hymn to Apollo*. Leiden.

Miller, D. G. 1982a. *Homer and the Ionian Epic Tradition*. Innsbrucker Beiträge zur Sprachwissenschaft 38. Innsbruck.

———. 1982b. *Improvisation, Typology, Culture, and "The New Orthodoxy": How Oral Is Homer?* Washington, D.C.

Minnis, A. J. 1984. *Medieval Theory of Authorship: Scholastic Literary Attitudes in the Later Middle Ages*. London.

Monroe, J. T. 1972. "Oral Composition in Pre-Islamic Poetry." *Journal of Arabic Literature* 3:1–53.

———. 1979. "Prolegomena to the Study of Ibn Quzmān: The Poet as Jongleur." In *El Romancero hoy: Historia, Comparatismo, Bibliografía crítica*, 77–127.

Monsacré, H. 1984. *Les larmes d'Achille*. Paris.

Moon, W. G., ed. 1983. *Ancient Greek Art and Iconography*. Madison, Wis.

Moran, W. 1975. "*Mimnēskomai* and 'Remembering' Epic Stories in Homer and the Hymns." *Quaderni urbinati di cultura classica* 20:195–211.

Morris, I. 1986. "The Use and Abuse of Homer." *Classical Antiquity* 5:81–136.

———. 1988. "Tomb Cult and the 'Greek Renaissance': The Past and the Present in the Eighth Century B.C." *Antiquity* 62:750–761.

Muellner, L. 1976. *The Meaning of Homeric EYXOMAI through Its Formulas*. Innsbrucker Beiträge zur Sprachwissenschaft 13. Innsbruck.

———. 1990. "The Simile of the Cranes and Pygmies: A Study of Homeric Metaphor." *Harvard Studies in Classical Philology* 93:59–101.

Murray, G. 1909. *The Interpretation of Ancient Greek Literature*. Inaugural lecture delivered before the University of Oxford, January 27, 1909. Oxford.

———. 1934. *The Rise of the Greek Epic*. 4th ed. Oxford.

Murray, P. 1981. "Poetic Inspiration in Early Greece." *Journal of Hellenic Studies* 101:87–100.

Nagler, M. N. 1974. *Spontaneity and Tradition: A Study in the Oral Art of Homer*. Berkeley and Los Angeles.

———. 1977. "Dread Goddess Endowed with Speech." *Archeological News* 6: 77–85.

Nagy, G. 1974. *Comparative Studies in Greek and Indic Meter*. Cambridge, Mass.

———. 1979. *The Best of the Achaeans: Concepts of the Hero in Archaic Greek Poetry*. Baltimore.

———. 1981. "An Evolutionary Model for the Text Fixation of Homeric Epos." In Foley 1981:390–393.

———. 1982. Review of Detienne 1981. *Annales économies sociétés civilisations* 37:778–780.

———. 1983. "*Sēma* and *Noēsis:* Some Illustrations." *Arethusa* 16:35–55. [Rewritten as Chapter 8 of N 1990b.]

———. 1985. "Theognis and Megara: A Poet's Vision of His City." In Figueira and Nagy 1985:22–81.

———. 1986a. "Ancient Greek Praise and Epic Poetry." In Foley 1986:89–102. [Rewritten as part of Chapter 6 in N 1990a.]

———. 1986b. "Poetic Visions of Immortality for the Hero." In Bloom 1986: 205–212.

———. 1986c. "The Worst of the Achaeans." In Bloom 1986:213–215.

———. 1988. Review of Shive 1987. *Phoenix* 42:364–366.

———. 1989a. "Early Greek Views of Poets and Poetry." In *Cambridge History of Literary Criticism*, Vol. 1, ed. G. Kennedy, 1–77. Cambridge. Revised paperback edition, 1993.

———. 1989b. Foreword to Martin 1989:ix–xi.

———. 1990a. *Pindar's Homer: The Lyric Possession of an Epic Past*. Baltimore. Revised paperback edition, 1994.

166 ———. 1990b. *Greek Mythology and Poetics*. Ithaca, N.Y. Revised paperback edition, 1992.

———. 1990c. "Death of a Schoolboy: The Early Greek Beginnings of a Crisis in Philology." *Comparative Literature Studies* 27:37–48. [Reprinted in *On Philology*, ed. J. Ziolkowski, 37–48. University Park, Pa., 1990.]

———. 1992a. "Homeric Questions." *Transactions of the American Philological Association* 122:17–60.

———. 1992b. "Mythological Exemplum in Homer." In *Innovations of Antiquity*, ed. R. Hexter and D. Selden, 311–331. New York and London.

———. 1992c. Introduction. In Homer, *The Iliad*, translated by R. Fitzgerald. Everyman's Library no. 60. New York.

———. 1992d. "Authorisation and Authorship in the Hesiodic *Theogony*." In *Essays on Hesiod*, Vol. 2, ed. A. N. Athanassakis. *Ramus* 21:119–130.

———. 1993. "Alcaeus in Sacred Space." In *Tradizione e innovazione nella cultura greca da Omero all' età ellenistica: Scritti in onore di Bruno Gentili*, Vol. 1, ed. R. Pretagostini, 221–225. Rome.

———. 1994a. "An Evolutionary Model for the Making of Homeric Poetry: Comparative Perspectives." In *The Ages of Homer: A Tribute to Emily Townsend Vermeule*, ed. J. B. Carter and S. P. Morris, 63–179. Austin.

———. 1994b. "The Name of Achilles: Questions of Etymology and 'Folk Etymology'." *Illinois Classical Studies* 19 (*Studies in Honor of Miroslav Marcovich*, vol. 2): 3–9.

———. 1994c. "The Name of Apollo: Etymology and Essence." In *Apollo: Origins and Influences*, ed. J. Solomon, 3–7. Tucson.

———. 1996. *Poetry as Performance: Homer and Beyond*. Cambridge.

Nagy, J. F. 1983. "Close Encounters of the Traditional Kind in Medieval Irish Literature." In *Celtic Folklore and Christianity: Studies in Memory of William W. Heist*, ed. P. K. Ford, 129–149. Santa Barbara, Calif.

———. 1985. *The Wisdom of the Outlaw: The Boyhood Deeds of Finn in Gaelic Narrative Tradition*. Berkeley and Los Angeles.

———. 1986. "Orality in Medieval Irish Narrative." *Oral Tradition* 1:272–301.

Nettl, B. 1956. *Music in Primitive Culture*. Cambridge, Mass.

———. 1964. *Theory and Method in Ethnomusicology*. New York.

———. 1965. *Folk and Traditional Music of the Western Continents*. Englewood Cliffs, N.J.

———. 1983. *The Study of Ethnomusicology: Twenty-Nine Issues and Concepts*. Urbana, Ill.

O'Brien, J. V. 1993. *The Transformation of Hera: A Study of Ritual, Hero, and the Goddess in the Iliad*. Lanham, Md.

Öhler, R. 1929. "Mythologische Exempla in der älteren griechischen Dichtung." Diss., Basel.

Okpewho, I. 1979. *The Epic in Africa: Toward a Poetics of the Oral Performance*. New York.

Ong, W. J. 1977a. *Interfaces of the Word: Studies in the Evolution of Consciousness and Culture.* Ithaca, N.Y.

———. 1977b. "African Talking Drums and Oral Noetics." *New Literary History* 8:411–429. [Reprinted in Ong 1977a:92–120.]

———. 1981. *Fighting for Life: Contest, Sexuality, and Consciousness.* Ithaca, N.Y.

———. 1982. *Orality and Literacy.* London.

———. 1986. "Text as Interpretation: Mark and After." In Foley 1986: 147–169.

Opland, J. 1988. "Lord of the Singers." *Oral Tradition* 3:353–367.

———. 1989. "Xhosa: The Structure of Xhosa Eulogy and the Relation of Eulogy to Epic." In Hainsworth and Hatto 1989:121–143.

Page, D. L. 1955a. *Sappho and Alcaeus: An Introduction to the Study of Ancient Lesbian Poetry.* Oxford.

———. 1955b. *The Homeric Odyssey.* Oxford.

———. 1959. *History and the Homeric Iliad.* Berkeley and Los Angeles.

———, ed. 1962. *Poetae melici graeci.* Oxford. [Abbreviated as *PMG.*]

———, ed. 1974. *Supplementum lyricis graecis.* Oxford.

———, ed. 1975. *Epigrammata graeca.* Oxford. [Abbreviated as *EG.*]

Palmer, L. R. 1979. "A Mycenaean 'Akhilleid'?" In *Serta philologica Aenipontana,* vol. 3, ed. R. Muth and G. Pfohl, 255–261. Innsbrucker Beiträge zur Kulturwissenschaft 20. Innsbruck.

———. 1980. *The Greek Language.* Atlantic Highlands, N.J.

Parry, A. M. 1966. "Have We Homer's *Iliad*?" *Yale Classical Studies* 20:175–216. [Reprinted in A. M. Parry, *The Language of Achilles and Other Papers* (Oxford, 1989), 104–140.]

Parry, M. 1928a. *L'épithète traditionnelle dans Homère: Essai sur un problème de style homérique.* Paris. [Translated in Parry 1971:1–190.]

———. 1928b. *Les formules et la métrique d'Homère.* Paris. [Translated in Parry 1971:191–234.]

———. 1930. "Studies in the Epic Technique of Oral Verse-Making, I: Homer and Homeric Style." *Harvard Studies in Classical Philology* 41:73–147. [Reprinted in Parry 1971:266–324.]

———. 1932. "Studies in the Epic Technique of Oral Verse-Making, II: The Homeric Language as the Language of an Oral Poetry." *Harvard Studies in Classical Philology* 43:1–50. [Reprinted in Parry 1971:325–364.]

———. 1971. *The Making of Homeric Verse: The Collected Papers of Milman Parry.* Edited by A. Parry. Oxford.

Parry, M., A. B. Lord, and D. E. Bynum, eds. 1974. *Serbo-Croatian Heroic Songs.* Vol. 3: *Avdo Medjedović: The Wedding of Smailagić Meho.* Translation, with introduction and commentary by A. B. Lord. Cambridge, Mass.

Pavese, C. O. 1974. *Studi sulla tradizione epica rapsodica.* Rome.

Peabody, B. 1975. *The Winged Word.* Albany.

Pearsall, D. 1984. "Texts, Textual Criticism, and Fifteenth-Century Manuscript

168   Production." In *Fifteenth-Century Studies,* ed. R. F. Yeager, 121–136. Hamden,
        Conn.

Pelliccia, H. N. 1985. "The Structure of the Archaic Greek Hymns." Doctoral
        diss., Yale University.

Peradotto, J. 1990. *Man in the Middle Voice: Name and Narration in the Odyssey.*
        Princeton.

Petegorsky, D. 1982. "Context and Evocation: Studies in Early Greek and San-
        skrit Poetry." Doctoral diss., Berkeley. Published by University Microfilms,
        Ann Arbor, 1982.

Petropoulos, J. C. B. 1994. *Heat and Lust: Hesiod's Midsummer Festival Scene Re-
        visited.* Lanham, Md.

Pfeiffer, R. 1968. *History of Classical Scholarship: From the Beginnings to the End of
        the Hellenistic Age.* Oxford.

Phillips, C. R., III. 1989. "Classical Scholarship against Its History." *American
        Journal of Philology* 110:636–657.

Pickens, R. T. 1977. "Jaufre Rudel et la poétique de la mouvance." *Cahiers de
        civilisation médiévale* 20:323–337.

———, ed. 1978. *The Songs of Jaufre Rudel.* Toronto.

Pinney, G. F. 1983. "Achilles Lord of Scythia." In Moon 1983:127–146.

Pötscher, W. 1961. "Hera und Heros." *Rheinisches Museum* 104:302–355.

Powell, B. B. 1991. *Homer and the Origin of the Greek Alphabet.* Cambridge.

Pozzi, D. C., and J. M. Wickersham, eds. 1991. *Myth and the Polis.* Ithaca, N.Y.

Pucci, P. 1979. "The Song of the Sirens." *Arethusa* 12:121–132.

———. 1982. "The Proem of the Odyssey." *Arethusa* 15:39–62.

———. 1987. *Odysseus Polytropos: Intertextual Readings in the Odyssey and the Iliad.*
        Ithaca, N.Y.

Rabel, Robert J. 1990. "Apollo as a Model for Achilles in the *Iliad.*" *American
        Journal of Philology* 111:429–440.

———. 1991. "The Theme of Need in *Iliad* 9–11." *Phoenix* 45:283–295.

Radloff, W. 1885. *Proben der Volksliteratur der nördlichen türkischen Stämme V:
        Der Dialekt der Kara-Kirgisen.* St. Petersburg.

———. 1990. Preface to Radloff 1885. Translated by G. B. Sherman and A. B.
        Davis. *Oral Tradition* 5:73–90.

Raible, W., ed. 1988. *Zwischen Festtag und Alltag: Zehn Beiträge zum Thema
        'Mündlichkeit und Schriftlichkeit'.* Tübingen.

Raphals, L. 1992. *Knowing Words: Wisdom and Cunning in the Classical Traditions
        of China and Greece.* Ithaca, N.Y.

Redfield, J. M. 1975. *Nature and Culture in the Iliad: The Tragedy of Hector.*
        Chicago.

Reichl, K. 1985. "Oral Tradition and Performance of the Uzbek and Kara-
        kalpak Epic Singers." In *Fragen der mongolischen Heldendichtung,* vol. 3, ed.
        W. Heissig, 613–643. Wiesbaden.

———. 1992. *Turkic Oral Epic Poetry: Traditions, Forms, Poetic Structure.* New York.

Renoir, A. 1986. "Oral-Formulaic Rhetoric and the Interpretation of Texts." In Foley 1986:103–135.

Reynolds, D. F. 1995. *Heroic Poets, Poetic Heroes: The Ethnography of Performance in Arabic Oral Tradition.* Ithaca, N.Y.

Risch, E. 1981. *Kleine Schriften.* Edited by A. Etter and M. Looser. Berlin.

———. 1987. "Die ältesten Zeugnisse für ΚΛΕΟΣ ΑΦΘΙΤΟΝ." *Zeitschrift für Vergleichende Sprachforschung* 100:3–11.

Ritoók, Z. 1987. "Vermutungen zum Ursprung des griechischen Hexameters." *Philologus* 131:2–18.

Robb, K. 1978. "Poetic Sources of the Greek Alphabet: Rhythm and Abecedarium from Phoenician to Greek." In *Communication Arts in the Ancient World*, ed. E. A. Havelock and J. P. Hershbell, 23–36. New York.

Rösler, W. 1980. *Dichter und Gruppe: Eine Untersuchung zu den Bedingungen und zur historischen Funktion früher Lyrik am Beispiel Alkaios.* Munich.

———. 1985. "Persona reale o persona poetica? L'interpretazione dell' 'io' nella lirica greca." *Quaderni urbinati di cultura classica* 19:131–144.

Rosen, R. 1991. Review of N 1990a. *Bryn Mawr Classical Review* 2.1:35–40.

Roth, C. P. 1990. *"Mixed Aorists" in Homeric Greek.* New York.

Rubino, C. A., and C. W. Shelmerdine, eds. 1983. *Approaches to Homer.* Austin.

Ruijgh, C. J. 1967. *Études sur la grammaire et le vocabulaire du grec mycénien.* Amsterdam.

Sacks, R. 1987. *The Traditional Phrase in Homer: Two Studies in Form, Meaning and Interpretation.* Leiden.

Saïd, E. W. 1978. *Orientalism.* New York.

Sapir, E. 1921. *Language: An Introduction to the Study of Speech.* New York.

Schapera, I. 1965. *Praise Poems of Tswana Chiefs.* Oxford.

Scheibner, G. 1939. *Der Aufbau des 20. und 21. Buches der Ilias.* Borna and Leipzig.

Scheid, J., and J. Svenbro. 1994. *Le métier de Zeus: Mythe du tissage et du tissu dans le monde gréco-romain.* Paris.

Schein, S. L. 1984. *The Mortal Hero: An Introduction to Homer's Iliad.* Berkeley.

Schmitt, R. 1967. *Dichtung und Dichtersprache in indogermanischer Zeit.* Wiesbaden.

Schnapp-Gourbeillon, A. 1988. "Homère, Hipparche et la bonne parole." *Annales économies sociétés civilisations:* 805–821.

Schomer, K. 1989. "Paradigms for the Kali Yuga: The Heroes of the Ālhā Epic and Their Fate." In *OEI* 140–154.

Scodel, R. 1982. "The Autobiography of Phoenix." *American Journal of Philology* 103:128–136.

Seaford, R. 1994. *Reciprocity and Ritual: Homer and Tragedy in the Developing City-State.* Oxford.

Sealey, R. 1957. "From Phemius to Ion." *Revue des études grecques* 70:312–355.

———. 1990. *Women and Law in Classical Greece.* Chapel Hill.

Searle, J. R. 1979. *Speech-Acts: An Essay in the Philosophy of Language.* Cambridge.

170   Segal, C. P. 1968. "The Embassy and the Duals of *Iliad* 9.182–98." *Greek, Roman, and Byzantine Studies* 9:101–114.

———. 1983. "*Kleos* and Its Ironies in the *Odyssey*." *L'antiquité classique* 52: 22–47.

Seydou, C. 1983. "The African Epic: A Means for Defining the Genre." *Folklore Forum* 16:47–68.

Shannon, R. S. 1975. *The Arms of Achilles and Homeric Compositional Technique.* Leiden.

Shapiro, H. A. 1983. "Painting, Politics, and Genealogy: Peisistratos and the Neleids." In Moon 1983:87–96.

———. 1990. "Oracle-Mongers in Peisistratid Athens." *Kernos* 3:335–345.

———. 1992. "*Mousikoi Agones:* Music and Poetry at the Panathenaic Festival." In *Goddess and Polis: The Panathenaic Festival in Ancient Athens,* ed. J. Neils, 53–75. Princeton.

———. 1993. "Hipparchos and the Rhapsodes." In Dougherty and Kurke 1993:92–107.

Sherratt, E. S. 1990. "'Reading the Texts': Archaeology and the Homeric Question." *Antiquity* 64:807–824.

Shive, D. M. 1987. *Naming Achilles.* New York and Oxford.

Sienkewicz, T. J. 1991. "The Greeks Are Indeed Like the Others: Myth and Society in the West African *Sunjata.*" In Pozzi and Wickersham 1991:182–202.

Sinos, D. S. 1980. *Achilles, Patroklos, and the Meaning of Philos.* Innsbrucker Beiträge zur Sprachwissenschaft 29. Innsbruck.

Slatkin, L. M. 1986. "The Wrath of Thetis." *Transactions of the American Philological Association* 116:1–24.

———. 1987. "Genre and Generation in the *Odyssey*." *ΜΗΤΙΣ: Revue d'anthropologie du monde grec ancien* 1:259–268.

———. 1991. *The Power of Thetis: Allusion and Interpretation in the Iliad.* Berkeley.

Slotkin, E. M. 1978–1979. "Medieval Irish Scribes and Fixed Texts." *Éigse* 17:437–450.

Smith, J. D. 1980. "Old Indian: The Two Sanskrit Epics." In *Traditions of Heroic and Epic Poetry,* ed. A. T. Hatto, 48–78. London.

———. 1989. "Scapegoats of the Gods: The Ideology of the Indian Epics." In *OEI* 176–194.

———. 1990. "Worlds Apart: Orality, Literacy, and the Rajasthani Folk-*Mahābhārata.*" *Oral Tradition* 5:3–19.

Smith, M. C. 1992. *The Warrior Code of India's Sacred Song.* New York.

Smith, W. C. 1993. *What Is Scripture? A Comparative Approach.* Minneapolis.

Snodgrass, A. M. 1971. *The Dark Age of Greece: An Archaeological Survey of the Eleventh to the Eighth Centuries.* Edinburgh.

———. 1987. *An Archaeology of Greece: The Present State and Future Scope of a Discipline.* Berkeley and Los Angeles.

Solmsen, F. 1981. Review of Nagy 1979. *American Journal of Philology* 102: 81–83.

Stiewe, K. 1962–1963. "Die Entstehungszeit der hesiodischen Frauenkataloge."
    Philologus 106:291–299; 107:1–29.

Stoddart, R. 1990. *Pindar and Greek Family Law*. New York.

Stolz, B. A., and R. S. Shannon, eds. 1976. *Oral Literature and the Formula*. Ann
    Arbor.

Sultan, N. 1993. "Private Speech, Public Pain: The Power of Women's Laments
    in Ancient Greek Poetry and Tragedy." In *Rediscovering the Muses: Women's
    Musical Traditions*, ed. K. Marshall, 92–110, 246–249. Boston.

Svenbro, J. 1976. *La parole et le marbre: Aux origines de la poétique grecque*. Lund.
    [Italian translation, with changes and corrections: Torino, 1984.]

———. 1982. "A Mégara Hyblaea: Le corps géomètre." *Annales économies sociétés
    civilisations* 37:953–964.

———. 1984. "La découpe du poème: Notes sur les origines sacrificielles de la
    poétique grecque." *Poétique* 58:215–232.

———. 1987. "The 'Voice' of Letters in Ancient Greece: On Silent Reading
    and the Representation of Speech." In *Culture and History*, ed. M. Harb-
    smeier and M. T. Larsen, 2:31–47. Copenhagen. [Recast as Chapter 9 in
    Svenbro 1988a.]

———. 1988a. *Phrasikleia: Anthropologie de la lecture en Grèce ancienne*. Paris.

———. 1988b. "Il taglio della poesia: Note sulle origini sacrificali della poetica
    greca." In Grottanelli and Parise 1988:231–252.

———. 1993. *Phrasikleia: An Anthropology of Reading in Ancient Greece*. Transla-
    tion by J. Lloyd of Svenbro 1988a, with additions by the author. Ithaca, N.Y.

Tambiah, S. J. 1981. "A Performative Approach to Ritual." *Proceedings of the
    British Academy, London* 65:113–169. [Reprinted in Tambiah 1985:123–
    166.]

———. 1985. *Culture, Thought, and Social Action: An Anthropological Perspective*.
    Cambridge, Mass.

Taplin, O. 1986. "Homer's Use of Achilles' Earlier Campaigns in the Iliad." In
    Chios, ed. J. Boardman and C. E. Vaphopoulou-Richardson, 15–19. Oxford.

———. 1992. *Homeric Soundings: The Shaping of the Iliad*. Oxford.

Taylor, M. W. 1991. *The Tyrant Slayers: The Heroic Image in Fifth Century B.C.
    Athenian Art and Politics*. 2d ed. Salem, N.H.

Thalmann, W. G. 1984. *Conventions of Form and Thought in Early Greek Epic Poetry*.
    Baltimore.

Thomas, R. 1989. *Oral Tradition and Written Record in Classical Athens*. Cam-
    bridge.

Tompkins, D. P. 1992. Review of Pozzi and Wickersham 1991. *Bryn Mawr Classi-
    cal Review* 3:152–157.

Turner, E. G. 1977. *Athenian Books in the Fifth and Fourth Centuries*. 2d ed.
    London.

Turpin, J.-C. 1980. "L'expression ΑΙΔΩΣ ΚΑΙ ΝΕΜΕΣΙΣ et les *actes de langage*."
    Revue des études grecques 93:352–367.

172   Ulf, C. 1990. "Die Abwehr von Internem Streit als Teil des 'politischen' Programms der Homerischen Epen." *Grazer Beiträge* 17:1–25.

Veneri, A. 1983. "Oralistica e questione omerica." In *Oralità, scrittura, spettacolo,* ed. M. Vegetti, 47–52. Torino.

Verdenius, W. J. 1985. Review of Nagy 1979. *Mnemosyne* 38:180–181.

Verdier, C. 1972. *Les éolismes non-épiques de la langue de Pindare.* Innsbrucker Beiträge zur Sprachwissenschaft 7. Innsbruck.

Vermeule, E. 1986. "Priam's Castle Blazing." In *Troy and the Trojan War,* ed. M. Mellink, 77–92. Bryn Mawr, Pa.

Vernant, J.-P. 1985. *Mythe et pensée chez les Grecs.* 2d ed. of the 1965 original, recast and repaginated. Paris.

Vine, B. 1977. "On the Heptasyllabic Verses of the Rig-Veda." *Zeitschrift für Vergleichende Sprachforschung* 91:246–255.

———. 1978. "On the Metrics and Origin of Rig-Vedic *na* 'like, as'." *Indo-Iranian Journal* 20:171–193.

Visser, E. 1987. *Homerische Versifikationstechnik: Versuch einer Rekonstruktion.* Frankfurt am Main.

Vodoklys, E. J. 1992. *Blame-Expression in the Epic Tradition.* New York.

Wade-Gery, H. T. 1952. *The Poet of the Iliad.* Cambridge.

Wadley, S. S. 1989. "Choosing a Path: Performance Strategies in a North Indian Epic." In *OEI* 75–101.

Watkins, C. 1963. "Indo-European Metrics and Archaic Irish Verse." *Celtica* 6:194–249.

———. 1977. "A propos de ΜΗΝΙΣ." *Bulletin de la Société de Linguistique de Paris* 72:187–209.

Waugh, L. R. 1982. "Marked and Unmarked: A Choice between Unequals in Semiotic Structure." *Semiotica* 38:299–318.

Webster, T. B. L. 1964. *From Mycenae to Homer.* 2d ed. New York.

West, M. L., ed., with commentary. 1978. *Hesiod: Works and Days.* Oxford.

———. 1988. "The Rise of the Greek Epic." *Journal of Hellenic Studies* 108:151–172.

———. 1990. "Archaische Heldendichtung: Singen und Schreiben." In *Der Übergang von der Mündlichkeit zur Literatur bei den Griechen,* ed. W. Kullmann and M. Reichl, 33–50. Tübingen.

West, S., ed. 1967. *The Ptolemaic Papyri of Homer.* Papyrologica Coloniensia 3. Cologne and Opladen.

———. 1988. "The Transmission of the Text." In *A Commentary on Homer's Odyssey: Introduction and Books i–viii,* ed. A. Heubeck, S. West, and J. B. Hainsworth, 33–48. Oxford.

Whitley, J. 1988. "Early States and Hero-Cults: A Re-Appraisal." *Journal of Hellenic Studies* 108:173–182.

Whitman, C. H. 1958. *Homer and the Heroic Tradition.* Cambridge, Mass.

Wickersham, J. M. 1991. "Myth and Identity in the Archaic Polis." In Pozzi and Wickersham 1991:16–31.

Wilamowitz-Moellendorff, U. von. 1884. *Homerische Untersuchungen*. Berlin.

Willcock, M. M. 1964. "Mythological Paradeigma in the *Iliad*." *Classical Quarterly* 14:141–154.

———. 1977. "Ad Hoc Invention in the *Iliad*." *Harvard Studies in Classical Philology* 81:41–53.

Wyatt, W. F. 1985. "The Embassy and the Duals in *Iliad* IX." *American Journal of Philology* 106:399–408.

Zink, M. 1972. *La pastourelle: Poésie et folklore au Moyen Age*. Paris.

Zumthor, P. 1972. *Essai de poétique médiévale*. Paris.

———. 1983. *Introduction à la poésie orale*. Paris.

———. 1984. *La Poésie de la Voix dans la civilisation médiévale*. Paris.

Zwettler, M. J. 1978. *The Oral Tradition of Classical Arabic Poetry*. Columbus, Ohio.

Index

DATE DUE

AUG 1 3 2004			